ST. HIPPOLYTUS

AND

THE CHURCH OF ROME

IN THE

EARLIER PART

OF

THE THIRD CENTURY.

FROM THE NEWLY-DISCOVERED PHILOSOPHUMENA.

BY

CHR. WORDSWORTH, D.D.

CANON OF WESTMINSTER,

AND FORMERLY FELLOW OF TRINITY COLLEGE, CAMBRIDGE.

Wipf and Stock Publishers

150 West Broadway • Eugene OR 97401

2001

St. Hippolytus and the Church of Rome
In the Earlier Part of the Third Century

By Wordsworth, Chr.

ISBN: 1-57910-763-X

Reprinted by *Wipf and Stock Publishers*
150 West Broadway • Eugene OR 97401

Previously published by Francis & John Rivington, 1853.

PREFACE.

THE present Work consists of two Parts. The former contains a Dissertation on the Authorship of the newly-discovered "Philosophumena," and on the Life, Times, and Works of the Writer, especially in reference to Christian Doctrine, and to the early History of the Church, particularly of the Roman Church, with some application to the circumstances of our own age.

The latter Portion of the Volume is occupied with the Historical Narrative, which is contained in the "Philosophumena," concerning the Church of Rome in the first quarter of the Third Century, and is the most ancient and ample record, now extant, of the condition of that Church in that early age. This Narrative is presented in the words of the Original, with an English Translation, and Notes.

The Notes are, for the most part, critical; some of the conjectural readings there proposed have been followed in the English Translation, in a few passages, where the Greek Text of the MS. did not appear to afford a clear sense. But none of these have been introduced into the Text itself.

In the Appendix will be found a Fragment of a Work by the Author of the "Philosophumena," from an Oxford MS. This is followed by a collation of passages in the "Philosophumena" with a Work of Theodoret, showing that the newly-discovered Treatise was recognized as an authoritative document in his age,—the fifth century,—and that considerable portions of the Tenth Book were adopted by him.

Cloisters,
Westminster Abbey,
March 23, 1853.

CONTENTS.

CHAPTER I.

CHAPTER II.

CHAPTER III.

CHAPTER IV.

CHAPTER V.

CHAPTER VI.

CHAPTER VII.

CHAPTER VIII.

CHAPTER IX.

CHAPTER X.

CHAPTER XI.

CHAPTER XII.

PART II.

APPENDIX.

ERRATA.

P. 87, line 11, *for* deny *read* denies.

P. 134, last line, *for* more *read* in ore.

DISSERTATION.

CHAPTER I.

ST. HIPPOLYTUS, BISHOP OF PORTUS.

RATHER more than a century ago, Cardinal OTTOBONI was BISHOP of PORTO,—the ancient PORTUS,—a maritime city, which is situated at the northern mouth of the Tiber, about fifteen miles from Rome, and had enjoyed considerable commercial celebrity in former times[1]. He possessed a noble library, and endeavoured to restore the architectural beauty of his

[1] See Dio Cass. in Claudio, lib. lx. num. xi. tom. ii. p. 949, ed. Hamburg, 1752, and Sir W. Gell's Vicinity of Rome, ii. p. 174-9, and Contorni di Roma, by Nibby, ii. p. 323, who has published a separate work on Porto. See also Westphal, Die Römische Kampagn, ep. 172. The harbour (Portus), whence the city derived its name and importance, had been constructed by the Emperor Claudius, and improved by Trajan, whence it was called "Portus Trajani;" and possesses an interest in Christian history, as the harbour at which St. Ignatius landed in his way from Antioch to his martyrdom at Rome. See Martyr. Ignat. § 5, § 6, p. 569, 570, ed. 2nd, Jacobson.

Episcopal City, which in the lapse of ages had fallen into decay.

In his zeal for the restoration of the ecclesiastical edifices of Portus, he did not forget the names of those among his predecessors, who had reflected honour on his See in earlier ages. Of these, one stood pre-eminent; one, whom he numbered in the lineage of his own episcopal ancestry,—had shed lustre not only upon the See of Portus, but on the Western Church, and on Christendom at large[2]. He had been celebrated for holiness and orthodoxy, for learning and eloquence[3]; he was reckoned among the Saints and Martyrs of the Western Church. He was also venerable for his antiquity; he had flourished in the second and third centuries of the Christian era. He had[4] been a scholar of St. Irenæus, who, in his youth, had listened to St. Polycarp[5], the disciple of St. John. This was St. HIPPOLYTUS.

It was the earnest desire of Cardinal Ottoboni, Bishop of Portus, to do honour to the memory of this great man. We may well sympathize with him

[2] Card. Baron. ad Ann. 229. "De Hippolyto hâctenus, in quo utraque conveniunt ut Orientalis et Occidentalis Ecclesiæ ingens decus meritò dici possit."

[3] He is called "Vir disertissimus" by St. Jerome ad Lucin. iv. p. 579, ed. Bened. "Sacratissimus et magnus Doctor Veritatisque testis fidelis," by Anastasius in Collectan. apud Galland. Bibl. ii. p. 469, and a "stream of living waters to the Church," ποταμὸς τῇ ἐκκλησίᾳ ζώντων ναμάτων, by Syncellus, ad A. D. 215, by Zonaras, Annal. p. 468, ἀνὴρ ἱερώτατος καὶ σοφώτατος.

[4] Phot. cod. 121.

[5] Euseb. v. 20.

in his wish, while we cannot but regret the means to which he resorted for its accomplishment.

The Bishop of Porto,—being a Suffragan of Rome, having the oversight of one of the churches anciently[6] called Suburbicarian, from their vicinity to the *Urbs*, or city of Rome, and one of those who are now designated "Cardinal Bishops," and being among those Prelates, whose office it has been from time immemorial to consecrate[7] the Bishop of Rome,—exercises considerable influence in the Roman Conclave. Cardinal OTTOBONI endeavoured to obtain a Pontifical brief for the sanction of a special Office

[6] See Ruffinus in Canon. Concil. Nicæn. 6, and Notitia Curiæ Romanæ, ed 1683, p. 17: "Consecrabant Pontificem Romanum Episcopi vii. ejus Suffraganei nimirum Ostienis, *Portuensis*, Sylvæ Candidæ sive Ruffinæ, Tusculanus, Prænestinus, Sabinensis, Albanensis, et dicebantur ante Leonis IX. tempora, Cardinales Episcopi." The first Bishop ever translated to the Papacy was a Bishop of Portus, Formosus, A. D. 891; ibid. p. 17. These Episcopi Suffraganei were formerly viii.; Eugenius III. reduced them to vi. by uniting the "Ecclesia Veliterna" to Ostia, and "Sancta Ruffina" to Portus. See Onuphr. de VII. Urbis Eccl., c. 1. Hence there are now Six Cardinal Bishops. The Roman Editor of the LXX Version of the Book of Daniel (Simon de Magistris), has shown some reasons for believing that the Suburbicarian Diocese of Portus, in ancient times, included the *Regio Tiberina* of Rome itself, and the *Insula Tiberina*. See the quotations in Lumper's Hist. Patrum, viii. p. 13—18.

[7] Liber Diurnus Romanorum Pontificum, cap. 2, art. 8: "Episcopus Portuensis dat orationem secundam." δίδωσι προσευχὴν δευτέραν.

in honour of St. Hippolytus; to be used annually in the diocese of Portus on the 22nd of August, the day in which he is commemorated in the Breviary and Martyrology of Rome[8]. Some circumstances, however, had then recently occurred, which obstructed the execution of his design. Many local traditions[9], it is true, were known to exist at Portus, connecting the name of St. Hippolytus with that city and See. He was, and is at this day, regarded as the Patron of the Diocese[1]. And the testimony of those who had applied themselves to the study of Ecclesiastical History, since the revival of letters in Europe, to the end of the seventeenth century, had been almost unanimous in favour of the claim of Portus to the possession of that inheritance. That St. Hippolytus, the scholar of St. Irenæus, had been Bishop of Portus Romanus, or the harbour of Rome, two miles to the north of Ostia,—had been affirmed by the most celebrated Church Historians and Divines of Rome,

[8] M. Bunsen places it, by a slight inadvertence, on the 21st of August. "Hippolytus and his Age," iv. p. 120.

[9] A building, called Torre di S. Ippolito, still stands at Porto. See Nibby, Contorni, ii. p. 320. The Church at Portus had been called "S. Hippolyti Ecclesia" from time immemorial, *e. g.* in a Bull of Pope Gregory IX., A. D. 1236.

[1] "Patronus totius Diœcesis." See the Pastoral Letter of Cardinal Giovanni Antonio Guadagni, Bishop of Portus, dated 26th September, 1756, requiring the recitation of an "Officium et Missam S. Hippolyti" annually by every Priest in the Diocese of Portus on the 22nd of August.

such as Cardinals Baronius[2] and Bellarmine[3], and had been acknowledged as indubitable by the most learned Theologians of other Churches, as, for example, by Archbishop Ussher[4], Henry Dodwell[5], Bishop Beveridge[6], and Bishop Bull[7].

But in the year 1685, a learned Theologian of Holland, Stephen Le Moyne[8], published at Leyden his "Varia Sacra," in which he controverted the ancient and generally received tradition concerning St. Hippolytus. He did not deny that Hippolytus was a Bishop: he acknowledged him as a Martyr: he admitted that he had flourished early in the third century. But he would not allow that he had ever sat in the Episcopal see of Portus, near Rome. Relying on certain notices occurring in some ancient writers, Le Moyne would have transferred St. Hippolytus from the genial clime of Italy and the banks of the Tiber, to the stern wilds of Arabia, and to the shores of the Red Sea. He would have made him a Bishop of the Roman Emporium at

[2] Card. Baron. Ann. ad A. D. 229.

[3] Card. Bellarmin. de Scriptoribus Ecclesiasticis, vii. p. 41.

[4] In notis ad Martyrium S. Ignatii, § 6, p. 570, ed. Jacobson.

[5] H. Dodwell, Dissertatio de Rom. Pontif. Success. p. 95, cap. 7, p. 202.

[6] Cod. Canon. Eccl., lib. ii. cap. 2, § v.

[7] Def. Fid. Nic., ii. 8. 1, p. 270, ed. Burton.

[8] Le Moyne, Proleg. in Varia Sacra. Vol. ii. p. 29, 30, ed. 2da, Lug. Bat. 1694. Le Moyne was a native of France, but composed this work in his capacity of Theological Professor at Leyden.

Aden, near what are called the Straits of Babel Mandeb, on the southern coast of Arabia [9].

Le Moyne's theory, which was defended with ingenuity and learning, found favour in various quarters. Dr. Cave [1] adopted it in England. Dupin [2] and Tillemont [3] in France, Spanheim [4] and Basnage [5] in Holland. Assemann, in Italy [6], appeared disposed to do the same. Portus was in danger of being deprived of its most illustrious ornament,—the Bishop and Martyr, St. Hippolytus.

Errors are not without use, as ministering occasions for the firmer establishment of truth. So it fared in the present case. It happened fortunately for the honour of Portus, and for the fame of Hippolytus, that the See of that city was filled at the time to which we refer, by a Prelate eminent for his love of literature, and distinguished by zeal and enthusiasm for the past, and by affectionate regard for

[9] Le Moyne, p. 30. Non Episcopus Portus Ostiensis (he appears to confound Ostia and Portus), sed Portus Romani in Arabiâ.

[1] Cave, Historia Eccl., i. p. 102.

[2] Dupin, Biblioth., i. p. 179.

[3] Tillemont, Mémoires, &c. Vol. iii. p. 104. 310, ed. 1732. See also Lardner, Credibility, i. p. 496, ed. 4to. 1815.

[4] Spanheim, Epitome Isagogica ad Hist. Eccl., p. 131, ed. Lug. Bat. 1689.

[5] Basnage, Annales Polit. Eccles. ad A.D. 222, Roterodami, 1706.

[6] Assemann, Biblioth. Orient. Clem. Vatican., iii. p. 1, c. 7, p. 15.

the memory of his own Predecessors, Cardinal Pietro OTTOBONI. It was also a happy circumstance that his rich Library was under the judicious care of one of the most accomplished Scholars and laborious Antiquarians that Italy could then boast, Constantino RUGGIERI.

Ruggieri had been invited from Bologna to settle at Rome, where he was intrusted with the superintendence of the Press of the Propaganda.

Cardinal Ottoboni requested him to explore the archives in his own princely collection, and in other depositories within his reach, for the examination or discovery of documents relating to the See of Portus, and to the history of St. Hippolytus; and he commissioned him to communicate the result of his enquiries in a Dissertation on that subject. A happier selection could not have been made; a more competent person for such a task could not have been found. Ruggieri undertook the work, and prosecuted it with vigour and assiduity. In the year 1740 his Dissertation was ready for the press, and it was thought worthy of being printed with the types of the Vatican. It was seen and eulogized by Cardinal Lambertini, afterwards Benedict XIV.[7] But unhappily before the entire volume could be printed Cardinal Ottoboni died. Ruggieri fell into distress,

[7] Lambertini, De Servorum Dei Beatificatione, lib. i. c. iv. n. 10. It was also seen and praised by Simon de Magistris See his preface to the Roman LXX Version of the Prophet Daniel.

and died also[8]. Eighty pages of the work had been printed, but, unfortunately, there the impression stopped. The edition was dispersed; a great part of it was consumed in fireworks for the Castel S. Angelo on St. Peter's Day, and, in fine, only five copies were saved. By a fortunate coincidence, one of these five, enriched with Manuscript notes, fell into the hands of a learned Abbate of the Diocese of Porto, Achille Ruschi. In the year 1771 he had prepared the Dissertation in a complete form for publication, and it appeared at Rome in that year, sanctioned with the approbation of the Maestro di Sagro Palazzo, and inscribed to the reigning Pontiff, CLEMENT XIV.[9]

This Dissertation of Ruggieri is distinguished by elaborate research, and critical accuracy; and is composed in a clear and flowing style of terse and elegant Latinity. It would be difficult to specify any work of the same description, which surpasses it in these respects. It throws much light incidentally on the history of St. Hippolytus. It also commends itself to the respect and gratitude of Englishmen by

[8] A.D. 1766.

[9] Its title is Constantini Ruggieri De PORTUENSI S. HIPPOLYTI, Episcopi et Martyris, Sede, Dissertatio postuma, ab Achille Ruschio Portuensis Diœcesis absoluta et annotationibus aucta. Romæ 1771, *Præsidum facultate.*

It is inserted in P. G. Lumperi Historia Sanctorum Patrum August. Vindel. 1791, Pars viii., where it occupies 255 8vo. pages.

the candid spirit and courteous temper with which it appreciates the learned labours of Anglican Divines, especially Bp. Pearson, Dr. Hammond, and Bp. Bull.

It appeared convenient and requisite to refer in this place to this important work, on account of its intrinsic merits; and because, though much has been recently written concerning the See of St. Hippolytus, little mention, if any, has been made of this Dissertation; and it seems almost to have been regarded as a modern discovery, that St. Hippolytus was Bishop of Portus near Rome. But the fact is, this matter was long since set at rest; and to write more upon it now would only be *actum agere.* The work of Ruggieri, published in 1771, exhausted that subject. It refuted in the most triumphant manner the theory of Le Moyne, and established beyond the possibility of a doubt, that St. HIPPOLYTUS, the scholar of St. Irenæus, the Bishop and Martyr of the third century, whose character and works were held in high esteem and veneration by the Christian Church in his own and succeeding generations, and whose memory is revered in a particular manner by the Church of Rome, was Bishop of Portus, at the northern mouth of the Tiber, and was consequently one of the Suburbicarian Bishops of the Roman Church in the third century after Christ, whence he is often called by Ancient Authors, not only "Bishop of Portus, or of the Harbour near Rome," but is designated frequently as 'a Roman Bishop,' and sometimes as "Bishop of the City," and even "Bishop of Rome[1]:" for the ancient Roman Province was sometimes called Rome[2].

This Dissertation also possesses a peculiar interest, and is entitled to particular regard, on account of its intimate connexion with the Diocese of Hippolytus, and with the See of Rome. It owed its origin to one of the Episcopal successors of Hippolytus; it was completed by one of the Clergy of the Diocese which he had governed; it was commended by one Bishop of Rome, Benedict XIV., and was dedicated to another, Clement XIV. It was produced, therefore, under the sanction of the Bishop of Portus, and under the auspices of the Bishop of Rome. It may be regarded as embodying the judgment of the Roman Church concerning St. Hippolytus. It may

[1] See Nicephor. Callist., iv. 31, and the Authorities in Fabricius Hippolyti Opera, i. p. viii.—x., and ibid. i. 42—47, and Ruggieri, p. 478—493, (cf. pp. 518. 520. 522. 525,) where numerous examples of these designations are given; Ruggieri sums up the testimony of Christian Antiquity concerning St. Hippolytus as follows, p. 493: "All doubt concerning his Episcopate will vanish, si disertissima Prudentii, Leontii, Anastatii aliorumque qui IV Ecclesiæ Sæculo usque ad Nicephorum XIII. sæculi Scriptorem floruerunt testimonia sedulo perpendere volumus, qui uno ore testantur magnum Hippolytum Episcopum et Martyrem, vel Portuensis Ecclesiæ Pastorem, vel Romanum, id est Romanæ Provinciæ Episcopum fuisse."

[2] Ruggieri, p. 522. Veteres "S. Hippolytum Episcopum Romanum vocant; quia Portuensis Episcopus fuit, quæ urbs in Suburbicaria Provincia sita est, quam Græci *Romam* vocant."

be considered as a mark of her respectful homage to his memory, and as a pledge of her readiness to receive with favour whatsoever comes before her, bearing the impress of his venerable name.

CHAPTER II.

THE "PHILOSOPHUMENA;" OR, REFUTATION OF HERESY.

THE discovery of a theological work, dating from so early a period as the first half of the third century, is an important event in the History of the Christian Church. It is one which we ourselves have been permitted to see.

A learned Greek, Minoïdes Mynas, having been despatched by M. Villemain, Minister of Public Instruction under King Louis Philippe, with a commission to make researches in Greek Monasteries for ancient MSS., brought back some literary treasures of this description from Mount Athos in the year 1842. Some of these were deposited in the Royal Library at Paris; and among them was a Greek MS., which was first carefully examined by M. Emmanuel MILLER, already known to the world from his official position in that national collection, and distinguished by the courtesy with which he has promoted the designs of foreigners desirous of access[1] to its literary riches, and by the publication of some remains of ancient Literature. The work in question was prepared for publication under the editorial superintendence of M. Miller, and was first printed at the instance and under the encouragement of the Delegates of the University Press at Oxford, where it appeared in the year 1851—rather more than sixteen centuries after its composition.

This Volume, thus resuscitated in a remarkable manner, has been found to possess special claims to public attention. It is valuable from its antiquity, and from its contents: it is valuable as a Philosophical work, and also as a Theological and Historical one.

It consisted, when perfect, of Ten Books. Of those ten, the second and third, and the commencement of the fourth, do not appear to be now extant. The first Book is not contained in the Parisian MS., but had been already known to the world from a MS. of Cardinal Ottoboni, and from three other MSS., and had been printed in the Benedictine edition of the works of Origen[2].

The design of its Author was to give an account in the first four Books, of the various systems of ancient Philosophy, physical and ethical[3]. This portion was

[1] To which the writer of these lines had occasion to bear testimony some years since. Diary in France, p. 90. 101, 2nd edit. 1846.

[2] Vol. i. p. 872—909, ed. Paris, 1733. It was first printed from a Medicean MS. in vol. x. p. 579, of Gronovii Thesaurus Ant. Græc.

[3] The following is the Author's description of his own work,

intended to be introductory to the rest. The writer then proceeds to treat of the various heresies in order of time, which had appeared in the Christian Church, from the first promulgation of the Gospel, down to his own age. Here then, in the fifth book, the work becomes theological, and here it is his purpose to show that (as St. Irenæus[4] and Tertullian[5] had observed) the dogmatic systems of heretics had their foundation,—not in Scripture,—but in the schools of Heathen Metaphysics. He disputes their claim to originality, and treats them as plagiarisms from Pagan Philosophy.

The circumstances now stated, with regard to the materials of which this work is composed, will suggest the reason why it bore a double title. It is inscribed "PHILOSOPHUMENA; *or*, a REFUTATION of all HERESIES[6]." The former of these two titles describes the contents of the first four Books: the second title designates the succeeding five; and both titles are

lib. x. p. 311: *συμπεριλαβόντες τὰ πάντων τῶν παρ' Ἕλλησι σοφῶν δόγματα ἐν τέσσαρσι βιβλίοις, τὰ δὲ τοῖς αἱρεσιάρχαις ἐν πέντε, νῦν τὸν περὶ ἀληθείας λόγον ἐν ἑνὶ* (Cod. *ἕνα*) *ἐπιδείξομεν, ἀνακεφαλαιούμενοι πρῶτον τὰ πᾶσι δεδοκημένα.*

[4] S. Iren. ii. xiv. 2.

[5] Hæreticorum Patriarchæ Philosophi, says Tertullian adv. Hermogen. c. 8, illi sapientiæ professores de quorum ingeniis omnis hæresis animatur. De Animâ, c. 3. 23. De Præscr. Hæret., c. 30. See also S. Jerome, Epist. 84, where he speaks of Tatian and others, who had traced heresies to philosophical sects.

[6] *φιλοσοφούμενα, ἢ κατὰ πασῶν αἱρέσεων ἔλεγχος.*

applicable to the last or tenth Book, which is an Epitome of the others; and concludes with a declaration of the truth, in an address to the Gentile world.

In the sixth and seventh Books the Author is often treading on the same ground as that traversed by St. Irenæus in his work on Heresies, to whom he acknowledges his obligations (p. 202. 222), and from whom he frequently transcribes, either verbatim, or with some modifications. And here we may observe, in passing, is a circumstance which imparts a peculiar value to the newly discovered Treatise. In some instances it presents to us the original Greek of Irenæus, where till now we possessed only the Latin Version. The recovery of this work is a recovery, in part, of the text of Irenæus. In some places, it will enable a future Editor of Irenæus to restore Irenæus to himself[7].

The two last Books of this Volume are those which impart to its discovery an historical importance, which it is not easy, at present, adequately to appreciate. Time alone can show in all its bearing the full importance of this work, composed sixteen centuries ago, and discovered in the nineteenth century in a monastery of Greece, by a Greek sent from Paris by the French Government, and presented to the world for the first time, under the

[7] Some evidence of this may be seen in p. 203 of the Philosophumena, and following pages. See also the passages cited in the Ecclesiastic, LXVII. p. 47.

editorship of a French scholar, in an English University. Time, it is probable, will prove that the hand ofan all-wise and merciful Providence may be distinctly seen in its preservation, and also in its publication at the present critical juncture in the History of the Church and the World.

On what grounds, it may be enquired, do we entertain such anticipations? Because, we would reply, this newly discovered work unfolds to us, in the ninth Book, a portion of ancient Church-History with which hitherto we have had comparatively but little acquaintance, from the lack of materials for an accurate knowledge with respect to it. The writer lived at a period prior to that of our most ancient Ecclesiastical Historians. He was anterior to Eusebius by a century. He does much to fill up a chasm in the Annals of the Western Church. And the portion of Church-History with which he deals is one of great importance to us, on account of its relation to certain questions of Christian Doctrine and Church Discipline, which possess more than ordinary interest, and exercise more than common influence, at the present time.

The writer places us at Rome; he describes, with graphic exactness, events which took place in the Church of Rome in the second and third centuries after Christ. He does not speak on hearsay; but as an eye-witness. And not only so, he represents himself as occupying an important position in the Church of Rome at that time, and as taking a prominent part in the occurrences which he narrates. In a word, we have here a Suffragan Bishop of the Roman Church, in the third century, presenting us with a Memoir of his own Time.

Inasmuch as this portion of the work is of a special character, and forms a substantive whole, and possesses peculiar claims on public attention at present, it appeared to deserve consideration, whether it might not be detached from the rest, and offered separately to the English reader in his own language, as well as in the original Greek.

Hence the present publication.

The Author of the newly-discovered work might now be left to speak for himself, and to recite his own history—and it would be irrelevant and almost presumptuous to anticipate him, even by a brief summary of his narrative. But, as has been already observed, we have here an Author professing to be a Roman Bishop, and presenting us with a "History of his own time." Have we here a Roman Huet? Have we, some may say, a Roman Burnet of the third century? Is his recital trustworthy? This is an important question. The reply must depend on the writer's character. And to determine this, we must ascertain, who is the Author? what is the evidence of his veracity?

This let us endeavour to do.

CHAPTER III.

THE PHILOSOPHUMENA; OR, REFUTATION OF HERESY—ITS AUTHOR.

THE Treatise now before us bears on its exterior the name of ORIGEN[1]. It has the same name inserted in its title, and inscribed on its back. Some of the copyists, also, who transcribed it many centuries ago, assigned it to Origen. And we read, also, the words "doctrine of Origen," noted by an ancient hand in the margin of the Volume[2]. And the *first* book of it, which (as was before observed) had been already known to the world, has been ascribed to him in no less than four MSS., and had been admitted into Editions of that Father's Works[3].

Is it then from the pen of ORIGEN?

[1] Its title is, Ὠριγένους φιλοσοφούμενα, ἢ κατὰ πασῶν αἱρέσεων ἔλεγχος. Origenis Philosophumena, sive Omnium Hæresium Refutatio: e Codice Parisino nunc primum edidit Emmanuel Miller. Oxonii, e Typographeo Academico, 1851, p. 339.

[2] P. 334. Ὠριγένης καὶ Ὠριγένους δόξα.

[3] Origenis Opera, ed. Car. Delarue, iv. voll. Paris, 1733. Vol. I. pp. 873—909.

We must reply to this question in the negative.

1. It has been a common practice, in ancient and modern times, to ascribe works,—especially anonymous works,—to illustrious persons. A book, wandering about the world without a name, is, and ever has been, an unattractive thing. Such Books had a tendency to *acquire* for themselves the name of a creditable author, just as, in course of time, nameless pictures assume the name of some well-known Master. The same motives which tempted some persons, who possessed more leisure than honesty, to compose works, and then to father them on great men, induced Copyists and Dealers in Manuscripts to assign celebrated names to the works which they themselves had transcribed or had purchased, and exposed to sale[4]. The name of Origen was the likeliest to occur to a person who was in quest of an Author for the present Treatise. Origen lived at the time from which this Treatise dates, and at which its Author flourished. Origen wrote in Greek. Origen was also a voluminous Writer. It would be more difficult to say what he had *not* written, than what he *had*. He was well versed in systems of Philosophers, as well as in theories of Heretics; and, therefore, it would appear probable, that *any* anonymous Greek treatise—such as that before us—might be more safely assigned to Origen than to any one else; and that it would pass under his

[4] See Bentley, Dissert. on Phalaris, pp. 6—8, ed. Lond. 1777.

name without further enquiry. A list of works, erroneously assigned to Origen, may be seen in the "Origeniana" of Huet[5], who states various reasons for such an ascription. We shall have occasion to observe hereafter, that another anonymous work, similar in some respects to the present, *was* from the pen of the same writer as composed the present Treatise, and that *it* was ascribed to Origen.

2. With regard to the words "*Doctrine of Origen*," inscribed by some ancient Copyist on the margin of a passage in this Treatise,—these do not appear to afford any argument (as has been supposed by some) for the ascription of this work to Origen, but rather the contrary. Silius Italicus, it is well known, was an admirer and imitator of Virgil, as Virgil was of Ennius. We should be much surprised to find, in MSS. of the "Punica" of Silius, the words "Versus Silii" noted at the side of one of the lines in that Poem, as we should be surprised to find a marginal note, "Versus Maronis," annexed to a line of the Æneid. But we should not be astonished to find the words "Versus Virgilii" appended as a marginal comment to a line of Silius; or to read the words "Versus Ennii" annexed to a line of Virgil. But we should not thence infer that the "Punic War" was written by Virgil, or that the Æneid was composed by Ennius, or that the marginal annotator had ima-

[5] Appendix to lib. iii. in the ivth Volume of the Benedictine Edition, p. 321. See also the Preface to that edition, p. xiii.

gined that this was the case—but the contrary. And so the words, "*Doctrine of Origen,*" do not appear to intimate, that in the copyist's opinion "the Philosophumena" was written by Origen, but that it was composed by some person who (in his view) had imitated or expressed the opinion of Origen, in that particular passage to which the marginal note was annexed.

3. The first book of the Philosophumena has, it is true, been inserted in editions of Origen's works. But the editors of Origen have avowed their belief, that the Treatise is not his[6]: and the recent discovery of the main portion of the remainder has corroborated their judgment.

Their opinion that the work is not by Origen was grounded on a passage occurring in the first Book[7], where the Author describes himself as "a successor of the Apostles, a partaker with them in the same grace and principal sacerdocy, and doctorship[8], and as numbered among the guardians of the Church." These words, they very justly observe, could only have been employed by a *Bishop*, speaking of himself. Origen was *not* a Bishop; and he was distinguished by modesty, as well as by learn-

[6] Origenis Opera, i. p. 873, ed. Bened. 1733. Huet. Origeniana, iii. Appendix xi. vol. iv. p. 527.

[7] Philosophumena, p. 3, l. 63, ed. Miller.

[8] ἀρχιεράτεια. Compare the language of Tertullian de Bapt. c. 17: "Dandi baptismum quidem habet jus *summus sacerdos*, qui est *Episcopus*."

ing. He would not, therefore, have written thus. Therefore, the Author of the Philosophumena is not Origen.

4. Again: Origen, it is true, visited Rome at a particular time which falls within the period described in the present Volume. He *came* to Rome in the Pontificate of Zephyrinus; but his visit was of brief duration[9]. Origen was only a sojourner at Rome for a short stay. The Author of the Philosophumena appears to have spent the greater part of his life at Rome, or near it. It is clear, from the narrative contained in the portion of the Philosophumena laid before the reader in this Volume, that the Writer was at Rome, or its neighbourhood, *before* the Pontificate of Zephyrinus, that he remained there during that Pontificate—which was not a short one, but lasted nearly twenty years—and that he continued there till after the death of Callistus, the Successor of Zephyrinus. Therefore, this Treatise was not written by Origen.

5. Besides: the Author of the Philosophumena describes himself as holding an important office in the Roman Church; he represents himself as having exercised ecclesiastical discipline there, and as having

[9] ἔνθα οὐ πολὺ διατρίψας, says Euseb. vi. 14. Origen is said, by St. Jerome (de Vir. Illust. c. 61, and by Nicephorus Callist. iv. 31), to have been among the hearers who listened to a sermon by St. Hippolytus, who was Bishop of Portus near Rome. This was probably on the occasion of this visit.

separated certain persons from Church-communion by sentence of excommunication [1].

Nothing of this kind could be said of Origen; therefore we are again brought to the conclusion that the treatise before us was not written by him.

6. Men's opinions alter; their tempers are liable to change; but *facts* are immutable. Hence, in this question of authorship, it appears more safe to dwell on circumstantial evidence, than to lay stress on discrepancies of thought and manner as visible in this Treatise, when contrasted with what is seen in undoubted works of Origen.

Yet such characteristics merit consideration. And they serve to confirm the opinion already stated, that the Volume before us is not attributable to him.

7. For example; our Author [2] speaks at large of the Noetian heresy, and its adherents, who dwelt on certain detached and isolated words of Scripture, and, relying on them, contended [3] that the First and Second Persons of the Blessed Trinity are only two different Names of the same Divine Being. His language, concerning these parties, is that of one who had recently had experience of the evils to which their false teaching led, and who had been engaged in a painful struggle with the abettors of that heresy.

[1] Book ix. 12, pp. 290. 35.

[2] Lib. viii. pp. 276, 277; ix. pp. 278—291.

[3] S. Hippol. c. Noet. iii. apud Routh Script. Eccles. Opusc. p. 48. ταῦτα βούλονται οὕτω διηγεῖσθαι, καὶ αὐτοῖς μονόκωλα χρώμενοι,—

But how different is the tone of Origen when treating of the same subject! In a spirit of calm philosophy, of ingenious tolerance, and inventive charity, he suggests circumstances of extenuation, and almost pleads for the erring while he deplores their errors. He observes, what was doubtless true, that the Noetians recoiled from an opposite heresy, which disparaged the dignity of the Son, and degraded Him to the level of an ordinary man, animated by the Spirit of God, and that thus, through fear of an heretical dogma, they had lapsed unconsciously into heresy [4].

This was a liberal view. It was suited to the po-

[4] Origen, in Matth. T. xvii. § 14, says that they err *φαντασίᾳ τοῦ δοξάζειν χριστόν*, and in Johan., Tom. ii. c. 2, calls them *φιλοθέους εἶναι εὐχομένους*, and offers also some apology for them as *εὐλαβουμένους δύο ἀναγορεῦσαι θεοὺς, καὶ παρὰ τοῦτο παριπίπτοντας ψευδέσι καὶ ἀσέβεσι δόγμασι*, vol. i. p. 92. Lommatzsch. See also Origen, Fragm. ex libro in Epist. ad Titum, ed. Lommatzsch V. 287, ne videantur duos deos dicere, neque rursum *negare Salvatoris Deitatem*, unam eandemque subsistentiam Patris ac Filii asseverant, *i. e.* duo quidem nomina secundum diversitatem causarum recipientem, unam tamen *ὑπόστασιν* subsistere, *i. e.* unam Personam duobus nominibus subjacentem, qui Latine *Patripassiani* appellantur. Origen's success in dealing with Beryllus of Bosra is well known, Euseb. vi. 33. S. Jerom. de Viris. Illust. c. 60, and was probably due to his Christian temper not less than to his profound learning. *οὐκ ἂν ῥητὰ καὶ ἄῤῥητα λέγοιμεν ἂν τοὺς ἄλλα δοξάζοντας*, he says, c. Cels. v. p. 273, *οὐκ ἂν ἀποστυγήσαιεν τοὺς παραχαράττοντας τὰ χριστιανισμοῦ*, he says in a spirit which can hardly be reconciled with the language of the present Treatise.

sition and genius of Origen, who beheld the strife from afar. But it was not to be expected from one who was actively engaged in the battle. And, however this may be, certainly nothing can be more different than the temper and tone with which the Patripassian heresy and its promoters are regarded and described in the works of Origen on the one side, and in the Philosophumena on the other. He who wrote the former could hardly have written the latter. Therefore again it would appear that the Author of the Philosophumena is not Origen.

8. One more remark of this kind. The opinion of Origen with regard to future punishments is well known. The same feelings which induced him to palliate the errors of heretics, beguiled him into exercising his ingenuity in tampering with the declarations of Scripture concerning the eternal duration of the future punishment of sin [5]. Thus false charity betrayed him into heresy.

But the author of the Philosophumena speaks a very different language. He does indeed, at the close of his work, address an affectionate invitation to the heathen world. He portrays with glowing and rapturous eloquence, the dignity, blessedness, and glory of those privileges which would be theirs, if they were Christ's. He describes the immense love of God in Christ to the world, and His earnest desire for their salvation, and he exhorts them to

[5] See Origen, 19. Homil. in Jerem. Tom. iii. p. 267. De Princ. i. 6.

accept God's gracious offers, and to enter the Church of Christ. But he does not pause there. He presents to them in dark colours another alternative. He describes the woe and the anguish to which they will be doomed, if they refuse to hearken to God. He displays the boiling surge of the never-ebbing lake of fire [6], and the excruciating agonies of those who are lost. He labours to prevail on them to escape from the wrath to come, and to attain the happiness of the blessed, by declaring to them, in God's name, that the pains of hell and the joys of heaven are not temporal, but eternal [7].

Such is his mode of dealing with that solemn subject. He builds his charity on faith, and speaks the truth in love.

Probably enough has been said here and elsewhere, to satisfy the reader that the author of the Treatise before us is not Origen.

Let us pass to another name.

[6] Philosophumena, pp. 338. 4, βρασμὸν ἀενάου λίμνης.

[7] Compare the similar statements of doctrine by St. Irenæus, iv. 78; v. 27.

CHAPTER IV.

ANOTHER NAME CONSIDERED.

It is a remarkable circumstance, that very few of the Roman Poets were natives of Rome. Catullus, Virgil, Horace, Ovid, Juvenal, Persius, were born in provincial towns of Italy. Many, also, of the Roman Poets, as they are commonly called, were not even natives of the Italian soil. Africa gave birth to Terence; Lucan, Seneca, and Martial, were from Spain. The same is true also of the most distinguished Orators, Philosophers, and Historians, whose names are generally connected with that of Rome. Scarcely one of the most eminent Roman writers was born within the walls of Rome. A similar remark may be made with regard to the early Ecclesiastical writers and distinguished men of the Latin Church. Few were connected by birth, or even by residence, with Rome. Of the fourteen Bishops who governed the Church of Rome during the first two centuries, two only appear to have left any reputation for literary attainments: St. Clement, whose Epistle to the Corinthian Church still survives, and whose native country is uncertain; and Victor, supposed to have been of Africa, who is regarded as the first Ecclesiastical Author who wrote in the Latin tongue[1]. There are very few names, of literary celebrity, which are in any way connected with the Roman Church in the first three centuries of the Christian era[2].

Hence it would appear to be a not very difficult task to discover the Author of the Treatise before us. He also puts into our hands three clues for his identification—not to speak of others at present. He represents himself—

1. As a Bishop;

2. As taking an active part in the Ecclesiastical affairs of Rome; and

3. As having written other Works, whose titles he specifies.

Who was there, let us ask, that corresponded to this description?

The name of Origen, suggested by the title, being

[1] S. Hieron. de Viris Illust., c. 34. 40. 53.

[2] The Historian Sozomen, who wrote early in the fifth century, asserts that no Bishop of Rome nor any Ecclesiastic preached to the people in his age. Sozomen, vii. 19, and see the note of Valesius on the passage; and it is commonly asserted that no Bishop of Rome delivered Sermons or Homilies in public before Leo I., in the middle of the fifth century; but this seems to be hardly reconcilable with the statement of Prudentius (born A. D. 348), Hymn. xi. 25:—

> Fronte sub adversâ gradibus sublime tribunal
> Tollitur, *Antistes prædicat unde Deum.*

dismissed as untenable, perhaps the first person who would present himself to the mind of an enquirer as a candidate for the authorship of this Treatise, would be CAIUS. He is known to have been a Presbyter of the Roman Church in the episcopate of Victor, and of Victor's successor, Zephyrinus[3]; and the Author of this Treatise lived in the age of Victor and Zephyrinus. Caius is also known as a learned and eloquent man, and as having conducted a theological disputation, probably by the appointment of Zephyrinus[4], with Proclus, a leader of the Montanists at Rome, and to have gained honour by the ability which he displayed on that occasion. From the fragments which remain of his controversial argument, we learn that he wrote in Greek; and we are informed, that, being a Presbyter of Rome, he was promoted to the Episcopal order[5].

[3] Euseb. ii. 25; vi. 20. Phot. Cod. 48. Victor is generally supposed to have sate in the see of Rome from A.D. 192 to A.D. 202; Zephyrinus from A.D. 202 to A.D. 218. Jaffé Regesta Pontificum, p. 5.

[4] Hence, perhaps, the assertion of Optatus i. 9: Marcion, Praxeas, Sabellius, Valentinus et cæteri usque ad *Cataphrygas* temporibus suis a Victorino Pictaviensi, *Zephyrino Urbico* (*i. e.* Episcopo *Urbis* Romæ), et a Tertulliano Carthaginensi et aliis adsertoribus Ecclesiæ Catholicæ superati sunt.

[5] Phot. Cod. 48. *τοῦτον τὸν Γάϊον πρεσβύτερόν φασιν γεγενῆσθαι τῆς κατὰ Ῥώμην ἐκκλησίας ἐπὶ Οὐίκτορος καὶ Ζεφυρίνου ἀρχιέρεων, χειροτονηθῆναι δὲ αὐτὸν* ΚΑΙ ΕΘΝΩΝ *ἐπίσκοπον*, where Fabricius reads ΚΑΙ ΑΘΗΝΩΝ. A change in the reading may perhaps be necessary, since the Romans themselves were *ἔθνη*,

Thus he appears to satisfy some of the most important conditions of the present case.

Another point, also, may be noticed here.

Among the Works which the writer of this Treatise specifies as having been produced by himself, is one entitled "On the Substance of the Universe [6]."

Can we, then, ascertain the Author of that Work —"On The Universe?"

Photius, the Patriarch of Constantinople,—the Statesman, Scholar, and Divine, of the ninth century, in that rich storehouse of ancient literary lore, the "Library" or bibliographical record [7], which he wrote when on a diplomatic mission as an ambassador in Assyria, and in which he describes the contents of the books he had read, refers to a Work [8], called "The Labyrinth"—so named (it appears) because its Author endeavoured to track certain heretical teachers through their devious mazes, and to enable others, who might be entangled in their windings, to extricate themselves from them.

From the notice given by Photius of "The Labyrinth," we learn, that the Author of it referred his

and St. Paul calls himself *ἐθνῶν ἀπόστολον* with reference to *Rome*, Rom. xi. 13, and says *ὑμῖν τοῖς ἔθνεσιν* in writing to *Rome*. We might, therefore, perhaps read ΚΑΙ ΕΩΘΙΝΩΝ, *i. e.* though presbyter of *Rome*, Caius, as practised in writing and speaking *Greek*, was consecrated a Bishop of the *Easterns*.

[6] pp. 334. 78. *εἴσονται, ἐντυχόντες ἡμῶν βίβλῳ περιεχούσῃ περὶ τῆς τοῦ παντὸς οὐσίας.*

[7] See Fabricius, Harles. x. p. 678.

[8] Phot. Bibl. Cod. 48.

readers to another work of his own composition[9] —a work "On the Substance of the Universe[1]."

By whom then was "The Labyrinth" written?

If we can discover this, we shall have ascertained the Author of our own Treatise; and of the Treatise on the Universe. Indeed, if the question concerning the authorship of any one of these three Treatises is settled, the question also would seem to be decided concerning the other two.

[9] M. Bunsen says ("Hippolytus and his Age," i. p. 248), that the "Author of the 'Cause of the Universe' referred to the 'Little Labyrinth' as his." This is an oversight. Indeed the reverse was the fact. Photius informs us (Cod. 48) that the Author of the "Labyrinth" referred to the work on "the Universe." The ingenious author of "Hippolytus and his Age" is somewhat severe in his strictures on the Patriarch of Constantinople, and charges him not unfrequently, and not very fairly, with writing carelessly and inaccurately; but a little more attention to the words of Photius would have saved M. Bunsen from the error which has just been noticed, and from some others. A Constantinopolitan envoy in Assyria in the ninth century did not possess the advantages for the revision of his works which he would enjoy if he were resident in England in the nineteenth; and perhaps the distinguished Author of "Hippolytus and his Age" may have ample cause to ask for the indulgence which he has not been disposed to concede to Photius and to many others that might be named.

"Æquum est
Peccatis veniam poscentem reddere rursus."

[1] ἐν τῷ τέλει τοῦ λαβυρίνθου διεμαρτύρατο ἑαυτοῦ εἶναι τὸν περὶ τῆς τοῦ παντὸς οὐσίας λόγον. This work, says Photius (Cod. 48), was entitled in some MSS. περὶ τῆς τοῦ παντὸς αἰτίας, in others, π. τ. τ. π. οὐσίας: in others, περὶ τοῦ παντός. He appears to have seen various MSS. of it.

On reference to the words of Photius, already noticed, it would seem at first sight that we have there a solution of the problem.

The Labyrinth, writes Photius, has been *ascribed* to *Origen*[2], but "*they say* that it is by CAIUS[3]."

Photius then mentions that the Author of the Labyrinth referred to the Treatise on the Universe as written by himself[4].

Here our first impression would be that the question before us was now set at rest.

We feel disposed to acknowledge CAIUS, the celebrated Roman presbyter of the second and third century, as the author of the newly-discovered Treatise, and of the two other works that have been mentioned, from the same pen.

But when we proceed to examine the evidence more closely, we find reason to retract, or, at least to suspend, our judgment.

Photius appears to hesitate, except as to the identity of the Author of the Labyrinth and of the Treatise on the Universe.

He had the Treatise on the Universe as well as the Labyrinth in his Library. He describes its contents[5]. He says that this Treatise having been

[2] See also Theodoret. hæret. fabul. ii. 5.

[3] Phot. Cod. 48. Γαΐου, ὅν φασι συντάξαι καὶ τὸν λαβύρινθον. He is reporting *their* opinion when he adds, Γαΐου ἐστὶ πόνημα τῇ ἀληθείᾳ τοῦ συντεταχότος τὸν λαβύρινθον.

[4] Ibid. ἐν τῷ τέλει τοῦ λαβυρίνθου διεμαρτύρατο ἑαυτοῦ εἶναι τὸν περὶ τῆς τοῦ παντὸς οὐσίας λόγον.

[5] Cod. 48.

left anonymous, had been attributed by some to Josephus[6], by others to Justin Martyr, and by others to Irenæus, and that in a marginal note in his MS., it was assigned to Caius, "who, *they say*, wrote the Labyrinth, the author of which states at the end of it that he wrote the work on the Universe."

"*But* (says Photius) whether it was written by Caius, or by another,—*is not yet manifest to me*[7]."

Thus then, we do not feel justified in awarding

[6] The patriarch of Constantinople is charged with great want of discernment in ascribing a Christian work to a Jewish Historian. (Bunsen, pp. 151, 152.) It is not probable that such a notion was due to Photius. He expressly states, that he does *not* know *who* wrote the "Labyrinth;" which is tantamount to a declaration that he did not know who wrote the book on the Universe. Besides, the statements in Josephus concerning John the Baptist (Antiq. xviii. 5), concerning Christ (xviii. 3) (a passage generally regarded as genuine by the Christian Fathers), and concerning James the just (Ant. xx. 9), had rendered it not so improbable that Josephus should write in the tone of a Christian. After all, the other names with which that of *Josephus* is associated, viz. the names of Irenæus and Justin Martyr, afford a presumption that the name of Josephus had been introduced by an error of the copyists into the MS. seen by Photius. The word *Josephus* was often written by the ancients *Joseppus*. (See Vales. and Euseb., i. 10.) (Gr. Ἰώσηπος, Ἰώσηππος.) Whence (as I believe has been suggested by others) it is likely that the name of the Jewish Historian, Ἰώσηπος, had supplanted that of the *Christian* Historian Ἡγήσιππος. The names *Hegesippus* or (as sometimes written) *Egesippus*, and *Josippus*, are confounded in ancient MSS. (see Routh. Reliq. i. 254); and Hegesippus is often associated with Justin Martyr. Cf. Grabe, Spicileg., ii. 203—214.

[7] οὔπω μοι γέγονεν εὔδηλον.

this work, and the other two connected with it, to CAIUS, on the authority of Photius.

2. Other considerations also may deter us from making such an assignment.

Notices of Caius have been left by Eusebius and St. Jerome. It is their practice to specify the titles of the works written by the persons whom they commemorate. They mention the disputation of Caius against Montanism. But neither Eusebius nor St. Jerome mentions any one of these three works just specified, as written by Caius.

It would not be surprising that *one* of these three works should not have been noticed by them in their account of the author of the three; but it is very improbable that *all* the three should have been *omitted* by them *both;* especially in the case of such a person as Caius, who was a distinguished man, but not (as far as we know) a voluminous writer.

It is not, therefore, probable that Caius wrote these three works; and since they were all written by the same author, therefore none of them was written by Caius; and therefore it would seem, on this ground, that we must look elsewhere for the Author of the newly-discovered treatise before us.

3. Again; the Treatise before us was written *after* the Episcopate of Zephyrinus; for it speaks of his death [8].

Now the disputation of Caius with Proclus the

[8] P. 288. 96. μετὰ τὴν τοῦ Ζεφυρίνου τελευτήν.

Montanist took place in the Episcopate of Zephyrinus; and the impression we receive from Church History is, that the reputation of Caius was mainly derived from his success in that controversy. It appears to have been the principal public event of his professional life.

The Author of the newly-discovered Treatise, which, it is to be remembered, is designed to be a History of Heresies, as well as a Refutation of them, refers to other works written by himself.

Now, at the close of his Eighth Book, he comes to speak of Montanus, and of the Montanistic tenets. He treats their heresy very lightly and briefly; indeed he hardly regards it as a heresy[9]; and takes care to inform his readers that the Montanists are orthodox in the main articles of the Faith.

If a person had taken up arms against Montanism as Caius did, and if he had composed and published a Work in refutation of Montanism as Caius had done, and if his name had been honourably associated, and almost identified, with the controversy which the Church carried on against Montanus, it does not appear to be probable that he would have spoken of Montanism as the Author of this Treatise does speak.

And if the Author of this Treatise had written against Montanism, it is probable, that, since he says

[9] Philosophumena, p. 275. He calls them *αἱρετικώτεροι*, *subhæretici;* and adds, *οὗτοι τὸν μὲν Πατέρα τῶν ὅλων Θεὸν καὶ πάντων κτιστὴν ὁμοίως τῇ Ἐκκλησίᾳ ὁμολογοῦσι, καὶ ὅσα τὸ Εὐαγγέλιον περὶ τοῦ Χριστοῦ μαρτυρεῖ.*

so little on that subject in this Treatise, and since it is his practice to refer his reader to his other works as supplementary to the present, he would have referred to his work on Montanism for further information on that matter. In a word, either Caius would not have spoken of Montanism, as the Author of this Treatise speaks; or, if he had spoken as he does, he would have said something more on that subject than this Author does say.

Therefore, on this ground also, we may infer that this Treatise was not written by CAIUS.

4. Besides, the Author of this Treatise, as we have seen, touches briefly on Montanism in the Eighth Book. He then passes on to another heresy, that of the Encratites; and, after a few words upon them, he brings the Eighth Book to a close.

And how does he begin the Ninth?

With a special Preface, a somewhat elaborate one, in which he states, that having described various Heresies, and having refuted them in the *preceding* Books of this Treatise, he is now entering a new field in the *Ninth* Book, and is approaching the most difficult toil of all. And what is that? To refute the Heresies that arose *in his own time*[1].

It is clear then that he *does not* regard *Montanism* as a heresy of *his own time*.

But Caius took an active part in refuting Mon-

[1] See Book IX. pp. 278, 279. The English reader may see the passages at length in the Translation in the Second Part of the present Volume.

tanism. It was by his refutation of it that he had gained his renown. Caius would never have described Montanism as a heresy of *the past.* He would not, and could not have written, concerning it, as this Author writes.

Therefore, again, we are brought to the conclusion that this Treatise was *not* written by Caius.

5. Once more. The Montanists against whom Caius argued, referred to the *Apocalypse* of St. John, as affording Scriptural authority to their prophetical rhapsodies and millenarian reveries. Caius, who seems to have been eminent for zeal, not always guided by discretion, appears to have encountered this argument by questioning the genuineness of the Apocalypse[2]. And, there is too good reason for

[2] As this seems to be doubted by some learned persons, let it be observed that it is evident from the testimony of Dionysius, Bp. of Alexandria, in Euseb., vii. 25, when rightly punctuated, that the genuineness of the Apocalypse had been denied by some in the Church, and that it had also been ascribed by them to Cerinthus, who (they said) had assigned it falsely to St. John, in order to gain currency for his own millenarian opinions under the authority of St. John's name. And that *Caius* was among those persons in the Church to whom Dionysius refers, appears (I conceive) from Euseb., iii. 28, where, after mentioning that Caius had alleged that Cerinthus sought to gain credence for his Chiliasm under the authority of "Revelations, as if written by a great Apostle," he immediately proceeds to cite the words of Dionysius concerning *the Apocalypse of St. John*, as quoted also in another place (Euseb., vii. 25). See also Mill. Proleg. in N. T., 654; Grabe, Spicileg., t. i. p. 312; Gieseler, Eccl. Hist., § 59; who affirm that Caius attributed the Apocalypse to Cerinthus.

believing that he was carried so far in his animosity against the fanatical dogmas derived by the Montanists from the Apocalypse, that he was not satisfied with denying the genuineness of that Book, but he even proceeded to the length of ascribing it to a heretic, Cerinthus.

If it should appear improbable that such an error as this should be committed by a distinguished person like Caius, a presbyter of the Roman Church; let it be remembered that, as was before observed, the Church of Rome was not eminent for learning at that time. Let it be remembered also, that the Church of Rome herself was induced by a similar fear of erroneous consequences [3], to surrender another Canonical Book of Holy Scripture—The Epistle to the Hebrews [4]. The learning of the Church was then mainly in the East. It was by the influence of the East on the West, that the Church of Rome was enabled to recover that Epistle. It was also the influence of the Apocalyptic Churches of Asia, exerted particularly through St. Irenæus and his scholar St. Hippolytus in the West, that preserved the Apo-

[3] First of Montanism, then of Novatianism. Philastr. de Hæres., § 89.

[4] It does not appear in the ancient Canon of the Roman Church (Routh, Rel. Sac., iv. p. 2); and St. Jerome says, iii. p. 60 (ed. Bened.), "Epistola ad Hebræos quam *Latina* consuetudo non recipit;" he says, ii. p. 608, "Eam *Latina* consuetudo non recipit;" but he says "inter Scripturas Canonicas ab Ecclesiis *Orientis* suscipitur et ab omnibus retrò Ecclesiasticis Græci sermonis scriptoribus."

calypse, as an inspired work of St. John, to the Church of Rome.

It becomes then a question for consideration in reference to the present Treatise,—

Does the Author speak of the Apocalypse? If so, in what terms?

In the Seventh Book [5] he is describing the heretical opinions and licentious practices of the Nicolaitans.

He thus writes [6]. "Nicolas, one of the seven who was ordained to the Diaconate by the Apostles, was the cause of a great aggregate of evils, who, having fallen away from sound doctrine, taught indifferentism of morals and of knowledge."

The rest is important, but the text is somewhat corrupt.

The original in the Paris Manuscript is as follows: *οὗ τοὺς μαθητὰς ἐνυβρίζον τὸ τὸ "Αγιον Πνεῦμα διὰ τῆς Ἀποκαλύψεως Ἰωάννου ἤλεγχε πορνεύοντας καὶ εἰδωλόθυτα ἐσθίοντας* [7].

The sense clearly is, "Whose disciples, *i.e.* the disciples of Nicolas . . . . the *Holy Spirit* rebuked by the *Apocalypse of St. John*, committing fornication, and eating things offered to idols."

[5] P. 258.

[6] πολλῆς δὲ αὐτῶν συστάσεως κακῶν αἴτιος γεγένηται Νικόλαος, εἷς τῶν ἑπτὰ εἰς διακονίαν ὑπὸ τῶν ἀποστόλων κατασταθεὶς, ὃς ἀποστὰς τῆς κατ' εὐθεῖαν διδασκαλίας ἐδίδασκεν ἀδιαφορίαν βίου τε καὶ γνώσεως.

[7] P. 259. 95. M. Miller reads οὗ τοὺς μαθητὰς ἐνυβρίζοντας τὸ ἅγιον Πνεῦμα διὰ τῆς Ἀποκαλύψεως Ἰωάννης ἤλεγχε.

He refers to the Book of Revelation, ii. 6. 14, 15. He quotes it as inspired, and as the work of St. John [8].

But what is to be made of the words *ENTBPIZON TO?* M. Miller proposes ἐνυβρίζοντας; we may perhaps read *EN TBPEI ZΩNTAΣ*, *living in licentiousness.*

This passage, like many others in the Treatise before us, is almost a transcript from the work of St. Irenæus against heresy [1]: and thus, as was before noticed, it helps us to the original Greek of that venerable writer, in many places where we possess him now only in the old Latin version.

It may also be added, that the text of our Treatise may be often corrected from Irenæus.

[8] It is observable that the Author of the Treatise on the Universe appears to refer to the Apocalypse. See Fabric. Hippol., i. 220: λίμνη πυρός, κ.τ.λ.

[9] Another correction—perhaps more probable—is offered by a writer in the Ecclesiastic, LXVII. p. 57, ἐνυβρίζον τὸ ἁ. π. Some doubts may be felt concerning the propriety of the word ἐνυβρίζω, as applied to the Holy Spirit, and used with an accusative case; but perhaps they may be removed by reference to p. 265. 33, Θεὸς ἐνυβρίζων ἀεὶ τοῖς κατειλημμένοις, and p. 287. 50, οἱ Ἰουδαῖοι ἐνυβρίσαντες αὐτόν.

[1] The passage in Irenæus is i. 27: "Nicolaitæ magistrum quidem habent Nicolaum, unum ex VII, qui primi ad diaconiam ab Apostolis constituti sunt: qui indiscrete vivunt; plenissimè autem per Joannis Apocalypsim manifestantur qui sint, nullam differentiam esse docentes in mœchando et idolothyton edere. Quapropter dixit et de iis sermo *Sed hoc habes quod odisti opera Nicolaitarum quæ et ego odi.*" (Apoc. ii. 6.)

Irenæus, in the old Latin version, says of the Nicolaitans, *indiscretè vivunt;* which perhaps our Author represents by ἐν ὕβρει ζῶντας[2].

St. Irenæus, we know, had a great veneration for the Apocalypse, and quotes it very frequently (about thirty times) as inspired, and as the work of the holy Apostle and Evangelist, St. John. Our Author was evidently a diligent reader of St. Irenæus; and, in the passage before us, he follows Irenæus in acknowledging the Genuineness and Inspiration of the Apocalypse.

Here then, as it seems, we have sufficient proof, that the Author of this Treatise is not CAIUS of Rome.

[2] As well as by ἐδίδασκεν ἀδιαφορίαν βίου.

CHAPTER V.

ANOTHER NAME.

In the year 1551, some excavations were made on the Via Tiburtina, or road to Tivoli, not far from the church of St. Lorenzo, near Rome. The clearing away of the accumulations of an ancient Cemetery and Chapel on that site led to an interesting discovery. A marble statue of a figure sitting in a Chair was brought to light. The person there represented was of venerable aspect, bald, with a flowing beard, and clad in the Greek pallium.

The two sides and back of the Chair were found to be covered with Inscriptions in Greek uncial letters. The right side of the Chair exhibits a Calendar, which designates the days of the months of March and April, with which the xivth of the moon coincides. This Calendar, indicating the Paschal Full Moons, is constructed for seven cycles of xvi years each, dating from the first year of the Emperor Alexander Severus, which is proved from this Calendar to have been[1] A.D. 222. According to the

[1] See Clinton, Fasti Romani ad A.D. 222.

theory on which this Calendar is made, after the completion of one cycle of sixteen years, the full moons *recur* on the same day of the month, but one day earlier in the week; and the Table is formed so as to represent in seven columns the day on which the full moon falls during seven periods of sixteen years.

The other side of the Chair presents a Table, indicating the Day on which the Easter Festival falls in each year for the same period of seven cycles of xvi years, dating also from A.D. 222. When the xivth day of the moon falls on a Saturday, then the Easter festival is not to be celebrated on the morrow, or *following* Sunday, but on the Sunday after that. This regulation was in accordance with the Latin practice, but at variance with the Alexandrine custom[2], according to which the Paschal Festival might be solemnized from the xvth day of the moon. This Paschal Table, also, is constructed in seven columns of xvi years each, and indicates the day of the month in which the Paschal Festival would fall, from A.D. 222 to A.D. 333.

Many things in this Calendar betoken that it is the work of a Western[3], and that it was designed for use in the Western Church.

The carved Back of the Chair, which was some-

[2] See Ideler, Chronologie, ii. p. 220.

[3] Ideler, Chronologie, ii. p. 213: Dass er im Occident lebte wird durch die von ihm befolgte *römische* Zeitrechnung ausser Zweifel gesetzt.

what mutilated, presents a Catalogue of Titles of Works—composed doubtless by the person who occupies the chair.

This Statue thus discovered was in a fragmentary state, but was happily preserved by Cardinal Marcello Cervino, afterwards Pope Marcellus II., and was removed as a valuable monument of Christian Antiquity to the Vatican, and was restored by the aid of Roman Sculptors, as far as might be, to its pristine form, under the auspices of Pope Pius IV.[4]

The Paschal Table inscribed on the sides of the Chair dates, as has been stated, from the beginning of the reign of Alexander Severus.

He ascended the imperial throne A.D. 222, when Callistus was Bishop of Rome,—about two years after the death of Zephyrinus, the Predecessor of Callistus, that is to say, in the period described by the Author of the Treatise before us, who represents himself as living under Zephyrinus and his successor; and who in this work, which is entitled "A Refutation of *all* Heresies," mentions *no* heresy *subsequent* to that age[5].

Among the titles of Books inscribed on the Chair, we find the following—"On the Universe."

[4] A representation of the three sides of the Statue and of the inscription upon them may be seen in the edition of Hippolytus by Fabricius, pp. 36—38; p. 74, folio, Hamburgh, 1716. On the present position of the Statue in the Vatican, see Platner and Bunsen's Rome, ii. p. 320.

[5] Thus there is no mention of the Novatians, who date from A.D. 251.

Our Author (as was before noticed) refers to a book bearing *this* title, as written *by himself*.

Can we, then, ascertain who the personage, represented by the statue, is?

If so, we have a clue to the authorship of our Treatise.

In reply to this question, let it be observed, that Eusebius and St. Jerome[6] have left Catalogues respectively of Works composed by an eminent person of that age.

Suffice it to say, that in those Catalogues they specify a Paschal Cycle of sixteen years, similar to that on the Statue.

They specify also other Works, which tally in the main with the Catalogue on the Statue. Whatever discrepancies there may be in the Catalogues, arise from omissions in one of what is inserted in one or both of the other two: and thus these discrepancies are of service, as showing that the Catalogues are, in some degree at least, independent of each other.

Therefore, the Writer, whose works Eusebius and St. Jerome are describing, is the same as the Person represented in the Statue.

The Author whose Works Eusebius and St. Jerome are enumerating, is St. HIPPOLYTUS.

He then is the person represented in the Statue.

1. This conclusion is confirmed by other evidence. The person represented in the Statue is a venerable

[6] Euseb. vi. 22. S. Hieron. de Viris Illust. 61.

figure, sitting in a Cathedra,—as a Christian Teacher. Hippolytus, it is well known, was a Bishop of the Church[7]. The Statue was found on the spot described by the Christian Poet, Prudentius[8], as the site where, after St. Hippolytus had suffered martyrdom at Portus, a monument was erected to his memory. The Cemetery where the remains of St. Hippolytus were buried, was near the Church of Lorenzo, where the Statue was discovered. In the life of Pope Hadrian I.[9], it is recorded that "he repaired the Cemetery of St. Hippolytus, near the Church of Lorenzo, which had long fallen into decay." Hence, it is evident that the person represented in the Statue is the venerable Bishop of Portus, the Saint and Martyr of the Roman Church in the third century, St. Hippolytus.

[7] Euseb. and S. Jerome as before.

[8] Prudentius de martyrio Sancti Hippolyti, Peri Stephanôn, Hymn. xi. 152:

> "Roma placet sanctos quæ teneat cineres.
> Haud procul extremo culta ad pomæria vallo—
> Mersa latebrosis crypta patet foveis."

In v. 220 the author describes a neighbouring temple, of which the ruins are said by Baronius to have been extant in his time. See Fabric. Hippol. i. p. xix. note.

[9] Pope from A.D. 772—795. Anastasii Liber de Vitis Pont. in Hadrian. I. A church of St. *Hippolytus* is described by an ancient writer on the "Regiones Urbis," apud Mabillon Analecta Vetera, p. 365, as standing on the *Via Tiburtina*, near the church of S. *Laurence*. See also the authorities in Ruggieri, pp. 473, 474. 476.

Accordingly, when the Statue was removed to the Vatican, it was there received as a Statue of St. Hippolytus, and the following inscription (declaratory of its purport and discovery, and of its restoration by Pope Pius IV.) was engraved on its pedestal,

STATVA
S. HIPPOLYTI
PORTVENSIS EPISCOPI
QVI VIXIT ALEXANDRO
PIO. IMP.
EX VRBIS RVINIS EFFOSSA
A PIO. IIII. MEDICEO
PONT. MAX.
RESTITVTA.

2. The Catalogue on this Statue of Hippolytus specifies (as we have said) a work "On the Universe."

The Author of our Treatise on Heresy mentions such a Work as written by himself.

Therefore, on this ground we infer that the writer of our Treatise is St. Hippolytus.

3. Next, it may now be added, both Eusebius and St. Jerome mention "a Treatise on Heresy," as written by Hippolytus[1].

Hence it would seem to be very probable that the Author of the newly-discovered Treatise is St. HIPPOLYTUS.

And, if this is the case, then it appears that the

[1] Euseb. vi. 22. πρὸς ἁπάσας τὰς αἱρέσεις. S. Hieron. de Viris Illust. c. lxi.: "Adversus omnes Hæreses." The title of our work is, φιλοσοφούμενα, ἢ κατὰ πασῶν αἱρέσεων ἔλεγχος.

discovery of a mutilated Statue, near Rome, three hundred years ago, will have served us as a clue for ascertaining the Author of a Treatise disinterred from a Monastery in Mount Athos in 1842; and will have aided us in the attainment of certain important results (as we shall see hereafter) consequent on that fact.

Let us therefore proceed to consider whether the opinion, now stated as probable, that the present Treatise was written by St. Hippolytus, may be corroborated by other proofs.

Various works are now extant, which are attributed to St. Hippolytus, and they have been inserted as such, in the edition of his writings published by Fabricius. But, since their genuineness has been doubted by some learned men, it will be better not to draw any inferences from them, as if they were undoubtedly his. Let us reserve what is to be said on them to a later period in the enquiry, and let us construct our argument on what is unquestioned and unquestionable.

4. Let us bear in mind what is the time and place with which we are concerned in the present enquiry.

The Author, whoever he may be, lived in the Church of Rome, in the end of the second and beginning of the third century. He does not write in the language of Rome, but of Greece. And his work proves him to have been a learned and eloquent man. If what he narrates of himself be true, he had composed various other works; he was a copious writer. And he held a high position in the Roman Church for many years.

Few persons correspond to this description. Indeed we might almost say that no one does—except St. Hippolytus.

Our Treatise (as we have seen) divides itself into two portions.

1. A view of the Philosophical Systems that had prevailed in the Heathen World.

2. A Refutation of the Heresies that had arisen in the Christian Church.

Hence, the twofold title, "PHILOSOPHUMENA; *or* a REFUTATION of HERESIES."

1. With regard to the first of these titles; it is observable that St. Hippolytus is called by ancient writers "a sacred *Philosopher*[2]," and it is said, that he was eminent "in Christian *Philosophy*."

It would seem then that he had written some Philosophical work, which entitled him to this appellation. Such a work is the present, as its name intimates.

Let us now refer to the Second title, the "REFUTATION of all HERESIES."

As we have already seen, Eusebius and St. Jerome

[2] Georg. Syncell. in Chronog. ad A.D. 215, as quoted in S. Hippol. ed. Fabr., i. p. 42. See also S. Jerome Epist. ad Magn. 70, et ad Lucin. 71, where he celebrates Hippolytus for his proficiency in Philosophy.

attest that a Work "Against all Heresies" was written by Hippolytus.

The same is affirmed by numerous other Authors of antiquity [3].

2. We are also informed, that St. Hippolytus [4] spoke in strong terms of censure against Nicolas, one of the VII. Deacons, as well as against the Nicolaitans—an observable circumstance, because many of the ancient Fathers, viz. Ignatius, Clement of Alexandria, Eusebius, and Theodoret did indeed reprobate the Nicolaitans and their Heresy, but exempted Nicolas the Deacon from blame [5].

Now, in a passage already [6] cited from the Treatise before us, we have seen that the Author censures both Nicolas and the Nicolaitans; as Hippolytus is said to have done.

3. We have also seen that the Author, in that passage, as in many others of this Treatise, copies St. Irenæus.

Now, among the scholars of Irenæus, we are informed, was Hippolytus [7].

[3] Georgius Syncellus in Chronog. A.D. 215. Chronic. Paschal. Alexandrin. p. 6. Nicephorus Callisti Hist. Eccl., iv. 31, ascribes to Hippolytus, *σύνταγμα πρὸς πάσας τὰς αἱρέσεις βιωφελέστατον.* S. Epiphanius, Hær. xxxi. c. 33, refers to Hippolytus as one of his predecessors in refuting Heresy.

[4] Gobar. ap. Phot. Cod. 232, *ποίας ὑπολήψεις εἶχεν Ἱππόλυτος περὶ Νικολάου τοῦ ἑνὸς τῶν ζ διακόνων, καὶ ὅτι ἰσχυρῶς αὐτοῦ καταγινώσκει.*

[5] Gobar. ap. Phot. Bibliothec., Cod. 232. [6] See above, p. 39.

[7] Phot. Cod. 121, *Μαθητὴς Εἰρηναίου Ἱππόλυτος.*

The time in which our Author lived, the mode in which he deals with the work of Irenæus, make it probable that he was reared under his training. He writes like a scholar of Irenæus.

Again, we saw in the passage, just noticed, from our Treatise, a testimony to the genuineness and Inspiration of the Apocalypse. He speaks concerning the Apocalypse as a scholar of St. Irenæus would speak [8].

4. We have contrasted that testimony with the mode in which Caius the Roman Presbyter treated

[8] One word may be said here concerning the *date* of the Apocalypse. *St. Irenæus*, who had seen Polycarp, the scholar of St. John, asserts (v. 30) that the Revelation was seen by St. John at the end of the reign of Domitian, A. D. 96 (οὐδὲ γὰρ πρὸ πολλοῦ χρόνου ἑωράθη, ἀλλὰ σχεδὸν ἐπὶ τῆς ἡμετέρας γενεᾶς, πρὸς τῷ τέλει τῆς Δομετιανοῦ ἀρχῆς). Yet M. Bunsen declares (ii. 141), "At all events the book itself plainly says the contrary. The horizon of the Vision is the latter half of the year 68;" i. e. St. Irenæus made a mistake of about 30 years concerning what he says took place almost in his own age! In the same oracular tone, M. Bunsen pronounces (i. 25), that "the Romans knew better than any body, from their first regular Bishop, Clemens, that the Epistle to the Hebrews was not St. Paul's." Why Linus, to whom the Apostles St. Peter and St. Paul first committed that Church (Iren. iii. 3), is not to be regarded as a regular Bishop, does not appear. (Compare Bp. Pearson, Dissert., ii. v.) As to the Epistle to the Hebrews, St. Clement imitates it, and it is probable that he and the Romans knew from St. Peter (2 Pet. iii. 15), as well as from other sources, that the Epistle was St. Paul's. See the arguments of Bp. Pearson, Dissert. i. c. viii. pp. 357—359.

the same Book—the Book of Revelation. Caius, we know, flourished in the Episcopate of Zephyrinus, that is, he was contemporary with—perhaps a little senior to—our Author; and not merely was contemporaneous with him, but resided at the same place, that is, in or near Rome.

The Author of our Treatise received and revered the Apocalypse.

Let us now turn to the Catalogue of the titles of Works inscribed on the back of the Statue of St. Hippolytus [9].

There we read the following:—"A defence of the Gospel according to St. John and of *the Apocalypse* [1]."

Hence we see, that whatever might be the disposition of his Roman contemporary Caius, Hippolytus acknowledged the Apocalypse as a work of the Evangelist St. John.

Nor is this all. It appears to be probable, that St. Hippolytus wrote in defence of the Apocalypse,—*against* Caius.

For in the Chaldee Catalogue of the Works of Hippolytus [2], is one, entitled, "Chapters of St. Hippolytus, *against Caius.*"

[9] This Catalogue may be seen in Gruter. Inscript. 140; Le Moyne's Varia Sacra, i. p. 496; S. Hippol. ed. Fabricii, i. p. 38; Cave, Historia Eccl. ed. Basil, 1741, i. 104; Bunsen, "Hippolytus and his Age," i. pp. 288, 289.

[1] Ὑπὲρ τοῦ κατὰ Ἰωάννην Εὐαγγελίου καὶ Ἀποκαλύψεως.

[2] By Hebed. Jesu. See S. Hippol. ed. Fabric., i. p. 224.

It is true that Fabricius and some other learned men have conjectured that this is an erroneous transcript, and that the true reading is "against the Caianites[3],"—heretics of that name. For why, they ask, should Hippolytus have written against his contemporary Caius, who refuted heresies?

But why, we may reply, should we desert the received reading? The fact is clear, that *some* persons in the Western Church had questioned the authority of the Apocalypse. Why otherwise should Hippolytus defend it? If Caius, the Roman Presbyter, treated the Apocalypse as we have seen he did (pp. 37, 38), and yet enjoyed the reputation he did in the Church of Rome, it is probable, that many in the Roman Church (misled it is probable by zeal against Montanism) looked on the Apocalypse with suspicion. What more reasonable, then, than that Hippolytus his contemporary, the scholar of Irenæus the disciple of Polycarp the hearer of St. John the beloved disciple of Christ, when writing a defence (as we know he did) of the Apocalypse, should address it to Caius, in order to warn him and others of his error, and to endeavour to rescue them from it?

However this may be, certain it is, that the Author of our Treatise censured Nicolas, as well as the Nicolaitans; and that he had no doubts as to the genuineness and inspiration of the Apocalypse.

[3] Fabric. Bibl. Græc. Harles., vii. p. 197, ed. Hippol., i. p. 224.

Certain it also is, that in both these respects, as in many others, he followed Irenæus. It is also evident, that St. Hippolytus did the same; and that he was a Scholar of Irenæus.

Hence, then, we recognize some further confirmations of the previous probability that our Author is St. Hippolytus.

Lastly, let us consider, by way of recapitulation, the personal history of the writer of this Treatise.

5. He writes, and writes eloquently, in Greek, and yet he lived in the Western Church. Besides this Treatise against all Heresy, he wrote a Work "On the Universe." He resided at Rome, or near it, under three successive Bishops at least, that is, in the Episcopate of Zephyrinus, of Callistus, and of his successor, Urbanus, perhaps longer [4]. He was a Bishop, and speaks of his obligation as such to refute heresy, and to maintain the truth [5]. He exercised Church discipline, in resisting false doctrine, and in separating open and obstinate offenders from Communion with the Church [6]. He describes [7], with the graphic liveliness of one who had been a spectator, or had heard a description of those who were eye-witnesses of it, a remarkable scene which took place at Portus, the harbour of Rome.

[4] Book ix. passim. [5] Book i. p. 3.

[6] See p. 290, where the Author uses the plural *we*, speaking of *himself*. See the Rev. T. K. Arnold's Theol. Critic, vol. ii. p. 597. So p. 334, 78, ἡμῶν βίβλῳ. [7] P. 286.

All these and other particulars which might be noticed, correspond with what we know of Hippolytus. His name is not of Latin origin, but Greek. Being a scholar of Irenæus, he was probably of Eastern extraction. And all Antiquity witnesses that he wrote in Greek. He composed a "Refutation of Heresy," and a "Treatise on the Universe." He lived under Zephyrinus, Callistus, and his successor, probably later. He was, also, a Bishop. As has been proved in the learned Work of Ruggieri, mentioned at the commencement of this enquiry, his Episcopal See was PORTUS, the harbour of Rome. He was, therefore, a Suffragan Bishop[8] of the Roman

[8] M. Bunsen (pp. 12. 207. 214) asserts that St. Hippolytus was a member of the Roman *Presbytery*, by virtue of the office he held as Bishop of Portus. But it does not appear that in ancient times the Suburbicarian Bishops of Rome had (as such) parochial cures in the city of Rome. Nor does there seem to be any analogy, as M. Bunsen supposes, between the case of St. Hippolytus and that of the Cardinal *Priests*, who now derive titles from Churches in Rome. The present successor of St. Hippolytus, the Bishop of Porto, is *not* a Cardinal *Priest*, but is one of the Six Cardinal *Bishops*. M. Bunsen (p. 316) affirms also that Hippolytus was *Bishop of the Nations*, "For (says M. Bunsen) that *this* title is mentioned (by Photius) as given to *Caius* the Presbyter, is, as *we have seen, only a* consequence of his (Photius) having taken Caius to be the Author of the Treatise about 'the Cause of the Universe.'" Strange to say, in the sentence immediately preceding that to which M. Bunsen refers, Photius implies that he himself did *not know who* wrote that Treatise, οὔπω μοι γέγονεν εὔδηλον. (Phot. Cod. 48.) "*What Photius knew* (continues M. Bunsen) was that this author was

Church. Hence, he is often called by ancient writers, a Roman Bishop, and even (in the language of those days) a Bishop of Rome [9]. He is commemorated as such in the Roman Martyrologies. As such he was honoured by a Statue in ancient times. As such he is venerated in the Roman Breviary [10], and has been received into the Vatican, sitting in his marble Chair. He is there installed in episcopal dignity,—as a Teacher of the Western Church.

A Treatise, therefore, like the present, coming from St. Hippolytus, and recovered almost miraculously in the middle of the nineteenth century, is entitled to respectful attention, especially from the Western Church. And it may reasonably be expected, that it will not fail to receive it.

made Bishop of *the Gentiles*. *Consequently* this was a title given to Hippolytus."

Is this Church-History ?

[9] See above, cap. i. pp. 9, 10. [10] Aug. 22.

CHAPTER VI.

OBJECTIONS CONSIDERED.—PHOTIUS AND OTHERS.

A CONSIDERABLE amount of evidence may be adduced to authorize the ascription of a Work to a particular writer, and such evidence may be sufficient to produce conviction, when considered by itself; and yet, when the question is subjected to further examination, and arguments are adduced on the other side, that conviction may be weakened, and the mind may waver concerning the soundness of its former persuasion.

We have been engaged in considering the question,—

To whom is the newly-discovered Treatise on Heresy to be assigned?

We have been led to observe, that the Candidates for its authorship cannot be numerous. We have examined the pretensions of two Competitors—Origen, and Caius of Rome, who appeared at first to have strong claims on our attention. We have seen that the Work could not be adjudged to either of them.

Another name was then adduced,—that of St. Hippolytus. And there seemed to be sufficient reason for awarding this Volume to him.

This part of our task has been performed with comparative ease. Others have smoothed the way. More than a year ago, a learned English Theologian[1], speaking of this newly-discovered Treatise, assigned it to St. Hippolytus; and, since that time, a Work has been published, which adduces some cogent arguments in favour of the same opinion, by a writer long known to the world—the Chevalier Bunsen[2].

[1] Archn. Churton, page xxvii. of the Preface to his Edition of Bp. Pearson's Vindiciæ Ignatianæ, where he calls this Treatise "Opus nuper felicibus Academiæ Oxoniensis auspiciis publicâ luce donatum, Christianæ Antiquitatis cultoribus acceptissimum, *Origenis*, ut titulus præfert, sive ut mihi cum Viris compluribus bene doctis probabilius videtur, S. Hippolyti." This preface is dated vii. Kal. Feb. MDCCCLII.

[2] In the First Volume of "Hippolytus and his Age," by C. C. J. Bunsen, D.C.L., Four Volumes, Lond. 1852. It appears that this Volume was written in June and July, 1851. It is much to be regretted that M. Bunsen's work should be often marred by great confidence of assertion on very slender grounds, and sometimes on none at all. And some of those assertions concern the most vital articles of Christian faith and practice, as well as important questions of Church History. And these asseverations are accompanied with contemptuous insinuations against the literary honesty of others—especially of the dead*. It is with unfeigned reluctance that the writer of these lines expresses himself

* *E. g.* p. 316: "It is a *fable*, whether *invented* or picked up somewhere by Cave, that Hippolytus was Clemens' disciple." Again, p. 263, concerning Bp. Bull: "Bull *often* makes assertions also which have no foundation."

But "Audi alteram partem" is the counsel which is suggested by experience in questions of this description. We cannot justly feel satisfied with any conclusion, till we hear what may be adduced against it. And it is not to be denied, that, in the present case, there is much to be said which might seem at first to be of sufficient weight to constrain us to suspend our judgment, if not to incline it in another direction.

Let us, then, address ourselves to the consideration of this *other* evidence.

1. The learned Patriarch of Constantinople, Photius, had in his Library a Work ascribed to St. Hippolytus: and it was a Work "Against Heresy."

In his bibliographical Journal, composed in Assyria, Photius describes it thus [3].

"A biblidarion" (a diminutive of little book) "of Hippolytus—was read to me [4]. Hippolytus was a

thus. But a sense of obligation compels him to say, and he has considered it a duty to adduce reasons in the course of this volume for his conclusion, that his exhortation to the reader of M. Bunsen's Volumes must be, Νᾶφε, *καὶ μέμνασ᾽ ἀπιστεῖν.*

[3] Phot. Cod. 121. *ἀνεγνώσθη βιβλιδάριον Ἱππολύτου· Μαθητὴς δὲ Εἰρηναίου ὁ Ἱππόλυτος· ἦν δὲ τὸ σύνταγμα κατὰ αἱρέσεων λβ΄. ἀρχὴν ποιούμενον Δοσιθεανοὺς καὶ μέχρι Νοητοῦ καὶ Νοητιανῶν διαλαμβάνον* (sic Bekker, pro vulg. *διαλαμβανόμενον*) *ταύτας δέ φησιν ἐλέγχοις ὑποβληθῆναι ὁμιλοῦντος Εἰρηναίου, ὧν καὶ σύνοψιν ὁ Ἱππόλυτος ποιούμενος τόδε τὸ βιβλίον φησὶν συντεταχέναι.... λέγει δὲ ἄλλα τε τινὰ τῆς ἀκριβείας λειπόμενα, καὶ ὅτι ἡ πρὸς Ἑβραίους ἐπιστολὴ οὐκ ἔστιν τοῦ Ἀποστόλου Παύλου.*

[4] It is well known to have been a common practice of students

Scholar of Irenæus. This Book is a 'TREATISE against THIRTY-TWO HERESIES;' it begins with the Dositheans, and goes down to Noetus and the Noetians: and the Author says, that he composed it as a synopsis of Lectures[5] delivered *vivâ voce* by Irenæus, in refutation of these heresies. There are some things deficient in accuracy in this book,—one is the assertion, that the Epistle to the Hebrews is not by the Apostle St. Paul[6]."

Here, then, we are met by a difficulty.

Photius had a Work before him—a Work on Heresy—a Work written by St. Hippolytus. He proceeds to describe it. How does it correspond with the Treatise before us? *His* Volume is a little book—a single *βιβλιδάριον; ours* is a large one: it consists of ten *βιβλία.* His began with the Dositheans, and ended with the Noetians; ours begins its catalogue of heresies with the Naassenes, and

in ancient times rather to *hear* books *read to them* by slaves called *anagnostæ*, than to read them with their own eyes. The pathetic lament of Cicero for the death of his own *anagnostes* will occur to the reader. Hence the expression of Photius.

[5] These Lectures were probably prior to the V. Books,—or rather portions of V. Books,—of Irenæus against Heresies, now extant, which were published at intervals A.D. 180—185, according to Bp. Pearson, Diss. Post. ii. xiv. p. 527. Perhaps the date should be carried lower: the third book was written under Eleutherus (iii. 3), whose Episcopate is extended by some to A.D. 192. Jaffé, p. 4.

[6] Cp. Euseb., vi. 20, where he says that Caius also did not acknowledge the Epistle to be by St. Paul, and even yet (adds Eusebius) some at Rome do not receive it as St. Paul's.

ends with the Elchasaites. His professed to be a compendium of *oral* discourses by Irenæus[7]; ours makes no such announcement. In the Treatise which Photius read, Hippolytus said that the Epistle to the Hebrews was not written by St. Paul. In the books which remain of our Treatise, there is no such assertion[8].

2. Can, therefore, our Treatise be the same Work as that read by Photius?

Attempts have been made to prove them identical[9].

[7] It could not have been a compendium from the *written* Treatise of Irenæus against Heresy, in V. books; for no mention is made there of the Dositheans or Noetians.

[8] These difficulties have been well stated by a learned writer, the Rev. Robert Scott, in an able Article in the Rev. T. K. Arnold's Theol. Critic, vol. ii. p. 524.

[9] M. Bunsen says, p. 16: "The description (given by Photius) *tallies so exactly with the book before us, that it cannot have been given of any other.*" Again, p. 25: "The rest of the account given by *Photius is positive and accurate enough to prove* that we have the work he speaks of before us." And again, p. 26: "*Photius evidently* found these Judaic sects, as we do, at the head of his Treatise, but *expresses himself inaccurately*" (that is, Photius is to be taxed with carelessness, because M. Bunsen is confident). He then proceeds thus: "*Instead* of calling them Ophites (says M. Bunsen), Photius designates them as Dositheans." Again, p. 26: "The last of the heresies treated by Hippolytus, in the work read by Photius, was that of the *Noetians;* and so in fact *it is in our book.*" Again, pp. 120, 121: "Looking back to the points I undertook to *prove*, I believe I have *established* them *pretty satisfactorily.*" "Our work begins in fact, as Photius says, so too does it end."

It was requisite to notice these assertions of M. Bunsen, for the

And it has been asserted, without any hesitation, that they are one and the same Work. But, on consideration of the evidence, few persons, it is probable, will concur in that opinion. No Procrustean process of pressure can make a Treatise in *ten biblia* to coincide with the single *biblidarion* described by Photius.

3. Besides,—looking at the contents of our Treatise, we find a copious account of proceedings which took place in the Church of Rome in our Author's lifetime, and in which he had an active share. Considering the nature of those proceedings, any one who remembers the relation of Photius, Patriarch of Constantinople, to the Bishop of Rome and the Roman See, and who recollects his long and vigorous struggle against what he regarded as its usurpations, will feel a strong persuasion, that if Photius had ever had before him the narrative contained in this Treatise, he would not have failed to notice it in his account of the Work, and would have dwelt upon the events there recorded, in his controversies with the Roman See.

4. Once more: We have seen that the Author of our Treatise claims the Work, "On the Universe," as his own [1]. But Photius (as we have also seen [2])

purpose of putting the reader on his guard, and of showing that affirmations from the same quarter on more important matters cannot be received without caution, although they may be made without hesitation.

[1] P. 334.

[2] Above, p. 33; p. 55, *note*.

did not know who wrote that Work on the Universe. He says that it has been ascribed to Justin Martyr, Caius, and others;—but has no suspicion that it was written by Hippolytus. Hence, again, it is clear, that our Treatise is *not* the Little Book on Heresy by Hippolytus, which Photius saw and describes.

5. Here, let us candidly avow, is an embarrassment: it must not be disguised or extenuated. Let us not close our eyes to it. Rather let us meet it, in hope, that, if our former conclusion was right, this, which is now a difficulty, may eventually become an ally. St. Hippolytus, it is confessed by all, wrote a Treatise on Heresy. Photius read a Work on Heresy, written by Hippolytus. Our Treatise is a Treatise on Heresy, and is different from the Book read by Photius. And it is anonymous.

Has not, therefore, the Little Book read by Photius the fairer claim of the two to be regarded as *the* Work on Heresy written by Hippolytus, and mentioned by Eusebius and Jerome and others, and received by the world as such?

Again: if we ascend upward from the times of Photius to an earlier period, we find additional evidence of the existence of a Work on Heresy written by Hippolytus,—and a Work *differing* from the Treatise before us.

6. For example: Gelasius[3], Bishop of Rome at

[3] Gelas. ap. Bibl. Patrum Max. Lugd., viii. p. 704. Fabric. Hippol., p. 225.

the close of the fifth century (A. D. 492—496), in his Treatise "On the two Natures of Christ," refers to a Work by St. Hippolytus on Heresy, and cites a passage from it. He introduces his quotation thus[4]: "From Hippolytus, Bishop and Martyr, of the Metropolis of the Arabians, in his Memoria Hæresium." He then recites (not in the original Greek, but in Latin) an extract; a very beautiful passage, in which Hippolytus collects from Holy Scripture some of the proofs, displayed by our Blessed Lord upon earth, of His Humanity, and also of His Divinity.

The passage which Gelasius cites *does not appear* in our Treatise.

Here, however, it may be observed, that there is good reason for doubting, whether the work above mentioned, ascribed to Gelasius, Bishop of Rome, is really his. Cardinal Baronius[5] states some reasons for questioning its genuineness. And, in addition to the arguments used to that effect by the learned Cardinal, it may be observed, that it is hardly possible that Gelasius Bishop of Rome should not have known that St. Hippolytus was Bishop of Portus, or at least should have imagined that he was Bishop of

[4] Hippolyti, Episcopi et Martyris, Arabum Metropolis, in Memoria Hæresum. Hippolytus could hardly have been Bishop of Bozra, for that See appears to have been filled by Beryllus to the year 244. See Ruggieri, pp. 354, 355.

[5] Ad A. D. 496. See also Ruggieri ap. Lumper. Hist. Eccl., viii. 539.

the metropolis of Arabia,—that is, of Bosra [6]. It is true that St. Jerome, who was Secretary to Pope Damasus, did not know the name of the See of Hippolytus [7]. But of this more hereafter. And ignorance is one thing; error is another. St. Jerome, born in the West, but living in the East, might not know the name of a Bishop who had flourished in the West. But it is hardly possible that Gelasius, a Bishop of Rome, should not have known that St. Hippolytus had been a Suffragan of his own See; or, at least, that he should have imagined that Hippolytus, Bishop of Portus, near Rome, was Bishop of Bosra in Arabia.

The fact seems to be, as indeed has been already suggested by others [8], that this error in the designation of Hippolytus was derived from the erroneous Latin version, by Ruffinus, of a passage in the Ecclesiastical History of Eusebius, where speaking of the learned ecclesiastical writers flourishing at a particular period, he says: "Of these, Beryllus left Epistles, and various choice extracts [9] from other writings. He was Bishop of the Arabians in Bosra. And likewise Hippolytus,—who was president of some other Church [1]."

[6] See Bingham, ix. ch. 1, and Carolus a S. Paulo Geographia Sacra, p. 295, ed. 1703, where Bosra is called the Metropolis of Arabia in Episcopal subscriptions.

[7] S. Hieron. Script. Eccl., 61. Hippolytus cujusdam Ecclesiæ Episcopus; *nomen* quippe urbis scire non potui.

[8] Cotelerius, Monument. Eccl. Græc. ii. 639. Paris, 1681.

[9] φιλοκαλίας.

[1] Ἐπίσκοπος δ' οὗτος ἦν τῶν κατὰ βόστραν Ἀράβων, ὡσαύτως δὲ

But whether this extract was really made by Gelasius, Bishop of Rome, or no, (which is not of much moment to the question before us,) we must now revert to the fact, that we look in vain for the passage, in our Treatise on Heresy.

On the other hand, it may be remarked, that the same passage exists in the original Greek, not in the "Treatise of Hippolytus against Noetus," as has been affirmed [2], but in his Exposition of the Second Psalm, and is so cited by Theodoret [3].

We may offer one more remark on this quotation, by Gelasius, before we close this Chapter; but in the mean time perhaps it may be affirmed that not much can be inferred from the words of Gelasius, either for or against the genuineness of our Treatise.

7. We ascend to an earlier period than Gelasius, and enter the fourth century.

A Bishop of Alexandria, Peter, who lived early in that century, refers to St. Hippolytus, whom he calls "a witness of Godliness," (probably alluding to his

καὶ Ἱππόλυτος, ἑτέρας που καὶ αὐτὸς προεστὼς ἐκκλησίας, which is thus rendered by Ruffinus, "Erat inter cæteros et Beryllus scriptor præcipuus, qui et ipse diversa opuscula dereliquit. Episcopus hic fuit apud *Bostram Arabiæ urbem maximam, erat nihilominus et Hippolytus* qui et ipse aliquanta scripta dereliquit Episcopus." The Latin words of Gelasius, "Episcopus Arabum Metropolis," seem to be derived from this version by Ruffinus.

[2] M. Bunsen says, i. p. 206, "The passage (quoted by Gelasius) *exists* in the special Treatise against Noetus." A passage *like* it is found in that Homily, chap. xviii. vol. ii. p. 19, ed. Fabric., and bears marks of being from the same author.

[3] Theodoret, Dial. ἀσύγχυτος. Vol. iv. Pars i. p. 132, Halæ, 1772.

Martyrdom,) and Bishop of Portus, near Rome[4]. He then proceeds to adduce a citation from a Work[5] of "St. Hippolytus, Against all Heresies." The quotation refers to the error of the Quartodecimans (that is, of those who kept Easter as the Jews did the Passover, on the xivth day of the Moon), and Peter states that he quotes verbally[6] from that Work of Hippolytus.

Let us now refer to our own Treatise. We there find that the Author speaks of the Quartodecimans[7], and that what he there says, bears some resemblance to the quotation of the Alexandrine Bishop, but is not identical with it[8].

[4] Chronicon Paschale sive Alexandrinum, p. 6. See S. Hippol. Fabric. i. p. 224; cf. ibid. p. 43.

[5] σύνταγμα. [6] ἐπὶ λέξεως. [7] P. 274, 85.

[8] M. Bunsen says (p. 15), the passage quoted by Peter "*must* have existed in our work," *i. e.* in the Philosophumena; and he pronounces the text of the Philosophumena to be defective, because it does not contain the passage quoted by Peter, but only presents "an abstract of it carelessly made." (p. 110.) An Author who writes thus would seem to imagine himself to be like Tiresias among the Shades, who is said

Οἶος πεπνῦσθαι· τοὶ δὲ σκιαὶ ἀΐσσουσιν.

The reader may compare the two passages:—

Quotation from Hippolytus against Heresy in Paschal Chronicle, p. 6.	*Philosophumena, or Refutation of Heresies*, pp. 274-5.
ὁρῶ μὲν (read ὁρῶμεν) ὅτι φιλονεικίας τὸ ἔργον· λέγει γὰρ οὕτως, "ἐποίησεν τὸ πάσχα ὁ χριστὸς τότε, τῇ ἡμέρᾳ καὶ (ᾗ ?)	ἕτεροί τινες φιλόνεικοι τὴν φύσιν. . συνιστάνουσι δεῖν τὸ πάσχα τῇ τεσσαρεσκαιδεκάτῃ τοῦ μηνὸς φυλάσσειν κατὰ τὴν

Hence then it is manifest, first, that the Bishop of Alexandria had *some* work of Hippolytus on Heresy in his possession; and, secondly, it is evident that our Treatise was not that work.

To these considerations must be added another; namely, that the work to which these Authors refer,—namely, Photius, Gelasius, and Peter of Alexandria,—as written by Hippolytus, appears to have *borne his name;* and to have been generally received as his. But our Treatise has not the name of Hippolytus prefixed to it.

8. *If* then the alternative lay between the Book seen and quoted by Photius and others on the one side, and our Treatise on the other, it would seem requisite to ask for more time to consider, before we ventured to arbitrate between the two, and to reject the former work, and to receive the latter, as *the* Treatise against Heresy written by Hippolytus, and recognized by Antiquity as such.

ἔπαθεν, διὸ δεῖ κἀμὲ δεῖ ὃν τρόπον ὁ Κύριος ἐποίησεν, οὕτως ποιεῖν." πεπλάνηται δὲ, μὴ γιγνώσκων ὅτι τῷ καιρῷ (ᾧ?) ἔπασχεν* ὁ χριστὸς οὐκ ἔφαγεν τὸ κατὰ νόμον πάσχα. Οὗτος (Αὐτός?) γὰρ ἦν τὸ πάσχα τὸ προκεκηρυγμένον, καὶ τελειούμενον τῇ ὡρισμένῃ ἡμέρᾳ. τοῦ νόμου διαταγὴν ἐν ᾗ ἂν ἡμέρᾳ ἐμπέσῃ. . . οὐ προσέχοντες ὅ τι Ἰουδαίοις ἐνομοθετεῖτο, τοῖς μέλλουσι τὸ ἀληθινὸν πάσχα ἀναιρεῖν (Christum) τὸ εἰς ἔθνη χωρῆσαν, καὶ πίστει νοούμενον οὐ γράμματι νῦν τηρούμενον.

* Cf. S. Hippol. (fragm. lib. i. de Paschate) ibid. p. 6. τὸ Πάσχα οὐκ ἔφαγε, ἀλλ' ἔπαθε (sc. χριστός). Fabr. Hippol. p. 43.

9. *But* let us now pass on to observe, that this is *not* the case.

It may perhaps be allowed to be *probable*, that St. Hippolytus wrote *two* works against Heresy.

It is not uncommon for Authors to write a brief Essay on a subject, and then, subsequently, to expand it into a larger Treatise.

Cicero amplified, in his De Oratore, what he had before treated in his earlier works on Rhetoric[9]. St. Paul's Epistle to the Romans is an expansion of that to the Galatians. Tertullian goes over some of the same ground in his "ad Nationes" that he had previously traversed in his "Apologeticus." Origen composed three different editions of Scriptural Expositions[1]. St. Augustine composed twelve books, "de Genesi ad literam," as a development of what he had before previously written in one book[2].

Let us remember, also, the nature of the subject; Heresy. Heresy is not stationary; but is ever receiving new accessions, and showing itself in new forms. New refutations are requisite, as new errors arise. It is, therefore, not unlikely, that, if new heresies had arisen in his later years, and if the old ones were not

[9] De Oratore 1, 2. Vis enim, ut mihi sæpe dixisti, quoniam quæ pueris aut adolescentulis nobis ex commentariolis nostris *inchoata* et *rudia* exciderunt vix hâc ætate digna, aliquid *iisdem de* rebus politius a nobis perfectiusque proferri.

[1] Sedulius, in præfat. operis Paschal., "Cognoscant Origenem *tribus editionibus* prope cuncta quæ disseruit aptavisse." See Vales in Euseb. vi. 38.

[2] S. Aug. Retractationes, i. 18.

extinct, Hippolytus would have written in continuation and expansion of what he had formerly published concerning Heresy.

10. In the present case, however, we need not rest on probabilities. We have good reason for believing, that St. Hippolytus wrote *two* Treatises against Heresy: first, a Compendium; then, afterwards, a longer Treatise. In speaking thus, we think that we have the authority of St. Hippolytus himself[3].

In the Introduction to the newly-discovered Treatise, the Author thus writes:—"No fable of those who are famous among heathens is to be rejected. Their incoherent dogmas are rather to be regarded as credible, on account of the greater infatuation of heretics, who have been supposed by many to worship God, because they hide and disguise their ineffable mysteries. *Whose dogmas we expounded, some time ago*[4], *with brevity, not exhibiting them in detail, but refuting them rather in rude*

[3] I am indebted to the learned Author of the Papers in the Ecclesiastic, Nos. LXVI., LXVII., LXXXIV., for the first suggestion of this solution. See No. LXXXIV. p. 399. The same explanation has been also given by Duncker, as mentioned by Jacobi, de Basilidis Sententiis, Berlin, 1852. Let me add as a conjecture, that as the smaller and earlier work of Hippolytus, his *βιβλιδάριον* against Heresy was due to the oral discourses or Lectures of his master Irenæus, so the idea of this later and larger Treatise was suggested by the Work of Irenæus against Heresy, which we now possess, and that the "biblidarion" bore very much the same relation to the Lectures, that the "Philosophumena" does to the Ἔλεγχος of Irenæus.

[4] *πάλαι.*

generality; not thinking it would[5] *be requisite to drag their secrets to the light,*—in order that when we had shown their tenets as it were darkly, they being filled with shame lest we should speak out their mysteries plainly, and show them to be infidels, might in some degree relinquish their irrational principles and godless designs. But since I perceive that *they have no feeling of regard for our moderation,* and that they do not consider that God, Who is blasphemed by them, is long-suffering, in order that either through compunction they may repent, or if obstinate they may be justly punished, *I am constrained to come forward,* and to disclose their secret mysteries, which they deliver with great confidence to those who are initiated by them. And though the subject compels us to launch forth on a wide sea of demonstration, I do not deem it fit to be silent, *but will exhibit in detail the dogmas of them all.* And though our argument will be long, yet it seems right not to flag. For we shall bequeathe to posterity a no slight boon, so that they may no longer be deceived, when all behold manifestly the secret orgies of heretics, which they deliver only to their neophytes."

11. Let us remember, also, that, as we learn from Photius, the biblidarion of Hippolytus terminated with Noetus and the Noetians.

[5] μὴ ἂν ἄξιον, Codices depravatè, says M. Miller, who has substituted ἀνάξιον, which, however, does not seem necessary, and gives a doubtful sense.

Now it appears from our Treatise, that *after* Noetus, another Heresy broke forth, derived in part from that of Noetus,—namely, the CALLISTIAN Heresy; and that it made great havock in the Roman Church, and that our Author had the principal share in checking its progress. Accordingly, in the Ninth Book, he begins as it were afresh, and devotes a great part of that Book to the Callistian Heresy, and to another still later Heresy, which he describes as owing its progress at Rome to the Callistian, viz.,—the Heresy of the Elchasaites.

We see, then, that our Author had written an earlier work on Heresy; and, in the History of the Callistian and Elchasaite Heresies *subsequent* to the Noetian, we perceive another very good reason why he should have written a Second Treatise on Heresy, if the former Work which he had written had *ended* with Noetus.

12. Thus, then, we find it stated as a fact by our Author in the newly-discovered Treatise,—

1. That he had already, some time since (πάλαι), written a book against Heresy;

2. That the former Work was a compendious one; and

3. He states some reasons for writing *another* Treatise more in detail.

13. We are, therefore, now led to enquire, whether we can find an earlier and shorter Work on Heresy which we may assign to our Author.

Now, supposing our Author to be St. Hippolytus

—(which we have good reason to do, from our Author's age and position in the Western Church, and from his authorship of a "Work on the Universe," quoted in this Treatise as written by our Author, and known from the list on the Statue to be written by *Hippolytus*)—we find that a shorter work on Heresy is ascribed to him, corresponding in character to that of which we are now in search.

Such a Work, we say, was written by Hippolytus[6]; it was inscribed with his name, and was read by Photius. It was a *short* Work—for it is called *biblidarion.* It was probably not in several successive Books, like our Treatise, but contained in a *single Book,* like[7] that annexed to the Præscriptiones of Tertullian. And it is not unlikely that the Heresies were *numbered* in it consecutively, and that each was despatched in a few paragraphs respectively, as is the case in the work on Heresy by Philastrius[8] (circ. A.D. 350). Otherwise, we can hardly see why Photius should call it "A Little Book against *thirty-two* heresies." For would he have taken the pains to *count* them? Would he have described it as such? It seems also to have been written a considerable time *before* our work, for it was not formed from

[6] It may be observed here, that Trithemius de Script. Eccles., No. XXXVI., A.D. 1494, in his catalogue of the works of Hippolytus, enumerates, "Contra Omnes Hæreses, lib. iii."

[7] Which, in a MS. of Semler, is entitled "Adversus omnes Hæreses."

[8] Bibl. Pat. Max. v. p. 701.

the Work of Irenæus against Heresy, but from his *lectures*, and was published as a compendium of them. The work of Irenæus was finished about A.D. 190, and he died about A.D. 202; whereas our Author refers to facts that did not take place till about A.D. 220. It also *ended* with the Noetians, and does not appear to have said any thing of the Callistians, and certainly did not go on (as ours does) to describe the Heresy of Elchasai.

14. Hence, therefore, the description by Photius of *another* work on Heresy by *Hippolytus*, *different* from our Treatise, so far from invalidating the evidence already adduced to show that our Treatise was written by Hippolytus, comes in as an additional proof that the newly-discovered Treatise is from him.

Our Author wrote *two* works on Heresy. The present Work is described by him as the latter and longer work of the two. If then our Author is Hippolytus, we may expect to find another earlier and shorter work than the present written by Hippolytus. We do find such a work. Therefore a new argument thence arises—that our Author is Hippolytus.

15. Here, also, the other difficulties vanish which were noticed in this chapter.

Gelasius—or whoever is the Author of the Treatise above mentioned as bearing his name—certainly did not quote from our Treatise: we have seen good reason for thinking that he did not quote from a Treatise on Heresy by Hippolytus, but from another work of his. It may be, however, that the passage he cites was in the shorter Treatise seen by Photius, as well as in the Exposition of the Psalms by Hippolytus. And the term by which he describes the work from which he quotes, viz., "*Memoria* Hæresium," would be very applicable to a brief Notice of Heresies, such as that which Photius describes.

The same may be said of the passage cited by Peter of Alexandria. It proves that there was a work on Heresy by Hippolytus, *different* from ours. His extract is from that work. It *differs* from what is said on the Quartodecimans in our Treatise, and yet in some degree *resembles* it in argument and language. It looks as if it came from the same pen as that which wrote our Treatise, though it is itself not the same as what is written there on the same subject. The author of our Treatise had written another Treatise on Heresy. Therefore this quotation by Peter, Bishop of Alexandria, comes in also as an additional proof that our Treatise was written by Hippolytus.

We may find perhaps, hereafter, that the "Little Book" of Hippolytus, seen and described by Photius, may prove of still more service to us yet. But let us pause here for the present.

CHAPTER VII.

OBJECTIONS CONSIDERED.

NARRATIVE CONCERNING THE CHURCH OF ROME.

A CONSIDERABLE portion of our Author's Ninth Book is occupied with a narrative of what he himself saw and did at Rome in the beginning of the third century. This part of his work, in the writer's own words, accompanied with an English translation, will be found in the second portion of the present volume, and the reader's attention is now requested to that narrative.

On reference to it, he will see that the author begins with describing a particular heresy, the NOETIAN. This consisted mainly in a denial of the distinct Personality of God the Father and God the Son, and in an assertion, that the words Father and Son were merely different appellations assigned to the same Divine Being accordingly as He existed in different relations, or manifested Himself in different modes[1]. Hence, its promoters were called *Patripas-*

[1] See Philosoph. pp. 284, 285.

sians; in other words, they were charged with affirming that it was the *Father Who suffered* in fact, although He whose Passion is described in Holy Scripture is called the Son. Hence, also, they were regarded as originators of the heresy which afterwards became more notorious under the name of Sabellianism, from its principal promoter SABELLIUS, who followed in the track of Noetus [2].

Our Author traces the course of Noetianism from Smyrna to Rome. It is said by him to have made its appearance in the Italian capital when Zephyrinus was Bishop of the Church there. It was not altogether a new dogma at Rome, for, according to Tertullian, a heresy had been there propagated by Praxeas, who afterwards passed over into Africa, which resembled that of Noetus. Perhaps it was received at Rome with less suspicion [3], because Praxeas

[2] Sabelliani (says S. Aug. de Hæres. XLI.) a Noeto defluxisse dicuntur, nam et discipulum ejus quidam perhibent fuisse Sabellium.

S. Augustine says that in his days the name of Noetians was almost obsolete (de Hæres. XLI.). Noetiani difficile ab aliquo sciuntur, Sabelliani autem sunt in ore multorum. Nam et Praxeanos eos a Praxeâ quidam vocant, et Hermogeniani vocari ab Hermogene potuerunt: qui Praxeas et Hermogenes eadam sentientes in Africâ fuisse dicuntur. Nec tamen istæ plures sectæ sunt, sed ejusdem sectæ plura nomina . . .; and of the Sabellians he says, Patripassiani quam Sabelliani pluries nuncupantur.

[3] Tertullian, adv. Praxeam I., Praxeas Episcopum Romanum agnoscentem jam prophetias Montani . . . coëgit literas pacis revocare. Ita duo negotia diaboli Praxeas Romæ procuravit:

had made himself conspicuous by the part he took against the Montanist heresy, which was obnoxious to the Roman Church, and which was combated by the Roman presbyter Caius, in the time of Zephyrinus[4].

However this may be, our Author relates[5], that the Noetian heresy obtained great success at Rome. Its principal teacher, Cleomenes, organized a congregation there, and attracted numerous disciples. At length, partly by persuasion, partly by corruption, he won over the Bishop of Rome, Zephyrinus, whom our Author represents as covetous and illiterate; and so he obtained Episcopal sanction for the heresy of Noetus.

The principal agent in this unhappy work of apostasy, according to our Author's relation, was Callistus. He represents Callistus as an ambitious person, aspiring to the Episcopal chair at Rome. He exhibits him as the confidential counsellor of Zephyrinus, and as exercising a dominant influence over his mind. In a word, he intimates that Zephyrinus was Bishop only in name, while, in fact, Callistus administered the affairs of the Roman Church.

Our Author introduces an episode concerning the early career of Callistus; which the reader may

prophetiam expulit et hæresim intulit. Paracletum fugavit et Patrem crucifixit.

Praxeas and Noetus are mentioned as distinct persons by Philastrius de Hæresibus LIII., LIV.

[4] See above, p. 29. [5] See his narative below, Pt. II.

see, in the Author's words, in the latter part of this volume [6].

During the Episcopate of Zephyrinus, according to our Author's recital, there were two parties in the Roman Church. One the orthodox, the other consisting of those who inclined to the opinions of Sabellius, who, it seems, was then in person at Rome. Our Author describes his own intercourse with Sabellius, and he had (as he informs us) almost prevailed on him to renounce his errors, and to embrace the truth. But Callistus stood in the way. He, to increase his own influence, and to promote his own designs, communicated with both parties, and endeavoured to ingratiate himself with both. With the orthodox he professed orthodoxy, and with the Sabellians he was a Sabellian. Callistus inveighed with great virulence against our Author [7], who (it appears) stood almost alone on the opposite side, and publicly denounced him with slanderous appellations, calling him a Ditheist, a believer in two Gods. So great, however, was the address of Callistus, and so successful were his manœuvres in dealing with both parties, and in gaining them over to his own interests, that on the death of Zephyrinus, when the See became vacant, Callistus (to use our Author's words) "thought that he had attained the object of his ambition," which, we learn from another passage, was no less than the Episcopal chair at Rome [8].

[6] See below, Pt. II. [7] See p. 286, 1.

[8] P. 288, 96. μετὰ τὴν τοῦ Ζεφυρίνου τελευτὴν, νομίζων τετυχη-

Upon this, "Callistus threw off Sabellius as heterodox, through fear of me (says our Author), and because he supposed that he would thus be able to wipe off the stain of obloquy to which he was exposed in the eye of the Churches [9], as not being of a sound faith."

Being, however, pressed by Sabellius on the one side, and by our Author on the other, and being ashamed to retract his opinion, and to profess the true faith, Callistus made a compromise, and devised a new Heresy, denying the divinity of the Son as a distinct Person from the Father, and yet not professing that the Father had suffered in the Son.

Our Author proceeds to say, that in the time of Callistus [1], corrupt doctrine in the Church was accompanied with laxity of discipline; and he affirms that the popularity of Callistus was due, in a great measure, to the indulgence he gave to the vicious passions of those who were under his charge. And yet, says our Author, they whose life and belief is such, "venture to call themselves a Catholic Church [2]." Our writer, however, treats them as Heretics. He calls

κέναι οὗ ἐθηρᾶτο, compared with p. 284, 77. *ταύτην τὴν αἵρεσιν ἐκράτυνε* Κάλλιστος—*θηρώμενος τὸν τῆς ἐπισκοπῆς θρόνον.*

[9] Perhaps, as was usual with Bishops in ancient times, Callistus had sent missives to other Churches to notify to them his election; and some enquiries or remonstrances may have been addressed by them, and some requisition may have been made that he should clear himself from the charge of heresy.

[1] P. 290, 42. *ἐπὶ τούτου.*

[2] P. 291, 72.

their congregation their school, and says that it survived at the time he was writing, which was after the death of Callistus, and that they were named Callistians[3].

Such is our Author's account of the CALLISTIAN HERESY.

In the perusal of this narrative, two questions arise. We know that from about A.D. 192 to A.D. 222[4], the See of Rome was occupied in succession by Victor, Zephyrinus, and Callistus;—

I. Does then the Author intend to convey to his readers the impression, that the CALLISTUS whose Heresy he is describing, was Callistus the BISHOP of ROME who succeeded Zephyrinus?

II. If so, is this narrative worthy of credit? could it have been written by Hippolytus, scholar of Irenæus, and Bishop of Portus, near Rome, who is now venerated as a Saint and Martyr by the Roman Church?

[3] P. 292, 80.

[4] Jaffé (Regesta Pontificum, Berlin, 1851,) arranges their Episcopates thus, pp. 4, 5:—

S. VICTOR, A.D. 190 or 192?—202.
(Euseb. v. 20. 22, 23.)
S. ZEPHYRINUS, A.D. 202—218.
(Euseb. v. 28; vi. 21.)
S. CALLISTUS, A.D. 218—223.
(Euseb. vi. 21.)

See also Labbé, Concilia, i. pp. 591—615, ed. Paris, 1671.

These are grave questions. It is scarcely possible to overrate their importance, in religious and civil respects.

1. As to the former of these two enquiries, it will be observed that the Author no where ascribes to Callistus, whom he charges with Heresy—the style and title of Bishop of Rome. He appears, in some respects, to regard him rather as a professorial teacher, than as an Ecclesiastical Primate. He calls his disciples "a *School*"—but never gives them the name of "a *Church*." This is the more remarkable, because when speaking of Victor, who was Bishop of Rome, from A.D. 192 to A.D. 202, and who was succeeded by Zephyrinus, he uses no such reserve. He openly and explicitly calls him "the blessed Victor, *Bishop of the Church*[5]." And when in the course of his narrative he comes to the death of Zephyrinus, and we expect to hear it recorded, perhaps with an exclamation of sorrow and indignation, that Zephyrinus was succeeded by Callistus the Heretic, we seem to be put off with a vague and equivocal phrase; "After the death of Zephyrinus," we read[6], "he (Callistus) *imagined that he had gained* the object of his ambition"—which we learn from another part of the narrative to have been the Bishoprick of Rome.

There is something almost mysterious in this

[5] P. 288, 70. [6] P. 288, 96.

seeming ambiguity of language, which at first excites suspicion. If Callistus—Callistus the Heretic—was really Bishop of Rome, why does not our Author say so? Why does he seem to decline the assertion? Is it because it was not true? Did he mean to convey the idea that Callistus attained the place to which he had aspired? If so, why this faltering, why this hesitation? Why does he not say plainly,—Victor was succeeded by Zephyrinus, and Zephyrinus was succeeded by Callistus, in the Roman See?

2. In considering these enquiries, let us remember that our Author's narrative was written *after* the death of Zephyrinus, Bishop of Rome. He mentions that event [7]. Our Author, living at Rome, must have known that *a* Callistus had succeeded Zephyrinus in the Roman See. And, if Callistus the Heretic was not Callistus the Bishop, he would (we may suppose) have taken good care that no one should confound the two. But he has not done this. On the contrary, *he produces the impression* on his reader's mind, that they are one and the same person. He speaks of the *succession* of Zephyrinus and Callistus [8]; he mentions that *on the death of Zephyrinus,* Callistus thought he *had attained* the object of his wishes. He thus intimates that, however Callistus might be regarded by others, he *imagined himself to be Bishop of Rome.*

3. Again, he uses the expression—"such events

[7] P. 288, 96. [8] P. 279, 37.

took place *under him* [9]," that is, in the time of his rule, meaning the rule of Callistus; and the events which he is describing are Episcopal Consecrations and Ordinations of Priests and Deacons; by which he seems to indicate that Callistus exercised Episcopal and Metropolitan jurisdiction. And, he affirms that the adherents of Callistus were the majority of Rome, and he says that they called themselves "*a Catholic Church* [9]."

4. Besides, *if* Callistus the Heretic was not Callistus the Bishop, then, living at Rome as he did *after* Zephyrinus, he lived *under Callistus the Bishop;* for Callistus succeeded Zephyrinus, A.D. 218; and Callistus the Heretic propagated his Heresy under him. And no mention whatever occurs of any opposition being made to Callistus the Heretic by Callistus Bishop of Rome. On the other hand, the followers of Callistus are represented as forming a majority at Rome.

5. On the whole then we are led to conclude that —according to our Author,—Callistus the Heretic was Callistus, Bishop of Rome.

But why then does our Author use such an ambiguous expression as this, "Callistus *imagined* himself to have attained the object of his ambition?" Why does he not say that he *did* actually attain it?

6. To this question we may answer—No one doubts, we suppose, that Zephyrinus—the Zephyrinus men-

[9] ἐπὶ τούτου. P. 290, 42. and p. 291, 72.

tioned by our Author—was Bishop of Rome. No one questions that *he* succeeded Victor, and sat in the See of Rome for about eighteen years. No one doubts that our Author intends us to understand that the Zephyrinus of whom he is speaking, was Zephyrinus, Bishop of Rome, and no other.

Now, what we may here observe is, that our Author uses almost the same term when he is speaking of Zephyrinus, as that which he uses when he is speaking of Callistus. "Zephyrinus," he says, "*imagined* that he governed the Church (of Rome) at that time[1]." And "Callistus (he says) *imagined* that he had attained the object of his wishes," which he had before told us was "the Episcopal Chair."

Each of these two expressions illustrates the other. Zephyrinus *imagined* himself to be Bishop, and he *was* Bishop of Rome. Callistus *imagined* himself to have attained the Bishoprick; and he also *was* Bishop of Rome.

7. But *why* did our Author say that they *imagined* themselves to be Bishops? why did he use such expressions as these?

The reason, probably, was this: He wished to contrast the orthodox Victor with his unworthy successors. He therefore calls *him* "Victor of blessed memory, *Bishop of the Church*." But, according to our Author, Zephyrinus and Callistus were *heretics*. They *imagined* themselves Bishops. But our Author, when speaking of their false teaching, would not *call*

[1] P. 279, 30.

them Bishops. He would not profane the title of Bishop, by assigning it to patrons of heresy, who denied the Divine Personality of Christ.

8. Such would be our reply to the first question proposed. Let us offer some further remarks in support of this explanation.

It does not appear that the Author of this treatise affirmed that the ministerial acts of Zephyrinus[2] and Callistus were null and void. But he prefers to resort to a circumlocution, rather than to call them Bishops of the Church.

The validity of Episcopal and priestly ministrations, when performed by Bishops and Priests in heresy, was a subject which tried the patience, and exercised the charity, of the Christian Church in the next age to that of Hippolytus, particularly in the controverted question of heretical baptism, under St. Stephen of Rome on the one side, and St. Cyprian of Carthage on the other. It was afterwards illustrated by the learning of St. Jerome in his disputation with the Luciferians, and was elucidated by the wisdom, and adorned by the piety, of St. Augustine, in his dealings with the Donatists.

[2] In the extract from the "Little Labyrinth," quoted by Eusebius, v. 28, and written by Hippolytus, concerning which more will be said in the next Chapter, Zephyrinus is called a *Bishop* (προσπεσεῖν Ζεφυρίνῳ τῷ ἐπισκόπῳ), but the incident there recorded might have occurred before Zephyrinus had given way to Callistus; and it is probable that our Author would have called Zephyrinus a Bishop, when not speaking of his heresy.

It has been argued in later times in our own Church, in her intercourse with opposite parties on both sides; and it is a topic which requires to be handled with great prudence, calmness, and discretion, as has been made abundantly manifest by the evil results which have arisen, on the one side, from that latitudinarian laxity which carelessly connives at false doctrine in those who hold office in the Church; and on the other, from that unrelenting rigour which rejects the ministration of some who bear rule in the Church, and deny the validity of the office itself, when the doctrine of those who hold it is not altogether exempt from serious admixtures of error.

Our present purpose is to note facts, and to derive inferences from them bearing on the question before us.

9. We were at first somewhat staggered by the manner in which our Author speaks of Callistus. A reason has been suggested for that language. Callistus, and we may add Zephyrinus, are not fully recognized by our Author in this narrative as *legitimate Bishops* of the Church—*because* they were *abettors of Heresy*.

10. Let us now observe, that this language of reserve in speaking of Bishops in heresy, was characteristic of a celebrated school which traced its succession from St. John.

St. John himself, in the Apocalypse (a portion of Scripture which appear to have been studied by this school with special attention) had said in his address to his own Church of Ephesus, "I know thy works, and thy labour, and thy patience, and how thou canst not bear them which are evil: and thou hast tried them which *say* that they *are Apostles, and are not,* and hast found them *liars* [3]."

The teachers of this School inculcated the duty of holding communion and fellowship with those who possess, what they termed *the Charisma,*—grace or gift,—of *Apostolical Succession* [4].

They also lay great stress on succession of *sound doctrine.* The idea is admirably expressed in the following sentences, from the pen of one among the most eminent teachers of that School;—

"Genuine gnosis," or knowledge—says St. Irenæus, Bishop of Lyons [5],—(as opposed to the false philosophy of the Gnostics who professed to be the only wise) "is the doctrine of the Apostles, according to the ancient constitution of the Church in the whole world, and the badge of the body of Christ, according to the *succession of Bishops,* to whose care they (the Apostles) delivered the Church in every place: in which [6] (Church) has been transmitted to us, guarded

[3] Rev. ii. 2.

[4] Iren. iv. 45. Ubi charismata Domini posita sunt, *ibi* oportet discere Veritatem apud quos est ea quæ est ab *Apostolis Ecclesiæ successio,* et id quod est *sanum* et irreprobabile *conversationis,* et *inadulteratum* et *incorruptibile sermonis,* constat.

[5] S. Iren. iv. 63.

[6] The reading of the old Latin Version is *quæ:* for which we ought perhaps to read *quâ,* i. e. *where,* or *in which.*

without adulteration, the plenary use of SCRIPTURE, *admitting neither addition nor curtailment*, and the reading of Scripture without corruption, and legitimate and diligent Preaching, according to the WORD of GOD."

Again, he says, "We must obey those presbyters in the Church, who have the *succession* from the Apostles, and, *together with the Episcopal succession*, have received the *genuine Charisma of Truth* [7]." And again, "Every word will be established to him who has diligently read the SCRIPTURES, among those presbyters who are in the Church, and with whom is *Apostolical doctrine* [8]."

Such is the teaching of St. Irenæus.

11. Let us now listen to one of his most distinguished scholars.

As to the grace of ministerial succession from the Holy Apostles, together with sound doctrine: "No one" (he says) "can rightly refute the dogmas of Heretics, save only the HOLY SPIRIT, given in the Church; which Spirit the Apostles first received, and communicated to those *who believe aright*, whose *Successors we* are, partakers of the same grace, principal sacerdocy, and doctrine [9]."

Again, he thus speaks in another place:

"Let not a Bishop domineer over the Deacons or Presbyters, or the Presbyters domineer over the People. For the constitution of the Church is

[7] S. Iren. iv. 43. [8] S. Iren. iv. 52.

[9] Philosophumena, p. 3, 60.

formed of them all. Not every one who prophesies is pious, nor every one who casts out devils is holy. Even Balaam prophesied, who was a godless man; and Caiaphas,—*falsely named a high priest.* The Devil himself and his angels reveal many things that are future. A Bishop who is burdened with *ignorance* or *malice* [10] *is no longer a Bishop,—but is falsely so called.*"

Such is the teaching of a scholar of St. Irenæus.

And that Scholar is St. Hippolytus [11].

12. Thus, then we perceive that those expressions in this narrative, which at first caused us embarrassment, are explained by reference to the teaching of the school in which St. Hippolytus was trained, and to

[10] ἀγνοίᾳ ἢ κακονοίᾳ πεπιεσμένος. St. Hippolytus seems to refer to his own personal experience in these two terms, ἄγνοια and κακόνοια, ignorance and malice; the first was the case of *Zephyrinus*; the second, of *Callistus.*

[11] In περὶ χαρισμάτων, a work mentioned in the Catalogue on the Statue; and embodied in the VIIIth Book of Apostolic Constitutions, whence it is transcribed in Hippolyti Opera, I., ed. Fabricii, p. 247. See also Præfat. ibid. p. vii., and Le Moyne's Observations, Varia Sacra, p. 1074, and Fabr. Hipp. I. 260. Cp. Pearsoni Vind. Ignat. P. i. c. 4. It is ascribed to St. Hippolytus in a Vienna and an Oxford MS. The title of this work as described in the Statue, περὶ χαρισμάτων ἀποστολικὴ παράδοσις. The mention of its being derived from "Apostolic Tradition" may have commended it to the special regard of the compilers of "the Apostolic Constitutions;" or perhaps the Title, as engraved on the Statue, may describe the recension of the work as embodied in the "Apostolic Constitutions" themselves.

the language used by himself in another place; and thus our difficulties have befriended us, and do in fact confirm the proof already stated, that the newly-discovered "Refutation of Heresy" is from the pen of Hippolytus.

CHAPTER VIII.

OBJECTIONS CONSIDERED.

NARRATIVE CONCERNING THE CHURCH OF ROME.

LET us now resume the enquiry;

Whether it is probable that the narrative contained in the Ninth Book of the Treatise before us, came from the pen of Hippolytus?

1. In reading that portion of the Treatise, we observe indications of personal animosity: it is characterized by a spirit of sternness, almost of asperity. And it would appear to have been written and published *after* the death of Callistus [1].

Supposing the narrative to be *true* (a question which may be reserved for future consideration), are we authorized to believe that Hippolytus, the Scholar of St. Irenæus, the Bishop and Doctor of the Church, who is called, by an ancient writer [2], "a person of very sweet and amiable disposition," and laid down

[1] See pp. 291, 2; and p. 330.

[2] S. Chrysostom (?) de Pseudoprophetis, tom. viii. p. 79, ed. Montfaucon. Ἱππόλυτος γλυκύτατος καὶ εὐνούστατος.

his life as a Martyr for Christ, would have expressed himself in the language of this Treatise, concerning Zephyrinus and Callistus, who had been Bishops of the Church, and had now been called away by death, from a world of strife, to render up their accounts to God?

In our Author's narrative there are some symptoms of self-sufficiency, which may appear to be hardly consistent with the character of a Christian Bishop eminent for holiness, as St. Hippolytus is believed to have been. He records his own acts (it may perhaps be said) with something like self-complacency, and even with boastful ostentation. "*We* (he says) resisted Zephyrinus and Callistus[3]." "*We* nearly converted Sabellius[4]." "All were carried away by the hypocrisy of Callistus except *ourselves*[5]." "Callistus threw off Sabellius through fear of *me*[6]."

May it not be said that this is the language of vain glory and egotism? Could it be the language of Hippolytus?

2. Besides, in perusing this history, the reader will not fail to observe that the tendency of some of the Author's observations has something of a sectarian character. He is vehement in his denunciations of Callistus for laxity of discipline, as well as for unsoundness of doctrine. If his narrative is true, this is not surprising. But then his own arguments, with respect to Church discipline, do not appear

[3] P. 279, 39. [4] P. 285, 88.

[5] P. 285, 2. [6] P. 289, 98.

to be unexceptionable. He seems to doubt whether the Church Visible on earth is a society in which there will ever be evil men mingled with the good. He scarcely seems to admit that the Ark, containing clean and unclean animals, was a figure of the Church in her transitory character. He is not disposed to recognize the Church Visible in the Field of Wheat and Tares[7]; he seems almost eager to imitate the Servants in the Parable, and pluck up the tares before the time of harvest; and he appears to indulge a hope that the Church on earth can be a field of wheat, and of wheat alone.

Here we see signs of impatience. And we know what evil results followed from the workings of a spirit similar to this in the next age to Hippolytus. It produced the schism of Novatian at Rome, who was offended with the facility with which the Roman Church re-admitted to communion heinous offenders, and especially the *lapsi*, who had apostatized from Christianity in persecution; and who procured himself to be consecrated Bishop of Rome, in opposition to Cornelius[8], and so (to adopt the language of modern times) became the *first Anti-pope*[9]. Novatianism propagated itself from Rome throughout a great part of the world, and distracted Christendom. The same spirit displayed itself in feuds and factions,

[7] P. 290. [8] Euseb. vi. 43. 45.

[9] A.D. 251. Jaffé Regesta Pontificum, p. 8, Berolini, 1851; a work which may be consulted on the chronology of the Bishops of Rome.

in outrage and bloodshed, in the African Church, in the fourth and fifth centuries; and it has never ceased to operate with disastrous energy, and to produce calamitous effects even to this day.

Again—

3. Suppose this Narrative to be written and published by Hippolytus. What impression would it have produced at Rome? Here is a Work in which the Author speaks of two Roman Bishops in terms of censure and even of abhorrence. He represents himself as their antagonist. He reprobates them as false teachers. One of them connives at heresy; the other founds an heretical school. Such are the terms which he applies to Zephyrinus and Callistus. Both of them were Roman Bishops. Both have been canonized by the Church of Rome. Both are venerated in her Breviary as Saints and Martyrs [1].

Can he who writes thus have been a Suffragan Bishop of the Roman See? Can he be Hippolytus, Bishop of Portus, near Rome? If so, how is it to be explained that his name has been venerated for many centuries by the Roman Church? Would

[1] See Breviarium Romanum S. Pii V. jussu editum in Aug. 26 and Oct. 14. More will be said on this subject in the course of this chapter. Compare Bianchini in Anastas. Bibliothec. de Vit. Rom. Pontif, where the date of the martyrdom of *Zephyrinus* is said to have been 26th July, A.D. 217. In some Roman Martyrologies it is placed on 20th Dec., A.D. 218. Concerning Callistus, see Mansi Not. in Baron. ad A.D. 226, and Lumper de Romanis Episcopis Sæc. iii. § ii. The date of his martyrdom is placed by some authorities on 14th Oct., A.D. 223.

she have permitted a Statue to be erected in his honour in a public place in one of her own cemeteries? Perhaps she erected it herself. In a word, if two of her Bishops had been denounced by him as heretics, and if, after their death, he had published the history of their heresy to the world,—would she have revered Hippolytus as a Saint?

Let us consider these points.

1. As to our Author's demeanour and language towards heretics.

The Apostle and Evangelist St. John was the beloved disciple. The mainspring of his teaching was Love. When in his old age he was brought into the church at Ephesus, the constant theme of his discourse was "Little children, love one another[2]." And yet in his Epistles, when he writes concerning heretics, "who abide not in the doctrine of Christ," St. John says, "If there come any unto you, and bring not this doctrine, receive him not into your house, neither bid him God speed: for he that biddeth him God speed is partaker of his evil deeds[3]." And tremendous are the denunciations of his Apocalypse against the abettors of heresy and corrupt doctrine, and against those who communicate with them in their errors[4].

The prevalent opinion of the Church, with regard

[2] S. Jerome in Galat. vi. [3] 2 John 10, 11.

[4] *E. g.* Rev. ii. 15. 20—23; xiv. 9, 10.

to St. John's sentiments and example with regard to heretics, is well indicated by the record of the incident related by St. Irenæus[5] concerning the Apostle. He quitted the bath at Ephesus, we are told, when he heard that Cerinthus was there, and exclaimed, "Let us make haste to flee the place, lest the house fall on our heads, since it has under its roof Cerinthus, the enemy of truth."

St. John was full of the Holy Ghost—the Spirit of Truth and Love. He, doubtless, in his own person, combined the Christian graces, Faith and Charity, in harmonious proportion. Among his scholars he numbered St. Ignatius and St. Polycarp. In the Epistles of the one we see love for the Truth; but love of Unity appears to be the master bias. In St. Polycarp we behold ardent zeal for the Faith, with vehement antagonism to Error. "Knowest thou me?" said Marcion the heretic to Polycarp, whom he met, as it seems, at Rome, whither Polycarp had come from Smyrna, to visit Anicetus, Bishop of Rome, "Yes," was the reply, "I know thee well, —the first-born of Satan[6]."

St. Ignatius seems to have sought for Truth through Unity, St. Polycarp aims at Unity through Truth.

St. Irenæus, when a boy, had seen "the blessed Polycarp;" he treasured his sayings in his memory, and has recorded them with affectionate veneration. And in imitation of the frankness of Polycarp, and

[5] iii. 3, p. 204, Grabe. [6] Iren. iii. 3. Euseb. iv. 13.

of his sternness of speech, when dealing with Heretics, he tells Florinus,—the heretic,—that if the holy Polycarp, whom both of them had known in youth, had heard the strange dogmas which Florinus was broaching, he would have stopped his ears, and exclaimed—"O merciful God, to what times hast thou reserved me!" and would have fled from the spot with execration [7].

2. Let us now, for argument's sake, be allowed to suppose that our Author's narrative is true. Let us see whether there is any thing in it inconsistent with the character of St. Hippolytus.

St. Hippolytus was trained in this school to which we have referred, as tracing its succession from St. John. He was a disciple of Irenæus, had heard his lectures, and has shown himself to have been a diligent reader of his works. He trod in his steps, and dwelt on the subjects which had been before handled by Irenæus [8]. He firmly asserted the continuity of spiritual grace, derived by succession from the Apostles in the laying on of Episcopal hands. Thus he affirmed the principle of Church Unity inculcated in the Epistles of St. Ignatius. He possessed also, in abundant measure, the masculine vigour and dauntless courage and fervent zeal of Polycarp. He loved the truth; he fought manfully for it; and abhorred Heresy. He had seen its bitter fruits, he beheld it

[7] S. Iren. ap. Euseb. v. 20. Routh, Opuscula, i. p. 32.

[8] As a comparison of the catalogues of their works respectively will show.

flourishing and dominant, in one of its most hateful forms, making havock far and wide in the fairest Church of the West. Under such circumstances as these, it required something more than the spirit of an Irenæus, an Ignatius, or a Polycarp—it demanded the spirit of a ST. JOHN, the divinely-inspired Apostle and Evangelist, so to contend against Error, as not to violate Charity; and so to resist Heresy, as not to execrate Heretics. And let us bear in mind, that though Zephyrinus and Callistus were dead at the time when our Author wrote, yet their Heresy was *not* dead: Callistus had passed away, but he had left Callistians behind him [9].

Our Author had been engaged in a conflict with Callistus, and was still at war with his disciples. That conflict had been a public one. Callistus and his adherents had denied the Divine personality of Christ as distinct from the Father. Our Author asserted it, and Callistus had reviled him openly as "a worshipper of two Gods [1]." Hence this controversy was a personal one. No one (says a great Father of the Church) should remain patient under

[9] P. 292, 80, and 329, 37. αἵρεσιν ἕως νῦν ἐπὶ τοὺς διαδόχους διαμείνασαν. From the terms in which Sabellius is mentioned in this Treatise (pp. 285. 289, 290), it may be inferred that it was written at a time when the name of Sabellius and of his heresy had become notorious; and, according to our Author, the existence of that heresy was due in great measure to Callistus.

[1] Pp. 285. 289.

a charge of Heresy. If Callistus was right, our Author was wrong. If Callistus, Bishop of Rome, did not impose sinful terms of Communion, our Author was a Schismatic. If Callistus was orthodox, our Author was a Heretic. Nay, he was worse than a Heretic; he was a Polytheist. He must therefore vindicate himself. He had been accused publicly, he must exculpate himself publicly. And he could not otherwise show that he himself was not heterodox, than by proving Callistus a Heretic.

When we consider these circumstances, and that men, however holy, are men, and are liable to human infirmities, especially when agitated by strong passions, or engaged in personal struggles concerning the most momentous articles of the Christian Faith, it may not seem to be improbable that one eminent in the Church, like Hippolytus, should have written as our Author has done.

3. When we remember also the particular school in which Hippolytus had been reared, and when we add to this the fact, observed by an ancient writer, that Hippolytus gave evidence of a fervid temperament [2], and was probably of Asiatic origin [3], we see no reason

[2] Phot. Cod. 202. θερμοτέρας γνώμης. See also some pertinent remarks by Lardner, Credibility, i. p. 488, on the style and character of the Author of the Little Labyrinth, *i. e.* on Hippolytus.

[3] A learned friend suggests a parallel in the strong language of St. Chrysostom against Eudoxia. Similar instances might be easily collected from every age.

to think that such a narrative as the present could not have been written by Hippolytus.

4. We do not dispute the fact that there is a tone of self-confidence in this narrative.

But let us remember the circumstances of the case. Our Author, whoever he was, was a learned and eloquent man. Few persons in his age in Christendom, none probably in the West, could have composed the Volume before us. It is rich in human learning as well as divine. The style is somewhat turgid, but it displays solid erudition, as well as luxuriance of language. Let us imagine such a person as this residing at Rome in the second and third centuries. He was well qualified to be Bishop of Portus, because it was the principal harbour of the imperial City, and was thronged with strangers, Greeks, Asiatics, and Africans, merchants, shipmen and soldiers, Philosophers, Physicians, Ambassadors, and Astrologers, Christians, Jews, and Pagans flocking to Rome.

But let us suppose such a person as this associated with such Ecclesiastics—and placed under the rule of such Bishops—as he represents Zephyrinus and Callistus to be: the one illiterate, the other profligate, both promoters of heresy. Let his account of their doings be exaggerated—though it is not easy to say why an Author who writes like the Author of the Philosophumena (and who appears to be no other than St. Hippolytus, a Bishop and Doctor of the Church) should be accused of misrepresentation,

—yet this we know, that the Western Church at that time was not endowed with erudition—especially such learning as that in which our Author excelled. He had the misfortune to be placed under men far inferior to himself. And "knowledge puffeth up." His own superiority was a stumbling-block; their inferiority was a snare. Suppose such a person as this to have been formerly intimate with the holy and learned Irenæus, suppose him to have been elated with his ancestral dignity of doctrinal succession, derived through Irenæus and Polycarp from the blessed Apostle St. John,—What a contrast would he see at Rome! What a severe trial of his temper would be there—what a perilous ordeal to pass through! Shall we be surprised that under such circumstances as these, expressions of conscious superiority, or even of vituperative indignation, should have escaped the lips of Hippolytus?

5. But, it may be said, Is there not a sectarian bias in this narrative? Is not the Author almost a Novatian before Novatianism,—a Donatist before Donatus? Can this be Hippolytus?

There is doubtless a *tendency* to Novatianism in this portion of our Author's work. Some of his principles, carried out without reserve or restraint, would no doubt lead to schism. But, when we consider human frailty, we may perhaps allow, that this might have been expected.

Almost all the evils in the Church are due to excess of reaction. Hippolytus flourished in the end of the second and beginning of the third century, when the evils had *not* arisen which afterwards flowed from the development of those principles which have some countenance from our Author. He represents himself as living at Rome when the discipline of that Church was very lax. His remedy lay in severity. The Roman Church had extended the range of communion too widely: he would have restrained it too strictly. Her practice was latitudinarian, and gave somewhat of a sectarian tendency to his principles. What is there here that does not occur, even in the best times, among the best men? It is the common course of human affairs. His contemporary, Tertullian, was offended by the same licentiousness in the Ecclesiastical system of Rome, and lapsed into Montanism[4]. Even Dionysius of Alexandria, in his zeal against Sabellius, is said by St. Basil[5] to have sown the seeds of Arianism. St. Chrysostom, in his ardour against a barren faith, may have prepared the way for the doctrine of merit; and St. Augustine, in his strenuous struggle against Pelagianism, may have been a precursor of Calvin.

But shall we charge those holy men with the consequences which *others* deduced from their principles after their death? Shall we not rather suppose that those principles would have been modified by them, *if* they had known the consequences which

[4] S. Hieron. Scr. Eccl. on Tertullian, 53.

[5] S. Basil, Epist. ix. 2.

others would draw from them; and if they had witnessed the results to which those principles might lead?

Our Author, whoever he was, *wrote before* the Novatian Schism. For he was a contemporary of Callistus, who died in or about A. D. 223. And his book appears to have been written at Rome when the memory of his conflict with Callistus was still fresh. The Novatian Schism did not appear at Rome till near thirty years afterwards (A. D. 251). Our Author, being at Rome in the position which he appears to have occupied, would either have taken part with Novatian, or against him. And, according to his own views of the case, the Novatians, or their adversaries, would have found a place in the Volume before us; as is the case with the Montanists and Quartodecimans, whom he acquits of heresy, and commemorates on disciplinarian grounds[6]. When, therefore, he acted and wrote as he did, our Author had not seen the development of the principles to which he gives some countenance. He had not witnessed the evils which arose from the rending of the Church by the schism of Novatian.

If, then, we reflect on the religious state of the Roman Church as displayed in this Volume, if we recollect the painful provocations which such disciplinarian laxity and heretical pravity as he describes rarely fail to minister to pious minds, and if

[6] Pp. 274, 275.

we remember that *we*, living in the nineteenth century, have seen the results of reactions in the opposite direction, but that *he* lived and wrote *before* the rise of Novatianism, we shall not judge our Author from our own circumstances, but shall endeavour to place ourselves in his age and country, and shall attribute his vehement language against laxity of discipline to his zeal for the holiness and purity of the Spouse and Body of Christ.

On the whole, then, we see nothing here inconsistent with the character of St. Hippolytus, who flourished *before* Novatian.

6. Rather, let us now add, we find in these very expressions, to which we have now referred, an additional confirmation of the proof that this Treatise is from him.

We have already adverted[7] to the HYMN of the Christian Poet who wrote at the beginning of the fifth century, PRUDENTIUS[8]. He there describes (as it seems) the cemetery and crypt near Rome to which the remains of St. Hippolytus were consigned after his martyrdom at Portus, and in which his Statue was disinterred, in A. D. 1551.

It is remarkable, that in that Poem Prudentius mentions that Hippolytus, the Bishop and Martyr of Portus, whose death he is describing, and for whose memory he expresses the deepest veneration, had

[7] Above, p. 46. Prudentius was born in Spain, A. D. 348.

[8] Hymn. peri Stephanôn, xi.

participated in the schism of Novatus. Prudentius dwells on this circumstance with studious and elaborate exactness. He brings it forward, somewhat abruptly, almost at the commencement of his poem, as if it was uppermost in his mind. He desires the friend to whom he addresses it [9], not to be surprised that Hippolytus, though formerly entangled in a perverse dogma, was afterwards enriched with the prize of the Catholic faith—the Martyr's crown. For (says the Poet [1], whose words shall be rendered literally) "when he was hurried away by the furious foe to death, he was attended by numerous followers, through the affection of his flock; and, being consulted—'Which way was the best?'—'Fly,' he replied, 'the execrable schism of the miserable Novatus, restore yourselves to the Catholic people. Let one faith thrive, which is built on the ancient temple, which faith Paul holds, and the chair of Peter. It grieves me to have taught what once I taught. Now a Martyr, I perceive *that* to be venerable which once I thought to be far from the worship of God.' When he had thus recalled his flock from the left road, and had taught them to follow where the right way leads, and when he, who before had drawn them astray, now guided them aright, having renounced the devious path, he is brought before the furious Governor, who was then persecuting the Christians, near the mouth of the Tiber" (*i. e.* at Ostia

[9] Valerian, Bp. of Zaragoza. [1] Hymn, xi. 19.

and at Portus, the See of Hippolytus), "and who, having made an excursion from Rome, on that self-same day, had extended his rage to the shores of the Etrurian Sea, and to the neighbourhood of the maritime PORTUS."

Such is the exordium of the Poem of Prudentius on the Martyrdom of St. Hippolytus, Bishop of Portus.

He then describes the circumstances of the Martyrdom; he recites the last prayer of the Martyr, when his aged limbs were torn in pieces by the wild horses to which (the Poet says) he was tied. He describes the conveyance of his remains to Rome; and their interment in a crypt or catacomb, and mentions a fresco on which the Martyrdom was delineated, and the erection of a chapel on the spot, and the concourse of people, high and low, from far and wide, from Alba and Samnium, and even from Nola and Capua, on the Anniversary when his Martyrdom was commemorated in that age—the 13th of August.

In perusing this interesting Poem which extends to near 250 lines, the reader can hardly fail to observe, that the recantation imputed to Hippolytus is made a main topic, not inferior to the Martyrdom itself.

It would appear from the Poet's words, that the memory of St. Hippolytus was venerated throughout Italy in the fifth century; and that it was generally known that he had occupied a position of antagonism to a Bishop of the Roman Church. Prudentius endeavours to account for this seeming incongruity. He says that St. Hippolytus *had* been in schism, that he had led his people astray, and had formed a separate congregation; but that *just before his death* he renounced his error, and exhorted his people to return to the Church.

This Poem was written more than a century and a half after the death of Hippolytus. Some persons have been perplexed by the application of the name "Presbyter" in this Poem to Hippolytus, who was a Bishop. But there is no difficulty here; though a Presbyter is not called a Bishop by ancient Authors, yet a Bishop is often called Presbyter[2]. And Prudentius sufficiently declares that the Martyr Hippolytus, whose death he describes, was a Bishop, by saying, that he was the *Head* of a Christian Church[3]. It is evident, also, that Prudentius means us to understand, that whatever the nature of the schism was with which Hippolytus is charged, he renounced it at his death—but not *before*. For why should the people have consulted him *then*,

[2] *E. g.* Irenæus is twice called μακάριος πρεσβύτερος in this Treatise, pp. 202. 222, and never Ἐπίσκοπος: and, after all, the Vatican MS. reads, Invenio Hippolytum qui quondam schisma Novati *Presbyteri* attigerat, for *Presbyter*, and that reading is received by Arevali, in his edition, Rom. 1805. In the Catalogus Liberianus, sect. iv., and Catalog. Felician. sect. vi., we read: "Eo tempore (A.D. 235) Pontianus Episcopus et *Hippolytus Presbyter* exitio sunt deportati in insulam Sardiniam." This was probably St. Hippolytus.

[3] Ipsum Christicolis esse *Caput* populis, v. 80.

which way they ought to go, if he had previously informed them? And why should he say that as a *Martyr* he recognizes the truth, and desires them then to *return* to the Catholic Church?

But the question arises—

Could Hippolytus, the Bishop of Portus, have been an adherent of Novatian, the first anti-Pope, or, as Prudentius calls him, Novatus—a confusion of names common in the Eastern Church, and excusable in a Western Poet writing in Elegiacs, and having to deal with a word, 'quod versu dicere non est?'

No, we may reply, Hippolytus could not have been a follower of Novatian. He could hardly have survived to so late a period as that of the Novatian schism, which did not appear till A. D. 251. And since we have minutely accurate details, in the works of St. Cyprian, concerning the history of the Novatian schism, and since it is not possible that so eminent a person as St. Hippolytus should have sided with Novatian, and no mention be made of the fact in any of those details, we may conclude that he was not among his adherents [4].

[4] This argument is well stated by Ruggieri, pp. 415—439, of his elaborate work described above, chapter i., where he has proved that St. Hippolytus could not have been implicated in Novatianism. Besides, Hippolytus, we are told by Photius (Cod. 121), was of opinion that the Epistle to the Hebrews was not written by St. Paul. The Novatians appealed to it as his; and grounded their stern discipline upon it. Philast. Hæres. 41.

The Church of Rome herself affirms, that St. Hippolytus, *Bishop of Portus*, was *not* chargeable with Novatianism. For she records in her Breviary (Aug. 22), that he was martyred "*Alexandro Imperatore*," whose reign ended A. D. 235, and Novatianism did not appear till fifteen years afterward.

She also affirms, that Prudentius in his hymn has confounded one Hippolytus with another [5]. For Prudentius says, that St. Hippolytus, *Bishop* of *Portus*, was torn in pieces by wild horses, but the Church of Rome in the Breviary assigns *that* mode of martyrdom to *another* St. Hippolytus, whom she commemorates on August 13; and she also relates in the Breviary, that St. Hippolytus, Bishop of Portus, was martyred in a very different manner [6].

But is there *no* foundation for the statement of Prudentius? Yes, we may believe, there is. Let us suppose, for argument's sake, that Hippolytus, though not a Novatian, had put forth some sentiments seeming to have some tendency to Novatianism. It would not have been wonderful, that he should be *afterwards*

[5] Cardinal Baronius was also of this opinion. Ad A. D. 229, No. 9. "Hæc Prudentius, qui errore lapsus tres in unum confudit Hippolytos." See also his Martyrol. 30. Jan. : "Prudentius tres Hippolytos conflavit in unum." The same is stated with much learning and ability by Ruggieri, p. 444.

[6] Ad Aug. 22. Apud Ostia Tiberina Hippolytus Episcopus Portuensis ob præclaram fidei confessionem manibus pedibusque ligatis in altam foveam aquis plenam præcipitatus martyrio coronatus est.

called a Novatian. The seven Sons and their Mother who suffered martyrdom under Antiochus Epiphanes, are commonly called "Maccabees," although they died many years *before* the standard of Judas was raised, which gave rise to the name of Maccabee. Such cases of anticipatory appellations are common. Hippolytus would have been cited by the promoters of Novatianism as favouring their views. Suppose him to have severed himself from communion with certain Bishops of Rome. Suppose him to have denounced them as patrons of heresy and immorality, and to have treated with indignation and scorn their claim, and that of their people, to be "a Catholic Church." Suppose him to have resisted them openly. Then it is very probable that the Novatians would appeal to him, as a venerable Bishop and Martyr, who had countenanced their cause. They would avail themselves of his name and reputation—perhaps of his writings. The Church of Rome would not have been unwilling that he should pass for a Novatian; for his antagonism would be rendered comparatively innocuous by being identified with a sect, and probably it would be taken for granted, that he retracted his opinions before he died, and that, with his last breath, the venerable Bishop and Martyr conjured his flock at Portus to return to the Roman Church.

Let us add to this the following consideration. *Another* eminent person, bearing the name of *Hippolytus*, was known as an adherent of Novatian, and he was also a Martyr[7]; and the narrative of Prudentius concerning the *manner* of the martyrdom of St. Hippolytus, Bishop of Portus, is at variance with the other records of that event[8].

Therefore we are led to conclude, that there is an error in the details of the Hymn of Prudentius, particularly with regard to the imputation of complicity with Novatian to St. Hippolytus[9].

But we also believe there is a historical basis of truth, even in that particular.

In a word, the Narrative before us in the ninth book of the newly-discovered Treatise, detailing the circumstances of the conflict of St. Hippolytus with two Roman Bishops, explains and corrects the Poem of Prudentius. It is the key that opens the lock which baffled the skill of many critics of old. And thus those very sentiments, occurring in this narrative, which seemed to have a Novatian direction, do, when compared with the Poem, supply another proof that the narrative before us is from the pen of Hippolytus[1].

[7] See the Authorities in Ruinart. ap. Fabric. Hippol. i. p. x. and ibid. p. xiii. "Usuardus 3 Kal. Febr. apud Antiochiam passio beati Ypoliti martyris, qui *Novati schismate* aliquantulum deceptus, operante Christi gratiâ, ad Ecclesiæ charitatem rediit."

[8] See ibid. pp. xx., xxi.

[9] Such also is the conclusion of Ruggieri in his Dissertation on St. Hippolytus, pp. 415—447.

[1] We may here refer to the testimony of ancient authors, who state that there were certain things liable to reprehension in the writings of St. Hippolytus, but that he made amends for them by

Whether or no Hippolytus (for so let us be permitted to call our Author) did continue in a state of separation from the Bishop of Rome after the death of Callistus, is a question of much interest, and deserves careful investigation. We may hope that Urbanus[2], the successor of Callistus, brought back the Roman Church to the true Faith, and that the breach was healed; and there appears to be some reason for this belief in the circumstance, that in the year A.D. 235, Pontianus, Bishop of Rome, and Hippolytus, were (it seems) brother-exiles and confessors of the Faith in Sardinia[3]. But this is not the topic before us.

Let us, then, pass on to observe, that the Poem of Prudentius aids us also in the solution of the last question proposed for consideration in this Chapter.

his martyrdom. Nicephor. Callist. iv. 31, τινὰ τῶν συγγραμμάτων ἐπιλήψιμα ἔχων τῷ ὑπὲρ χριστοῦ μαρτυρίῳ τελειωθεὶς τὸν τῆς ἀγνοίας μῶμον ἀπετρίψατο.

It is true we do not know what these particulars were. Some have supposed them to have been certain points in his prophetical interpretation animadverted on by Photius. Or they may have been his approximations to the verge of Novatianism, as noticed in this chapter.

[2] Zonaras says, that Hippolytus flourished under Urbanus (Annal. Tom. ii. ap. Fabric. Hippol. p. x.). His words are remarkable: Οὐρβανοῦ τῆς Ἐπισκοπῆς τῆς Ῥωμαίων πόλεως προεστῶτος καὶ Ἱππόλυτος ἤνθει, ἀνὴρ ἱερώτατος καὶ σοφώτατος, Ἐπίσκοπος τοῦ κατὰ Ῥώμην Πόρτου γενόμενος.

[3] See the Authorities in Fabric. i. p. xxi. Lardner, i. 498, supposes that S. Hippolytus was martyred either A.D. 235 or A.D. 250. The former date is the more probable.

7. How is it possible that Hippolytus should have been honoured by a Statue at Rome, if he had resisted two Roman Bishops, who are canonized as Saints and honoured as Martyrs by the Church of Rome, and if he had denounced them as heretics?

Zephyrinus is indeed *called* a Saint and Martyr, and Callistus also, and they are venerated as such in the Public Liturgy of the Roman Church [4]. But our Author, who wrote very soon after the death of both, certainly does not regard either of them as a Martyr or a Saint. And it is generally acknowledged and deplored that the records of the earlier Bishops of Rome are very defective and erroneous. The history of that Church, during the second and greater part of the third century is almost a blank, in which little that is trustworthy has been inserted, except the names and dates of the Bishops. In course of time Writers arose, who filled up the vacant space with legendary tales; and Martyrdoms were recorded of Popes, who had died quietly in their beds [5]. The

[4] The Festival of Zephyrinus is Aug. 26, and we find the following Collect for that day in the Roman Breviary (p. 1055, ed. Ratisbon, 1840):—

Oratio.

"Præsta, quæsumus, omnipotens Deus, ut beati Zephyrini Martyris tui atque Pontificis, cujus gaudemus meritis, instruamur exemplis, per Dominum."

The festival of Callistus is October 14, and it is said in the Breviary, p. 1151, "Callistus . . . martyrio coronatus sub Alexandro Imperatore. . . . Corpus in Basilicam S. Mariæ trans Tiberim ab ipso ædificatam delatum, sub arâ majori *maximâ veneratione colitur*."

[5] "Recepta de primis Romæ Episcopis plerisque Martyribus

Church enjoyed peace and was not assailed by persecution during the times of Zephyrinus and Callistus. It is very improbable, to say the least, that either of them perished by Martyrdom. We must be on our guard not to form our estimate of the character and lives of Roman Bishops in the second and third centuries, from statements which did not see the light till four centuries after them [6].

8. Let us now turn to the STATUE. It is observable, that, though all Antiquity testifies that "a Refutation of all Heresies" was written by St. Hippolytus, yet *that* particular work is not specified in the catalogue on the Statue.

There must (we are led to conjecture) have been some reason for this omission.

There would be no ground for it, if, in the eyes of persons in authority at Rome, it had been altogether unexceptionable; and supposing the first eight books of our work to have formed the *whole* work, and supposing them to have been written by Hippolytus,

sententia erronea est," says Bp. Pearson, Dissert. Posth. i. c. iv. The whole of that chapter is very important in its bearings on the present subject, as showing the scantiness of materials, even in the sixth century, for any thing like an accurate knowledge of the Roman Church as it had existed in the second and earlier part of the third.

[6] See Bp. Pearson, i. c. xii. 4, who says, "Dico nullum Papam aut alium quemcunque fuisse auctorem Libri Pontificum sive gestorum Pontificalium ante *sextum* sæculum, *imò nullum ejusmodi librum in Ecclesiâ extitisse* ante annum CLX ab obitu Damasi Papæ" (*i. e.* ante annum DCCCIV).

then, when we consider the importance of the subject, and the learning and ability displayed in those books, we recognize cogent reasons for the *insertion* of this work in the catalogue on the Statue.

But it is *omitted*. And now, we would ask, Does not the narrative in the ninth book *explain* the omission? and does not that omission supply an additional argument in behalf of the genuineness of the narrative?

9. The existence of the honorary Statue is explained by the Poem of Prudentius. If the memory of Hippolytus, who had lived in the third century, and was *supposed* by some in the fifth century, to have been an adherent of Novatian,—the first Antipope, the Author of a widely-spread schism,—was so dear to the people of Rome and Italy, as Prudentius describes it to be, that they flocked from almost all parts of Italy to his grave, on the anniversary of his Martyrdom,—if Prudentius himself, "the Christian Maro and Flaccus" (as Bentley calls him), erected a Monument to Hippolytus, more durable than marble, in the interesting Hymn to which we have referred, there is no reason for surprise that some of those who resorted to his grave, among whom (as Prudentius states) were wealthy Patricians [7], admirers of his learning, his eloquence, his piety, and of his courage, displayed in his life, his writings and his death, should have united together in raising a Monument to his

[7] Urbs augusta suos vomit effunditque Quirites
Una et *Patricios* ambitione pari.—v. 200.

memory, and should have loved to see his venerable figure perpetuated in marble, and have inscribed its pedestal with his Paschal Calendar, and with the titles of his works. No wonder, we may say, that they paid this tribute to his memory, *although* he had resisted two Popes in succession. If Hippolytus, although *supposed* to have been an adherent of Novatian, who had withstood so holy a Pope as Cornelius, was honoured with a Poem and a Chapel, there is no ground for surprise that although he was *known* to have resisted a Callistus or Zephyrinus, he should have been honoured with a Statue. Perhaps some of those who erected it loved and venerated him the more, *because* he had stood firm and immovable, and almost alone, against a deadly Heresy, patronised by two Prelates of Rome [8]. When

[8] M. Bunsen places the erection of the Statue at some period between Constantine and the sixth century (p. 223). There seems reason for believing that it was earlier; for the Paschal Calendar inscribed upon it dates from A. D. 222. And as Turrianus (ap. Fabr. Hippolyt. i. pp. 164—171), and after him Ideler (Chronologie ii. p. 224) observe, the Calendar appears to have been intended for use in the period for which it was made, and could not have been long in use, on account of certain imperfections in its construction. After the lapse of one or two of its cycles of sixteen years it would have become obsolete. And after it was superseded, no one, probably, would have been at the pains to engrave it. If this reasoning be correct, the Statue is of greater interest and value as being almost a contemporary monument to the memory, and a contemporary tribute to the virtues, of St. Hippolytus.

in the next age to Hippolytus, Sabellianism (the natural growth of Noëtianism) became widely dominant in Christendom, and made great ravages in the Church, perhaps through the previous example and influence of Zephyrinus and Callistus as described in the narrative before us, then another Bishop of Rome, the great Dionysius (A.D. 259—269) came forward to stay the plague. He vindicated the true faith from the aggressions of Sabellianism on the one side, and of Tritheism on the other[9]. Then (it is very probable) the services that had been rendered by Hippolytus to the cause of Christianity by his gallant resistance to a pestilent Heresy, were gratefully appreciated by the Church and Bishop of Rome. Then his name was beloved, and his memory revered by her. Thousands flocked to the tomb of one who had contended for the honour of Christ in his life, and had glorified Him in his death. Then perhaps this Statue was erected. Then the infirmities of temper, the vehemence of language,

[9] For an excellent summary of his history in this particular respect, see Bp. Pearson, Dissert. i. c. 10. 5. See also Coustant, Notitia Epistolarum Dionys. Rom. (ap. Routh, iii. 114); Neander, ii. p. 369. Fragments of the work of Dionysius, called Ἀνατροπὴ, or Refutation, are preserved by St. Athanasius de decretis Synodi Nicænæ, § 26, and are contained in Routh, Reliquiæ, ed. 1815, iii. 179—183. ὁ μὲν Σαβέλλιος βλασφημεῖ αὐτὸν τὸν υἱὸν εἶναι λέγων τὸν πατέρα καὶ ἔμπαλιν· οἱ δὲ τρεῖς θεοὺς τρόπον τινὰ κηρύττουσιν εἰς τρεῖς ὑποστάσεις ξένας ἀλλήλων παντάπασι κεχωρισμένας διαιροῦντες τὴν ἁγίαν Τριάδα.

the scornful sarcasm, and acrimonious altercation were forgotten. The schism had been healed by death, and the memory of passionate conflicts was buried in the Martyr's grave.

CHAPTER IX.

OBJECTIONS CONSIDERED.

SILENCE OF CHURCH HISTORIANS.

We have already considered some of the various questions which occur to the reader when he first peruses our Author's narrative concerning Zephyrinus and Callistus.

Let us now proceed to examine some others.

1. We see in that narrative two Bishops of Rome, the greatest Church in the West, not only charged with Heresy, but with patronising and propagating it. And they are represented as disparaging those who were orthodox, and as assailing them publicly with calumnious appellations, and other contumelious indignities. If this had been the case, we feel disposed to ask, Would not the whole Church have sounded an alarm? Would not the world have rung with the fame of such doings as these? Let us consider some parallel cases. What a stir was made in Christendom, when Liberius, Bishop of Rome, lapsed into Arianism in the fourth century. And with what surprise and consternation did the Church Uni-

versal receive the intelligence, that Pope Honorius, in the seventh century, had communicated with the Monothelites? Notwithstanding all the extenuating circumstances pleaded in their favour, the names of Liberius and Honorius have been branded with the stigma of infamy, and have been generally regarded with sorrow mingled with abhorrence by a great part of Christendom, from their own times even to this day[1].

2. But who knows the name of Zephyrinus as connected with heretical doctrine? Who knows the name of Callistus as the founder of a sect? And if

[1] Especially Pope Honorius: anathematized *even by Popes themselves* as a heretic, on their accession to the Papacy. See the "Liber Diurnus Romanorum Pontificum" (ed. Paris, 1680), used in the eighth century at the consecration of Roman Bishops, who then made a solemn public declaration as follows: "Auctores novi hæretici dogmatis Sergium, Pyrrhum, Paulum et Petrum Constantinopolitanos, unà cum *Honorio* qui *pravis eorum assertionibus fomentum impendit* . . . cum omnibus hæreticis scriptis atque sequacibus nexu *perpetui anathematis* devinxerunt. Cum suprà fatis hæreticis, Sabellium, Paulum Samosatenum, Marim Persam, Montanum, Donatum, . . . *execramur ac condemnamus.*" This was a part of the profession of faith of the Roman Bishops in the ninth century.

It is observable that they then affirmed themselves to be *not* infallible. For not only did the Popes declare that *Pope Honorius had fallen* into *Heresy*, but their Profession of Faith goes on to say, "Unde et districti anathematis interdictioni subjicimus, si quis unquam, seu *Nos*, sive est alius, qui *novum* aliquid præsumat contra hujusmodi evangelicam traditionem et orthodoxæ fidei Christianæque religionis integritatem."

our Author's narrative is true, they were not only Heretics, but Heresiarchs. Would they not, therefore, have taken their place as such in the pages of Church History? Would not Eusebius have recorded their acts? Would not St. Jerome? Would they not have been enumerated in the copious Catalogues of Heretics, drawn up by the laborious diligence of Epiphanius, Philastrius, Augustine, and Damascene? If Liberius and Honorius attained such unhappy notoriety, surely some records would survive of the more miserable apostasy of two Bishops of Rome in succession—Zephyrinus and Callistus,—who propagated heresy, and proscribed those who were orthodox.

Such surmises as these have doubtless occurred to the reader of this narrative, and they have been propounded by some as objections to its credibility [2].

Let us then consider them. And

1. If in previous Chapters it has been shown to be probable, that the Work before us is from the pen of Hippolytus, if we have seen reason for believing that the narrative in the Ninth book is from his pen, then we have good ground for saying, that the narrative is deserving of credit. For it comes from a person of unimpeachable character, who was a Bishop of the Roman Church in the age of Zephyrinus and Callistus. Therefore we are bound to say, History is *not*

[2] Particularly in an article of an English Journal, which states also some of the objections considered in previous chapters.

silent on the subject of their apostasy. On the contrary, our Author informs us, that the Heresy patronised by Callistus produced "a very great confusion in the minds of all the faithful in all the world[3]." It did make a great noise: it excited a great commotion. It did not escape the notice of History. St. Hippolytus is its Historian.

But 2. It may be said, these considerations do not remove the difficulty. For if our Author is Hippolytus, if this narrative is from his pen, how is it that the facts narrated by him did not become generally known? If Zephyrinus and Callistus acted and taught, as our Author says they did, and if our Author was a Bishop of the Roman Church, how is it to be explained that the name and narrative of St. Hippolytus did not give notoriety to them?

3. Such questions, we may first observe, appear to proceed from a lack of adequate discrimination of times and seasons in the Church. They seem to arise from a habit of mind formed under the influences, literary and theological, *subsequent* in time to the epoch at which our Author wrote. The eyes of men have been so much dazzled with the splendour with which the Church of Rome has been invested since the tenth century, and they are so much impressed with the grandeur and magnificence which she displayed in mediæval times, that they are hardly able to see clearly what she was in the *first*

[3] P. 279, 17.

ages of Christianity. They reflect their own ideas back from the thirteenth century to the third. But it is for the calm and thoughtful student of History to emancipate his mind from the thraldom of these delusive impressions.

Each age has its own character. The ante-Nicene period is different from the Nicene. The Christianization of the Empire introduced a new era in the history and fortunes of the Church. *If* such events as our Author describes *had taken place* in the *fourth* or *fifth* centuries instead of the *third*, then indeed they would have been noised throughout the world, and the echo of them, sounding far and wide, would have been heard distinctly at this day.

4. If, again, the Scene of such events as these had been in the *East*, instead of the West, then it is probable the world would have heard much of them for some time. The Eastern Church, even then, was eminent for learning. But Rome was barren in Theological Literature. Noetus, an Eastern of Smyrna, was well known to the Church. But there were few comparatively in the world to record the acts of the Roman Callistus. Let us, then, bear in mind the place and time at which the events in this narrative are represented to have occurred,—Rome, in the beginning of the third century. Rome at that time did not contain fifty Presbyters. It was still a heathen city[4]. It has been asserted by Æneas

[4] Euseb. vi. 43, cp. Optat. ii. p. 49, who speaks of XL et quod excurrit basilicas.

Sylvius, who afterward became a Bishop of Rome as Pius II. (A. D. 1458), that "[5] *before the Council of Nicæa* little regard was paid to the Church of Rome, and that every one in Christendom looked after their own affairs," and cared little for the doctrine or doings of Roman Bishops. This is a strong statement; and we should be involved in serious error, if we estimated the importance of Rome and her Bishops in the third century by the influence which they *afterwards* acquired [6]. In external respects, there was almost as much difference between Callistus and Innocent III., as there was between Servius Tullius and Augustus Cæsar. And it was not more strange that Callistus, the Slave of Carpophorus, should become a Roman Bishop, than that Servius, the Slave of Tanaquil, should become King of Rome.

We may pursue the parallel further. To us the History of the Roman Church in the beginning of the third century has been hitherto almost an unex-

[5] Epist. 31, ad Martinum Mayerum. "Ante Nicænam Synodum unusquisque sibi vixit, et parvus respectus ad Romanam Ecclesiam habebatur."

[6] Neander justly observes, ii. 483, "Important as the Church of Rome *became* . . . yet it was from the beginning comparatively barren in respect to all theological science. . . . Two individuals only appear to have distinguished themselves as ecclesiastical authors among the Roman Clergy, the presbyter Caius the opponent of Montanism, and Novatian, whom Cornelius, Bishop of Rome, calls ὁ δογματιστής," Euseb. vi. 43, a name which, Neander well remarks, suggests that such a phenomenon was rare at Rome.

plored region. It has been what the history of Heathen Rome is under her Kings—almost barren of facts, and peopled with fables of a later age. We have had few materials whereby to form an accurate judgment concerning it. And in this consists the value of the present narrative in the recently-discovered Treatise. If it is genuine, if it is authentic, it may almost be called an historical revelation. It aids us in filling up a chasm in a very interesting period of Church History. The rescue of this single Volume from the monastic cloister of Mount Athos, is a more important event than the disinterment of a chest of ancient "Libri Pontificum," written under the Kings of Rome.

5. There is extant an ancient Dialogue of a Christian Author, written in the Latin language, composed with perspicuity and elegance of style, and dating as it would seem from nearly the same period as the recently-discovered Treatise on Heresy. And it is observable, that the Scene of that Dialogue is laid at Ostia—within a very short distance of our Author's residence Portus[7]. The reader will anticipate the name of Minucius Felix. This Dialogue, entitled "Octavius," from the name of the Christian interlocutor, who prevails on his heathen friend Cæcilius to renounce paganism for Christianity, af-

[7] It begins with a reference to the Temple of Serapis, which stood at Portus. See the ancient inscription in Spon. Miscell. erudit. Antiquit. Lugd. 1685, p. 329: M. Αὐρήλιος Ἥρων Νεώκορος τοῦ ἐν Πόρτῳ Σεράπιδος.

fords no information with regard to the doctrinal or disciplinarian condition of the Roman Church at that time. But it shows that it was then a poor and despised community, or, as Cæcilius calls it, a "latebrosa et lucifugax natio [8]"—it was a "Church of the Catacombs."

6. The History of the Western Church in the second and third centuries is, as we have said, almost a *terra incognita.* Let us consider some causes of this.

The Christians at that time were engaged in acting and suffering, and had but little leisure for writing. Apologies for Christianity against Paganism, Vindications of the Catholic Faith, and Refutations of Heresy, were their Literature. Being exposed to the peril of martyrdom, they had little means or inclination for the collection of materials for History. And even if Church Histories had been written in the second and third centuries, they would probably have been destroyed in the Decian and Diocletian persecutions. Church History is the produce of Peace. We may thank Constantine for it.

But it may be said, Have we not Church Historians who profess to describe the early period of the Roman Church? Have we not Eusebius? Have we not St. Jerome? Was not he secretary to Pope Damasus? and must not he have known the early history of the Roman Church? We have indeed such writers, and we have reason to be thankful for

[8] Minuc. Felix, p. 75, ed. Lug. Bat. 1672. See also p. 102, Pars vestrûm major et melior egetis, algetis, fame laboratis.

them. But let us consider their circumstances. Eusebius, who wrote his history about A.D. 325, informs us, that he was the *first* who attempted to compose a Church History. His words are remarkable. He claims indulgence because he is "the first to engage in this enterprise, and because he is entering on a desert and untrodden road, and is not able to find any print-marks of persons who had preceded him[9]." Eusebius wrote, a century *after* Hippolytus. Besides, Eusebius was an *Eastern;* he knew little of Latin[1]; his accounts of the early history of the Roman Church are very meagre. And St. Jerome, though a Western by birth, was an Eastern by residence in his maturer years, and did not much more for Church History than transcribe from the work of Eusebius.

7. We may here advert to a remarkable proof of the slender knowledge possessed by Eusebius and St. Jerome with regard to the earlier history of the *Western* Church. It is very significant. And, what is also worth notice, it is connected with Hippolytus.

Neither Eusebius nor St. Jerome knew that St.

[9] Euseb. i. 1.

[1] "Eusebius Latinæ linguæ perexiguam habuit cognitionem." See Vales. and Heinichen in Euseb. i. 13; ii. 2; ii. 25; iv. 8; viii. 2. "Eusebius" (says Bp. Pearson, Annal. Cyprian. Præf.) "scriptor in rebus Occidentis parum accuratus." Again: "Eusebiana Pontificum Romanorum Chronologia merito suspecta," says Bp. Pearson, Dissert. Posth. i. c. 10, p. 101. Again: "Eusebio res Occidentalis imperii parum cognitæ," says Dodwell, Dissert. p. 110.

Hippolytus was Bishop of Portus, near Rome. Neither of them knew the See of which he was Bishop.

Eusebius says that Hippolytus was Bishop of some Church without specifying the name, and St. Jerome states that he was not able to *discover* the name of his See[2], and Eusebius, when he wrote his history, does not appear to have known that St. Hippolytus suffered Martyrdom.

8. Let us here notice some other parallel instances. Eusebius, it is clear, did not know who was the Author of the "Little Labyrinth," from which he quotes a long extract[3]. We know that it was written by Hippolytus[4].

Eusebius mistakes Novatus for Novatian[5], and never mentions Lactantius or Minutius Felix. Theodoret never mentions St. Cyprian[6], and does not appear to have known the See of Hippolytus[7].

If then the Historians of the Church, the most learned men of their age, did not know these promi-

[2] Euseb. vi. 20. S. Jerome, de Viris Ill. lxi. "Nomen urbis scire non potui."

[3] v. 28.

[4] Ruggieri says very truly, p. 497, *Recentiores* Scriptores *multa* sciverunt quæ *Eusebio* et S. *Hieronymo* fuerunt incomperta, and he adduces various instances in proof, pp. 497—505.

[5] Euseb. vi. 43. 45, and the Variorum Notes, pp. 511. 534, ed. Oxon. 1842.

[6] "Theodoretus Cypriani utpote *Latini* nusquam meminit," says Bp. Pearson, Annal. Cyprian.

[7] He calls him ἐπίσκοπος καὶ μάρτυρ in several places—iv. 54. 130. 282, and in each of these cases he quotes him after Ignatius and Irenæus, whose sees he mentions, but he never mentions that of Hippolytus.

nent facts in the History of so celebrated a person as Hippolytus,—is their silence or the silence of others, with regard to *any* events in his life, or in the History of the Western Church in his age, to be regarded as of sufficient weight, to set aside, or countervail positive testimony from a credible source? Assuredly not.

When Ruffinus, presbyter of Aquileia, wished to give to Western Christendom a History of the early Church, he did not compose an original work, but translated the History of Eusebius. Sulpicius Severus, and Orosius writing in the West, show how little was known by Occidental Christians concerning their own early Church History; Socrates, Sozomen, and Theodoret, are Orientals [8].

Hence it has come to pass, that we have hitherto been obliged to study the early History of the West, in the pages of the East. The Easterns were not acquainted with the early History of the Roman Church, and we cannot learn from them what they themselves did not know.

Therefore (we may repeat), no argument can be derived against the credibility of the present Narrative from any silence of Church Historians.

9. Let us here notice two parallels to the events recorded in our narrative.

[8] How little have we heard of Rome except through the medium of Greece! What should we have known of the Scipios if Livy had not been preceded by Polybius. The names of Dionysius of Halicarnassus, Appian, Dio Cassius and other Greek writers suggest similar reflexions.

(1) A Bishop of Rome at the end of the third century, Marcellinus, who afterwards suffered Martyrdom, is said to have fallen away in the time of persecution from the Christian faith, and to have sacrificed to the gods of the heathen. This is generally stated by Roman writers, who have composed the lives of Roman Bishops[9]. But Eusebius says nothing of it; nor any Historian of that age.

(2) Again; A Bishop of Rome in the second century was induced to favour Montanism: he acknowledged the prophecies of Prisca and Maximilla, and communicated with Montanist congregations. And how do we know this? From a single passage of Tertullian[10]; if that had been lost, we should have heard nothing of this important fact. And to this day it has not been determined by learned men, *who* that Montanizing Bishop of Rome was[1]. But no

[9] *E.g.* Anastasius, and Platina. [10] Tertullian c. Prax. c. 1.

[1] Valesius in Euseb. v. 4, thinks it was Eleutherus. So does Bp. Pearson, Diss. ii. 9. Neander asserts that it was Anicetus (on Tertullian, p. 486); in another place he seems to lean to Eleutherus, Eccl. Hist. ii. 258; Baronius, that it was Anicetus. H. Dodwell affirms, with good reason, that it was Zephyrinus himself, Dissert. (ad A.D. 173) de Rom. Pont. Successione, xiv. § 9. Dodwell argues this from the close of the Catalogue of Heresies at the end of Tertullian's Præscriptiones, "*Post hos omnes,* i. e. *post* Theodotum Argentarium (who was certainly under Zephyrinus, Euseb. v. 28) *etiam* Praxeas quidam *hæresim* introduxit quam *Victorinus corroborare* curavit." Now, from Tertullian c. Praxeam, c. 1, it appears that Praxeas did *two* things at *Rome* at one and the same time: one was, he induced the Bishop

one doubts the fact. Whether it made a noise at the time, we cannot say, but

> Ad *nos* vix tenuis famæ perlabitur aura.

---

of Rome to revoke the letters of communion he had given to the Montanists; the second was, he broached his own heresy, *i. e.* the Patripassian heresy, which resembled that afterwards brought to Rome by the followers of Noetus, and encouraged by Zephyrinus. "Duo negotia diaboli Praxeas Romæ procuravit; prophetiam expulit et hæresim intulit. Paracletum fugavit et Patrem crucifixit."

The words "Praxeas hæresim introduxit, quam *Victorinus corroborare* curavit," have caused some perplexity. Who was this "Victorinus?"

Gieseler proposes "Victor" (§ 60, notes 5 and 7), supposing a reference to *Victor*, Bishop of Rome, who excommunicated the Theodotians, and therefore might be represented by some as favourable to the opposite heresy, that of Praxeas.

The sentence bears a remarkable resemblance to the words of S. Hippolytus speaking of Noetianism in our Treatise, p. 279, 29, *Κλεομένης ἐκράτυνε τὸ δόγμα κατ᾽ ἐκεῖνο καιροῦ Ζεφυρίνου διέπειν νομίζοντος τὴν ἐκκλησίαν*, and p. 284, 77, *ταύτην τὴν αἵρεσιν ἐκράτυνε Κάλλιστος . . . τὸν Ζεφυρῖνον . . . πείθων δόγμασι. . . .*

Perhaps we may suppose that the word *Victorinus* in the passage aforesaid is a reading *composed* of the *two* names, *Victor* and *Zephyrinus*, and that it proceeded from the doubts of the copyists wavering between one and the other, and that the true reading is *Zephyrinus*.

A learned friend communicates a conjecture first made by Dr. Allix (see Waterland, v. 227. Judgt. of Primitive Churches, chap. v.), that the List of Heretics at the end of Tertullian's Præscriptiones is only a Latin Translation of the *βιβλιδάριον* of Hippolytus, seen by Photius, see above, p. 59. If this is the case, then the supposition above-mentioned would be more probable.

These circumstances are important, as showing that, because Bishops of Rome erred in the second century, it does not necessarily follow, that a clear and circumstantial account of their errors is to be expected from the Church Histories which we now possess, or that, when we have such an account in a single writer of credit, we should look upon his narrative as apocryphal[2].

10. But we are understating the argument. Our Author is not *alone* in recording the errors of Callistus.

Theodoret, the Ecclesiastical Historian and Bishop of Cyrus in the fifth century, in his compendious account of Heresies, adds to his article on Noetus, a shorter one on *Callistus*[3].

"*Callistus* took the lead in propagating this Heresy after Noetus, and devised certain additions to the impiety of the doctrine[4]."

Here then is another witness. It is evident, as will be shown hereafter, from a comparison of Theodoret's Account of Heresies with the newly-discovered Treatise[5], that Theodoret, in composing his

[2] It is observable that Hippolytus in his Catalogue of Heretics never mentions *Praxeas*. Nor does Tertullian mention *Noetus*. Yet who doubts the existence of either?

[3] It is headed, in the Roman edition of Theodoret, περὶ Καλλίστου.

[4] Hærat. Fab. Comp. iii. 3, tom. iv. pt. i. ed. Hal. 1772, p. 343.

[5] See below, Appendix B. to this Volume.

own work, used our Author's Volume, and derived materials from it. He seems to have contented himself with referring to the *Tenth Book,* being an *Epitome* of the rest; perhaps he had not access to the other Nine. But from these facts it is clear, that the newly-discovered Treatise was written *before* the time of Theodoret; and that he regarded our Author as trustworthy, and followed him as such.

11. Let us also recollect the character of the Callistian Heresy, as described by our Author. It had no elements of permanence. For it arose from a compromise due to personal and local circumstances. It was an attempt to reconcile two incompatible systems—the system of Noetus and Theodotus. It was not therefore likely to make any great stir after the death of Callistus. It would soon be obsolete and forgotten [6]. It would be absorbed in Sabellianism, as even the more consistent theory of Noetus was soon merged in that Heresy. "The *Noetians,*" says St. Augustine [7], "are scarcely known by any one now; but the Sabellians are in many people's mouths." No wonder that the world soon forgot the Heresy of Callistus.

12. It may be here observed, that Theodoret states

[6] Sabellius is called a disciple of Noetus by Philastrius, Hæres. 54. See also S. Aug. Hæres. 41.

[7] Aug. de Hæres. xli. Noetiani difficile ab aliquo sciuntur Sabelliani autem sunt more multorum.

that no vestige even of Sabellianism remained in his age[8]. He is speaking of the East. And probably it was almost extinguished at Rome, by Dionysius, Bishop of that Church, in the middle of the third century[9]. Can we then be surprised that the doctrines and acts of Zephyrinus and of Callistus, should not have found a prominent place in the annals of the Church?

13. If History had been silent with respect to them, there would not therefore have been much cause for surprise. But, as we have seen, History is not silent. And let us proceed to observe that there are also various scattered notices in ancient ecclesiastical writers, which, though not directly adverting to the events recorded in this narrative, yet throw light upon them, and are illustrated by them.

Thus the laxity of discipline with which our Author taxes the Church of Rome in his own age is described in very similar terms by his contemporary, Tertullian[1].

14. Again, a passage has been preserved by Eusebius, which was written by St. Hippolytus[2]. It is from

[8] Hæret. Fab. comp. ii. xi.: *οὐ βραχὺ τούτων διέμεινε λείψανον.*

[9] See above, p. 118.

[1] The passages may be seen quoted below in notes to the translation of that portion of the Philosophumena.

[2] See Euseb. v. 28, compared with Theodoret ii. 4 and ii. 5. The ground of its ascription to St. Hippolytus is that its Author claimed as his own the Book on the Universe, which is known, from the statue of Hippolytus, to have been written by him.

the "Little Labyrinth," a work directed against the Heresy of Artemon and Theodotus, who affirmed our Blessed Lord to be a mere man.

These heretics had alleged, that their own opinions had been sanctioned by the Church of Rome, "*till the age* of Victor, but that from *the time* of *Zephyrinus*[3], his successor, the truth had been corrupted."

Here, then, it was affirmed, that, under the Episcopate of Zephyrinus, a *change* had *taken place* in the doctrine of the Roman Church.

Now, if (as the Author of our Treatise states) Zephyrinus lapsed into Noetianism, which was indeed the opposite extreme to the heresy of Artemon, as well as contrary to orthodoxy, then indeed there *was* a change in the teaching of Rome, and the truth was corrupted from the date of *his* Episcopate.

Thus the assertion of Artemon and his followers confirms this narrative, and is explained by it.

15. But this, it may be said, was an assertion of heretics.

True; but let us observe, How does Hippolytus himself meet the charge in the passage quoted by Eusebius[4]? Does he deny the accusation, by asserting the orthodoxy of Zephyrinus? *If* Zephyrinus had been sound in faith, and had been acknowledged as such, he could hardly have failed to repel so grave

And the date of the Author and his subject and style are confirmatory of this evidence.

[3] ἀπὸ Ζεφυρίνου παρακεχαράχθαι τὴν ἀλήθειαν.

[4] Euseb. v. 28.

an impeachment by an indignant appeal to the conscience of the Roman Church. But he does not thus speak. No; he uses the following words: "This charge would" (he allows) "perhaps *have been probable*"—this is a remarkable confession; it would perhaps *have been probable, if* something else had not been the case. And what was that? Does he say,—*If* Zephyrinus had not been orthodox, and known to be such [5]? No; he urges no such plea, he makes no such affirmation; but, waiving that question, he says, *If* the doctrines of Artemon were not contradicted by Scripture, and if the Divinity of Christ had not been taught by the *primitive* Church.

He therefore almost seems by implication to admit the charge against Zephyrinus, as countenancing an innovation in the doctrine of the Church; and this admission, if such it be, is explained by the narrative before us. And let us add, that, in the extract from St. Hippolytus, quoted by Eusebius, there is also an invective against an heretical Bishop, Natalius, who had lapsed into heresy through *avarice*, and there is an animadversion on and against "the vice of *covetousness*, as working the ruin of *the majority of men* [6]," a remark which was perhaps suggested by the besetting sin of Zephyrinus [7], as displayed in the Narrative before us.

[5] ἦν δ' ἂν τυχὸν πιθανὸν τὸ λεγόμενον.

[6] τῇ πλείστους ἀπολλυούσῃ αἰσχροκερδείᾳ.

[7] Where Zephyrinus is represented as having fallen into heresy through avarice. See Refutation of Heresy, p. 279. 30, 1,

16. Another topic of interest, which appears to be illustrated by the present Narrative, is the following.

When we read the annals of the savage persecution which raged under Decius the Emperor, in the middle of the third century (that is, a few years after the events described in our Author's narrative), we feel staggered and perplexed by the stern severity of that terrible judgment. Wherefore did it please the Almighty to pour out the vials of His wrath upon His Church? Why did He permit the heathen to rage so furiously against her?

The present History supplies the answer. It exhibits the greatest Church of the West corrupted by Heresy, sullied by licentiousness, and distracted by schism. *Οὐ νέμεσις*, we therefore say, No wonder that the Righteous Ruler of the World should have visited her with the scourge of persecution, in order to chastise her for her sins, and mercifully to call her to repentance.

Thus the present narrative is fraught with instruction. It vindicates the ways of God to man; and it reads a solemn warning to Christendom, by displaying the retributive consequence of false doctrine and of corrupt practices in a Church.

St. Cyprian, the venerable Bishop of Carthage, lived at the time of that persecution. In one of his writings[8], composed soon after its cessation, he has

Ζεφυρίνου ἀνδρὸς αἰσχροκερδοῦς, and *κέρδει προσφερομένῳ πειθόμενος*, and again, p. 284, 82, *Ζεφυρῖνον ὄντα δωρολήπτην καὶ φιλάργυρον.*

[8] De Lapsis, p. 435, cap. v.

expressed himself in language which affords a strong confirmation of our narrative, and an eloquent comment upon it, and admirably enforces the important moral which it suggests to the mind.

"The gloom of persecution," he says, "ought not so to blind the reason, as not to allow light to survive for the contemplation of the divine law. When the cause of the malady is ascertained, then a remedy for it is discerned. The Lord would try His household; and *because a long peace*[9] *had paralysed the discipline* which we had received from heaven, the divine chastisement *roused our Faith, which was lying prostrate and almost asleep;* and when we for our sins merited severer retribution, our most merci-

[9] *I.e.* from A.D. 210 to A.D. 235. Sulpicius Severus (lib. ii. p. 383) says, "Severo imperante Christianorum vexatio fuit; interjectis deinde annis XXXVIII *pax Christianis fuit*, nisi quod medio tempore Maximinus nonnullarum Ecclesiarum *clericos* vexavit." The Emperor Septimius Severus, at the beginning of his reign, A.D. 193, was not unfavourable to the Christians (Tertullian ad Scap. c. 4); but A.D. 203 he issued an edict forbidding them to receive proselytes; and persecutions, not however general, ensued. Euseb. vi. 7. Caracalla, A.D. 211—217, did not persecute. Heliogabalus and Severus Alexander favoured Christianity, so far as to regard it on a par with other religions. The successor of Severus, Maximin, A.D. 235, revived the rage of persecution, especially (Eusebius says *only*) against the Bishops of the Church. Euseb. vi. 28, where see the note of Valesius. Probably it was then that St. Hippolytus, as a Bishop, suffered martyrdom; and there may be some allusion to the fact stated by Eusebius in the line of Prudentius concerning Hippolytus (xi. 80), as a reason urged for his death, "Ipsum Christicolis esse *caput* populis."

ful Lord so tempered all things, that the storm which has now passed over us seemed rather an examination, than a Persecution.

"Every one among us was eager for the increase of his riches, and, forgetting how believers acted in the time of the Apostles, and how they ought to act in all ages, every one was anxious to augment his own wealth. No longer were Priests adorned with devout religion, nor Ministers by faith undefiled, no more was there mercy in acts, or discipline in conversation. Many Bishops, who ought to have given admonition and example to the rest, deserted their flocks, grasped at Secular gain from lucrative traffic, and coveted heaps of money, while their brethren in the Church were famished, and seized estates by wily frauds, and augmented the interest of their money with manifold usury."

Such is St. Cyprian's picture of the state of the Church [1] before the Decian persecution, that is, at the period described by our Author in the narrative before us. Thus the Bishop and Martyr of Carthage, bears testimony to the truth of the history written by the Bishop and Martyr of Portus.

17. An observation may be introduced here, which is suggested by this narrative, as applicable to our own times.

[1] A similar description of disciplinarian laxity in the Church is given by Commodian, who wrote in the third century. Instructiones, v. 873—v. 1057.

It seems to be imagined by some, that, in order to the maintenance of pure doctrine and wholesome discipline in a Church, it is almost indispensable that she should not be connected with the Civil Power by any ties of alliance; and, in cases where the Church is so associated with the State, they are desirous of seeing a disruption of that union, and cherish a confident hope that soundness of doctrine and effective administration of discipline will be obtained by the severance of the one from the other, and are not to be looked for without it.

Let attention be therefore paid to the condition of the Church of Rome, with regard both to doctrine and discipline, at the beginning of the third century, as presented in this Volume.

She was not hampered by any trammels of civil control, but was exempt from all secular restraints. Indeed, she was precisely in the position which has been selected as most favourable to dogmatic soundness, moral sanctity, and disciplinarian strictness, and which, it has been supposed, will, by a natural consequence, produce those inestimable benefits. Besides, she had some among her who were little removed in the line of succession from the holy Apostles. The teaching of Apostolic men sounded in her ears. She had an Hippolytus, the third in degree from St. John.

And yet, melancholy truth, she was corrupted with heresy, torn with schism, and polluted with vice. She was governed by a Zephyrinus and a

Callistus; and St. Hippolytus was stigmatized as a heretic. . . . Let not the warning be lost!

But to return.

18. We have been reviewing certain passages of ancient writers which incidentally reflect light on the Roman narrative of our Author, and receive light from it; and, in this manner, afford guarantees of our Author's veracity. More such illustrations might be added, and will probably suggest themselves to the reader, who may find profitable employment in observing such undesigned coincidences as these.

19. Let us now pass on to notice an objection, which has, in all probability, already occurred to his mind. How can it be explained, that a narrative of so much interest and importance as the present, contained in a work composed by so eminent a person as Hippolytus, should have escaped the notice of the world? How may we account for the fact, that it has been reserved to a felicitous enterprise in the middle of the nineteenth century to call it forth from the grave in which it had lain buried for 1600 years?

One reply, and one only, as it would seem, is to be made to this question. It has pleased Divine Providence that it should be so. And the ways of Providence are marvellous. The preservation, the discovery, and lastly the publication of this Volume, demand our grateful admiration. It may not be presumptuous to say, that the same Divine Power which sealed up the cities of Herculaneum and Pompeii in their graves of lava for seventeen centuries, and then raised them from the tomb and revealed them to our sight, that we might see in them a faint image of the sudden destruction from fire which will one day overtake the World while engaged in its business and its pleasures, has had some great purpose in view, in the wonderful burial and resurrection of this interesting Work. He Who allowed the copies of His Holy Word to be destroyed, and Who hid one, and one only, copy in his Sanctuary, may have had some great design in view, while He permitted the other transcripts of this work to perish, in concealing one copy in safe custody in the monastic cloister of Mount Athos. Perhaps, also, it may be said, that the form of the question ought to be modified. The real ground for surprise is not so much that the other transcripts should have perished, as that this one Manuscript should have been preserved.

Of the works written in the third century how small a residue survives! Of how many ecclesiastical authors, who lived at that period, we have nothing more than the names! Let us cast our eyes over the pages of Dr. Routh's "Reliquiæ Sacræ;" how many writers do they present to us of the Antenicene age, how many titles of works, and how few are the fragments there gathered together. In that Sacred Reliquary, in that spiritual catacomb of the Primitive Church (if we may be permitted so to call it), a little dust—precious indeed as gold—in a few sepulchral urns, is all that now remains[2].

The reason of this is clear; the Christians of that age were dispersed by the persecutions of Decius and Diocletian. Their churches were burnt; their houses were spoiled; they themselves were swept away by fire and sword. The Church was scattered to the winds. The rage of Diocletian was specially directed against Sacred Books. The Volumes which escaped from the perils of those days were like brands snatched from the fire.

If the work upon heresy now in our hands had been published in the *fifth* or the *sixth* century, when the storm of persecution had passed away, then, indeed, we might have been surprised that it should not have been known to subsequent ages, but now, we repeat, we ought rather to be surprised —that a single copy remains.

20. Let us observe, also, our Author's position as writer; it was very peculiar;

He was an Eastern writing in the West. He wrote at Rome in the language of Greece. And he published his work when the use of the Greek language was becoming less common in Western Christendom. As the Church of Rome grew in

[2] ———— βραχὺ
σμῆγμα δυσδάκρυτον ἀν-
τήνορος σποδοῦ γεμί-
ζον λέβητας εὐθέτου.
Æschyl. Agam. 430.

importance, so the language of Rome became more and more the language of the Western Church. In the third century, particularly by the influence of Tertullian and Cyprian, the Western Church began to possess a Literature of its own. Under such circumstances as these, the demand for our Author's work was not likely to be large. How little should we now possess of his master Irenæus, if his Work on Heresy had not been very early translated into Latin. How very scanty are the remains of any early Greek ecclesiastical writings that were first published in the West. Tertullian's Greek works are lost. A few paragraphs are all that remain of Caius. Hermas survives only in Latin. Clement of Rome probably owes the preservation of his Epistle to its having been sent into Greece. Our Author's Treatise being published in the West, but not in the language of the West, would soon cease to be transcribed. It would be superseded by other works on Heresy, such as those of Philastrius and Augustine, written in Latin, and soon sink into oblivion.

21. Besides, let us now revert to the fact already mentioned before, as established by the testimony of Photius[3], that a *smaller* work, *written* also by Hippolytus, as a Refutation of Heresy, was once in existence.

Now, let us observe, the newly-recovered Treatise on Heresy appears to have been either *anonymous*,

[3] See above, pp. 59—75.

or at least not to have retained the name of *Hippolytus*, and it is a much *larger* work than the *biblaridion* seen by Photius, and described by him as a Treatise of Hippolytus on Heresy.

It is very probable that the smaller work did much to throw the larger work into the shade.

Isaac Casaubon has well shown, in his admirable dedication prefixed to Polybius [4], that the making of Epitomes has tended to the destruction of the works epitomized. Justin has extinguished Trogus. The Excerpta made from Polybius have destroyed a great part of Polybius. It is not too much to say, that the learned Emperor Constantinus Porphyrogenitus innocently and unconsciously perpetrated a massacre of ancient Historians, by ordering their works to be abridged. Henceforth no one would purchase, no one could transcribe them. The imperial Abstracts superseded the voluminous and costly originals; just as it is to be feared, the cheap compendiums of Butler and Paley and Locke would have done, in days gone by, in our own Universities, if we had lived in an age of manuscripts, and not of printed books [5].

If a *small* Work and a *large* Work, bearing the name of the same Author and treating on the same

[4] Casaubon, Dedicatio ad Polyb. p. 18, vol. iii. ed. Amst. 1670. Accessit pestis alia, Compendiorum et Epitomarum confectio, quod genus Scriptionis publicè noxium et magnis scriptoribus semper fuit exitiosissimum.

[5] "Epitomes" (says Lord Bacon) "are the moths of History,

subject, were extant in ancient times, the chances of vitality were greatly in favour of the smaller. It was more portable, and less costly. It was first observed by Casaubon [6] that Eustathius, the Archbishop of Thessalonica, in his vast Homeric Commentary, rarely quotes from the *entire* work of Athenæus, but generally uses the *Epitome* of that Author; and Bentley has shown that Eustathius appears *never even to have seen* the entire Athenæus, but *always* to have used the Epitome [7]. Similarly it may be remarked, that Epiphanius wrote two works on Heresy, his "Panarium," a very voluminous one, and an Epitome of it, called "Anacephalæosis," or Recapitulation. St. Augustine has left us a work on Heresies, and he refers to Epiphanius; he copied from the "Recapitulation," but does not appear to have known the "Panarium [8]."

Our Author wrote two treatises on Heresy. The smaller, it is probable, superseded the larger, the more so because the smaller bore his name prefixed; the larger seems to have been without it. Four MSS. have been preserved of the First Book, which has been

which have fretted and corroded the sound bodies of many excellent Histories;" and, we may add, of many excellent works on Theology and Philosophy also.

[6] Casaubon in Athenæum, i. 1.

[7] Bentley, Dissertation on Phalaris, p. 95, ed. Lond. 1777.

[8] "Anacephalæosis sola sine Panario venit in manus Augustini," say the Benedictine Editors, viii. p. 47, ed. Paris, 1837, and see Lardner, i. p. 583.

published long ago[9], and we have this newly-discovered MS. of Six other Books. But not one of these five MSS. bears the name of Hippolytus.

Hence, it came to pass, that the narrative contained in the Ninth Book concerning the Roman Church, did not attract the attention that otherwise it would have done.

22. Nor is this all. Not only did a *smaller*, and *separate*, Treatise on Heresy by Hippolytus exist, which interfered with the circulation of the Larger Work; but the *Larger Work* itself was *epitomized* in the *Tenth Book:* and this Tenth Book, being a Recapitulation, had a tendency to supplant the other Nine.

There appears to be good reason for believing, that, as St. Augustine used only the Summary of Epiphanius, so likewise Theodoret, in his work on Heresy, used only this Recapitulation by Hippolytus[1].

And this Recapitulation, describing the Heresy of Callistus (p. 330), does *not* style him *Bishop of Rome*, but merely refers to the narrative of his doings already given in the Ninth Book.

Hence this summary also conduced to the same result as the "Little Book" of Hippolytus. It sheltered Callistus, and helped him to escape from the notice of History.

23. Further, may we not say, that such a book as

[9] In the Benedictine edition of Origen. See above, p. 18.

[1] See below, Appendix B.

this, published in the West, and containing such a narrative as that in the Ninth Book, concerning the Roman Church, was not likely to be regarded with favour in the region of Rome, where it was composed and published? It displays a picture, which no member, and especially no presbyter or Bishop, of that Church, could otherwise regard than with feelings of sorrow and shame. They would not be eager to transcribe it, or to purchase copies of it.

And all who are familiar with the History of ancient MSS., know well how soon a book perished, which was not often transcribed. And therefore the wonder is, not that the other copies of this work were lost, but that *one* copy was saved. Probably, under Providence, it owed its preservation to its having been transported by some friendly Greek from the West to the East, and lodged in a cell of Mount Athos. And now it has come forth from its place of refuge, and has been brought back by a Greek from the East to the West, and it speaks to the World at large.

24. On the whole, it appears, that this Narrative concerning the Roman Church in the early part of the Third Century, was written by St. Hippolytus, a scholar of St. Irenæus, Bishop of Portus, near Rome, an eminent Doctor and Martyr of the Church. He was an eye-witness of what he relates,—his relation, therefore, is entitled to credit; it is to be received as true.

No valid objection can be raised against this conclusion from the silence of History. History records facts corroborating this narrative, which is itself a most credible History, as coming from Hippolytus. And many causes contributed to render this Narrative less generally known. The *place* of its original publication, the *time* of its appearance in the world, the character of the Narrative itself, were unfavourable to its circulation. It was antecedent to Church History, and Church History was of *Eastern* growth, and knew little of the *West.* And Persecution soon followed the publication of this Narrative, and diverted the mind of the Church in another direction, and destroyed much of her Literature. The Work in which this Narrative is contained, and in which it lies almost obscured, had other literary rivals to contend with. *Other* Histories of Heresy, written in Latin, superseded it. Its own Author did much to supplant it. First, his smaller work, described by Photius; and, secondly, his own Summary in the Tenth Book, sufficed for the public demand: the rest was rarely transcribed, and was soon forgotten. The Heresy of Callistus had vanished from the world, and was of little interest to it. Thus the memory of him and his doings died away. And, in the course of a few centuries, Callistus, the promoter of heresy, became even a Saint and a Martyr in the Roman Church.

Therefore, the silence of Church Historians—such

as Eusebius and others, writing in the East, in the fourth century, and in later times—suggests to us another cause of thankfulness for the remarkable discovery of the Treatise in which this Narrative concerning the Roman Church is contained. It reminds us how much we have gained by this discovery. For this Narrative affords us new and most effective means for the successful resistance and refutation of novel and dangerous errors, and for the firmer establishment and maintenance of Scriptural and Catholic Truth.

CHAPTER X.

INFERENCES FROM THE FOREGOING ENQUIRY.—WORKS ASCRIBED TO ST. HIPPOLYTUS.

IN the year 1716-18, an edition of the works, or fragments of works, ascribed to St. Hippolytus, and then known to be extant, was published at Hamburgh, by Dr. John Albert FABRICIUS[1] of Leipsick, in two thin folio volumes; a great part of which was occupied with dissertations on the Paschal Chronicle, and other subsidiary matter.

The works collected by Fabricius, and published under the name of Hippolytus, had been attributed to him in ancient Manuscripts, and had been, for the most part, received as genuine by some eminent

[1] S. HIPPOLYTI Episcopi et Martyris Opera non anteà collecta et partem nunc primùm e MSS. in lucem edita Græcè et Latinè; accedunt Virorum Doctorum Notæ et Animadversiones.

The Second Volume, as far as it relates to St. Hippolytus, derives its value principally from the Homily against Noetus, in the Greek original, supplied by Montfaucon from a transcript of a MS. in the Vatican. In the former Volume the Homily had been given only in a Latin Translation by Francis Turrianus.

critics and divines. But others had expressed a doubt whether any of these writings, ascribed to St. Hippolytus, are really his.

Dr. Mill, the learned Editor of the Greek Testament, who had purposed to publish an edition of them, has intimated [2] an opinion that none of them are genuine, except perhaps the work upon Antichrist. H. Dodwell spoke with much hesitation. Dr. Grabe was scarcely more confident [3]. The Benedictine Editors of St. Ambrose seem to have imagined that all the writings of St. Hippolytus were lost [4].

Such being the opinions of some distinguished men concerning the writings ascribed to St. Hippolytus on the authority of some ancient MSS., and inserted as such in the edition of Fabricius [5], no arguments have been founded upon them in our enquiry concerning the Authorship of the newly-discovered Treatise on Heresy. We have abstained from deductions of this kind, as being of a precarious character, and liable to exception. And the question of Authorship has been examined on independent grounds.

But now at this stage of the investigation, when

[2] Proleg. in N. T., n. 655. See Lardner, Credibility, i. p. 499.

[3] Note on Bp. Bull, Def. Fid. Nicæn. c. 8. These passages were collected by Lardner. Cp. Bull, Def. F. N., iii. 8. 4, p. 596, and Waterland, iii. p. 102.

[4] Temporum iniquitate perierunt.

[5] See above, p. 48.

we have been brought by other considerations to the conclusion,—that the newly-discovered Treatise is rightly ascribed to St. Hippolytus,—it becomes a reasonable and interesting subject of enquiry;—

Whether the *other* writings attributed to Hippolytus on a certain amount of presumptive evidence, and inserted in the edition of his works, bear marks of being from the same hand, as the Treatise on Heresy?

If this is found to be the case, then we shall obtain a twofold result,

1. We shall be confirmed in our previous conviction that the newly-discovered Treatise is from Hippolytus. And

2. We shall also be disposed to give credence to the opinion of those who have accepted the *other* works—to which we have referred,—as genuine.

The evidence here applicable is partly external, and partly internal.

I. The Author of *this* Treatise affirms, that he wrote a Book on the SYSTEM of the UNIVERSE[6]. St. Hippolytus wrote a work bearing that title, as appears from various testimonies, and particularly from the Catalogue on his Statue, where it is described as being written "against the GENTILES[7], and against PLATO, or on the UNIVERSE." It was, in all probability, intended to be a Christian System of Cos-

[6] p. 334.

[7] πρὸς Ἕλληνας καὶ πρὸς Πλάτωνα ἢ περὶ τοῦ Παντός.

mogony, contrasted with that propounded by Plato in his dialogue bearing a similar title—"ON THE UNIVERSE, or Timæus[8]," which had been rendered familiar to the Roman literary world through the translation made by Cicero, of which some portions remain.

([1]) One very interesting fragment, from a Work having this title, "On the Universe," and bearing the name of St. Hippolytus, was discovered in a MS. in an Italian Library, and thence first printed by David Hœschel, in a note to Photius[9], and subsequently by Stephen Le Moyne, in his Varia Sacra[1], and by Fabricius, in his edition[2] of Hippolytus[3].

On examining this fragment, we find much resemblance, both of thought and language, between it and the latter part of the recently-discovered Treatise on Heresy[4]. They mutually illustrate each other. And thus the proof that the Treatise is from Hippolytus, strengthens the belief that the Fragment has been rightly ascribed to him: and the ascription of the Fragment by ancient Manuscripts to St. Hip-

[8] Platonis Opera, vii. pp. 234—372, ed. Bekker, London, 1826. The remains of Cicero's translation are in his Works, vii. p. 930, and are entitled "Timæus seu de Universo," ed. Oxon. 1810.

[9] P. 923. [1] P. 1119. [2] I. p. 220.

[3] And also (in some respects more correctly) in the Sacra Parallela bearing the name of John Damascene, ii. pp. 755. 788, ed. Lequien, where a portion of the fragment is attributed to Meletius, and a portion to Josephus (Ἰώσηππος).

[4] The subject of both is the condition of departed spirits in

polytus, corroborates the proof that the Treatise is also from him.

another world. Some of the parallels are as follows concerning the place and punishment of the wicked:—

Fragments from the work "On the Universe," p. 220.	*"Refutation of Heresy," p. 339.*
χωρίον ὑπόγειον ἐν ᾧ φῶς κόσμου οὐκ ἐπιλάμπει; φωτὸς τούνυν τούτῳ τῷ χωρίῳ μὴ καταλάμποντος . . . ἐφ' ᾧ κατεστάθησαν ἄγγελοι φρουροὶ πρὸς τὰς ἑκάστων πράξεις διανέμοντες τὰς τῶν τρόπων προσκαίρους κολάσεις . . . . . ἐν τούτῳ τόπος ἀφώρισταί τις λίμνη πυρὸς ἀσβέστου. P. 221. οἱ ἄδικοιεἰς ἀριστερὰ ἕλκονται ὑπὸ ἀγγέλων κολαστῶν, μετὰ βίας ὡς δέσμιοι ἑλκόμενοι, οἷς οἱ ἐφεστῶτες ἄγγελοι διαπέμπονται ὀνειδίζοντες καὶ φοβερῷ ὄμματι ἐπαπειλοῦντες, τῆς γεέννης ἔγγιον ὄντες τοῦ βρασμοῦ ἀδιαλείπτως ὑπακούουσι.	ἐκφεύξεσθε ταρτάρου ζοφερὸν ὄμμα ἀφώτιστον ὑπὸ Λόγου φωνῆς μὴ καταλαμφθὲν, καὶ βρασμὸν ἀενάου λίμνης γεννήτορος φλογός, καὶ ταρταρούχων ἀγγέλων κολαστῶν ὄμμα ἀεὶ μένον ἐν ἀπειλῇ.

Other resemblances between the Treatise "on the Universe" and the "Philosophumena," indicating their common origin, and, by consequence, showing that the author of the "Philosophumena" is Hippolytus, may be seen in the notes accompanying the translation inserted in the latter portion of this volume. An argument might also be adduced in confirmation of the Hippolytean origin of this fragment from its similarity to the language of Irenæus on the same subject. See Iren. ii. 63, 64, on "the

This Fragment is of great value. It describes the place of departed Spirits, which it terms "Hades;" and it pourtrays the condition of the Souls, both of the wicked and the righteous, on their separation from the body by death. The former, it is there said, pass immediately into a state of misery, in which they suffer great pain, and have gloomy forebodings of the still greater and interminable woe and shame to which they will be consigned in Hell, at the general Resurrection and last Judgment, when their bodies will be reunited to them, and when they will receive their full and final sentence from the lips of their Everlasting Judge.

The Author of this work teaches also the following doctrine concerning the spirits of the righteous on their deliverance from the burden of the flesh.

Bosom of Abraham:" "*dignam* habitationem unamquamque gentem percipere, etiam *ante Judicium*."

This Fragment on the Universe (Hippol. Fabric. p. 221), speaks of the constituent parts of the dead body, decomposed and dissolved as in a crucible (χωνευτήριον), and all its elements, though mouldered into dust or scattered to the winds, to be gathered again together at the Resurrection. This passage has been printed among the fragments of St. Irenæus (p. 468, Grabe), whence, in one place, it may be emended. The Author is speaking of the union of the body with the soul in this world, and their reunion in the next: and he compares that union to the marriage tie, in the mutual affection which the body and soul ought to have for each other: ψυχὴ συγχαρήσεται καθαρὰ καθαρῷ παραμείνασα, ᾧ ἐν τῷ κόσμῳ νῦν δικαίως συνοδεύουσα, καὶ μὴ ἐπίβουλον ἐν πᾶσιν ἔχουσα. For νῦν δικαίως the MS. of Irenæus supplies νυμφίῳ δικαίῳ.

They then pass, he says, into a place of rest and refreshment, which is called "Abraham's Bosom [5]," they there join the society of other holy and blessed spirits, and enjoy a foretaste of the still greater bliss of which they will have a full fruition after the General Resurrection and Universal Judgment, in the glories of heaven, and which will be for ever theirs.

This Fragment is of a great doctrinal importance. It contains—

1. A protest against the dangerous doctrine of those who imagine a sleep of the soul, in the interval between Death and Judgment.

2. A no less clear warning against the Romish Doctrine of Purgatory.

3. A refutation of a popular error, which supposes that the *Souls* of the righteous, immediately on the departure from the *Body*, are admitted to the enjoyment of full felicity in heaven, and which thus sets at nought the transactions of the general Resurrection, and the Universal Judgment of quick and dead.

4. A proof that the notion of a Millennial reign of Christ on earth before the Resurrection, had no place in our Author's system. This is the more observable, because St. Hippolytus belonged to a theological school—that of Irenæus—in which Millenarian

[5] The doctrine and language of the Eighth Book of the Constitutions, cap. 41 (p. 423, ed. Coteler.) bears much resemblance to that of our Author; thus another proof arises, that portions of the Eighth Book are derived from Hippolytus.

opinions had previously shown themselves [6]; and it may therefore be concluded, that careful examination of Scripture, and subsequent discussion and closer scrutiny of the subject, had deterred him from adopting those opinions, or that he had seen cause to renounce them. Perhaps it may even be inferred, that his master, Irenæus, had seen reason to revise his own opinions in this respect *after* the publication of his work on Heresy, in which they are broached. However this may be, it appears that those opinions gradually died away.

5. A testimony to the Doctrine of the Anglican Church, concerning the state of departed souls, as declared in her Liturgical Formularies, particularly in her Burial Office, and in the writings of her ablest Divines [7].

The Writer also speaks thus clearly [8] concerning

[6] See on Irenæus, v. 34. M. Bunsen observes, p. 256, that St. Hippolytus did not fall into another error of his master Irenæus, *i. e.*, concerning the duration of our Lord's ministry, which Irenæus imagined to have extended beyond His fortieth year (Iren. ii. 39, ed. Grabe, p. 161). Lumper, who has noticed this, well adds that St. Hippolytus did more than this. St. Hippolytus (in Daniel, num. iv.) says that our Lord suffered in His thirty-third year. See Lumper, viii. 177.

[7] See, for instance, Bishop Bull's two admirable Sermons on the State of the Soul after Death. Sermons II. and III., vol. ii. pp. 23—82, ed. Burton, Oxf. 1827. Compare also Justin Martyr, Dial. c. Tryp. § 5. Tertullian. de Resurr. § 43.

[8] Ap. Joh. Damascen. ii. p. 775. πάντες δίκαιοι καὶ ἄδικοι ἐνώπιον τοῦ Θεοῦ Λόγου ἀχθήσονται τούτῳ γὰρ ὁ Πατὴρ τὴν πᾶσαν

the Divinity and Proper Personality of Christ, as the Word of God, and Judge of Quick and Dead. "All men, both just and unjust, will be brought before the Divine Word: for to Him hath the Father given all judgment, and He Himself, executing the counsel of the Father, is coming as Judge, whom we call Christ, God Incarnate."

In referring to this Fragment, "On the Universe," we feel no small satisfaction in the assurance, that we there read the words of one of the greatest Doctors of Antiquity, St. Hippolytus.

(2) Another important Fragment from the same work, "On the Universe," is contained in a Manuscript in the Bodleian Library, but was not printed by Fabricius. It will be found at the close of the present Volume[9]; and the reader will see that it resembles the latter portion of the Treatise on Heresy.

It also contains a valuable statement of the Doctrine of Repentance; and corroborates the proofs already adduced, that St. Hippolytus was not a Novatian.

II. Let us now advert to another Fragment, not included in the edition of Hippolytus by Fabricius.

The Author of a Work, which was written in the age of Zephyrinus, against the Heresy which denied the Divinity of Christ, and which was called the

κρίσιν δέδωκε, καὶ αὐτὸς βουλὴν Πατρὸς ἐπιτελῶν Κριτὴς παραγίνεται ὃν Χριστὸν προσαγορεύομεν Θεὸν ἐνανθρωπήσαντα.

[9] Below, Appendix A.

"LITTLE LABYRINTH," referred in that work, as we have seen (p. 30), to the Treatise "On the Universe," as written by himself.

An Extract from the "Labyrinth" has been preserved by Eusebius[1], and, as we have also seen, it reflects light on the Narrative concerning the Church of Rome, contained in the newly-discovered Treatise. We find, also, some similarity of manner between that fragment and the relation just mentioned.

The fragment is itself a narrative; it concerns the state of Ecclesiastical affairs, during the Episcopate of Zephyrinus; and it may be regarded as introductory to the history contained in the Ninth Book of our Treatise. It bears a strong resemblance to our Treatise in the general view that it takes of Heresies. It represents them as derived from ancient schools of Heathen Philosophy; and affirms, that they owe much more to the teaching of the Portico, the Lyceum, and the Academy, than to that of the Scriptures and the Church.

There is also a resemblance between the diction of this fragment and the works of Irenæus[2].

[1] Euseb. v. 28, and in Routh's Reliq. Sacr. ii. 7—12, ed. 1814. See there p. 19, where Dr. Routh well says, "probabiliter contendere quis possit opus, de quo agimus, Parvum Labyrinthum ascribendum *Hippolyto* esse." Dr. Routh was the first to ascribe the Labyrinth to Hippolytus; and time has shown the soundness of his conjecture.

[2] *E. g.* γραφὰς θείας ῥεραδιουργήκασι sc. hæretici. Compare St. Irenæus, Preface, ῥαδιουργοῦντες τὰ λόγια τοῦ Θεοῦ.

Let me take this opportunity of noticing a passage in the

In a doctrinal point of view it is valuable, as affirming (in opposition to the assertions of the Theodotian heretics), that the Divinity of Christ, the Word of God, is taught in Holy Scripture, and had been continually and constantly maintained by the Church from the first[3].

Proemium or Preface of St. Irenæus which appears to have caused much perplexity. He is speaking of the strange tenets of the Valentinian Gnostics, which he promises to disclose to his reader. *ἀναγκαῖον ἡγησάμην μηνῦσαί σοι τὰ τερατώδη καὶ βαθέα μυστήρια ἃ οὐ πάντες χωροῦσιν ἐπεὶ μὴ πάντες τὸν ἐγκέφαλον* ἘΞΕΠΤΥΚΑΣΙΝ. The latter words have not been explained. The word *ἐξεπτύκασιν* is corrupt, and ought, probably, to be corrected into ἘΞΕΠΤΙΚΑΣΙΝ, and the sense would be, "I have thought it necessary to expound to you these portentous and profound mysteries, which all men do not comprehend, because (forsooth, to adopt their expression) men have not *sifted* their brains." St. Irenæus alludes to the Gnostic notion derived from some medical theories (which may be seen in Stieren's edition), that the brain must be cleansed by the discharge of phlegmatic humours through the nasal membranes as through a sieve, that the mind might be clarified, and be competent to understand their subtle speculations. This they called *ἐκπτίσσειν* or *διαπτίσσειν τὸν ἐγκέφαλον*. The same correction is to be made in Ælian. Hist. Animal. xvii. 31. *ἐκπτυσσόμενον ἀέρα*, Perizon. p. 949, where the Medicean MS. has very nearly preserved the true reading *ἐκπτισσόμενον*. It has *ἐκπτισόμενον*. The false reading *διαπτήσαντες λεπτὰ* for *διαπτίσαντες* still remains in some editions of Theophrastus, Hist. Plant. ix. 17.

[3] *E. g.* ἀδελφῶν ἐστι γράμματα πρεσβύτερα τῶν Βίκτορος χρόνων ἐν οἷς ἅπασι θεολογεῖται ὁ χριστός· ψαλμοὶ δὲ ὅσοι καὶ ᾠδαὶ ἀδελφῶν ἀπ' ἀρχῆς ὑπὸ πιστῶν γραφεῖσαι τὸν ΛΟΓΟΝ τοῦ Θεοῦ τὸν ΧΡΙΣΤΟΝ ὑμνοῦσι θεολογοῦντες.

This Fragment,—not inserted in the edition published by Fabricius—will doubtless find a place in future collections of the works of St. Hippolytus.

III. Let us now pass on to another work ascribed to St. Hippolytus.

This is a CHRONICLE; or, rather, a Chronological Epitome, which exists (as far as is known) only in Latin, and was first printed at Ingolstadt, in 1602[4], from two Paris Manuscripts; whence it was transferred into the edition of Fabricius[5]. It does not bear the name of Hippolytus. But since it is apparent from internal evidence, that it was composed in the age of Alexander Severus (when Hippolytus flourished), and is continued to A. D. 235, and since the Catalogue on the Statue of Hippolytus attests that he had composed such a work; therefore it has been attributed to him by some learned persons[6].

[4] In Canisii Antiquarum Lectionum, tom. ii. p. 179. It was also printed by Labbé, Bibl. nov. MS. p. 298, Paris, 1657, from a third MS.

[5] i. pp. 49—59.

[6] It is entitled by Fabricius "Chronicon Anonymi quod ad S. *Hippolytum* viri docti referunt; certè scriptum illâ ætate," p. 49. Bp. Pearson, Dissert. Posthuma, i. cap. x. § 1, calls the author "quidam anonymus." See also Dodwell, Diss. c. xiv. § xix., doubts whether it is by S. Hippolytus. Bianchini argues that it cannot be a work of Hippolytus from certain discrepancies between it and the Paschal Canon on the Statue. Dissert. cap. iii. § vii.

The discovery of the present Treatise appears to remove all doubt on this subject.

Our Author informs us[7] that he had written a chronological work, and refers his readers to it. He then introduces an abstract of his chronological system, in regard to Jewish History. Suffice it to say, that the details in the Treatise harmonize in language and substance with those contained in the Chronicle[8]. They seem to be from the same hand.

Thus, then, the Treatise strengthens the evidence already existing, that the work in question is by Hippolytus[9].

IV. Another writing, attributed in Manuscript copies to Hippolytus, and inserted in the edition of Fabricius, comes next under consideration. It is entitled, "CONCERNING ANTICHRIST[1]." Such a work was written by St. Hippolytus, as we know from the testimony of St. Jerome[2] and Photius[3]; An-

[7] P. 331, 81.

[8] Compare Philosophumena, pp. 331—333, with the Chronicon in Fabricius' edition of Hippolyti Opera, i. pp. 50—53.

[9] Henry Dodwell supposes, with good reason, that the Chronology of St. Hippolytus with regard to the succession of Roman Bishops is embodied in the work of Syncellus, Dissertat. de Rom. Pont. Success. c. xiv.

[1] i. p. 4. It was first published by Marquard Gudius, from two French MSS., at Paris, 1661, and after him by Combefisius, in a Catena on Jeremia ii. p. 449.

[2] De Viris Illustr. 61.

[3] Phot. Bibl. Cod. 202.

dreas, of Cæsarea, and Arethas, refer to it in their comments on the Apocalypse [4].

On comparing this work with the Treatise on Heresy, we see good reason to believe that they are from the same hand [5]; and, therefore, it being granted that our Treatise is by Hippolytus, we are confirmed in the persuasion, that the Work on Antichrist is from him; and the ascription of *a* Work on Antichrist to Hippolytus by Ancient Authors, Jerome and Photius, and of *this* particular Work on Antichrist to him by ancient MSS., is a further proof that the Treatise on Heresy is by Hippolytus.

There is also considerable similarity in some passages of this Work to certain sections of the Work on Heresy by St. Irenæus, the master of St. Hippolytus, especially in those portions where our Author treats on the Apocalyptic prophecies [6]. Upon these, however, the reader may remark, that Hippolytus appears studiously to have avoided any approximation

[4] On the Revelation, xii. 18; xiii. 1; xviii. 10.

[5] E. g.

Work on Antichrist.	*Treatise on Heresy.*
p. 5, c. 2. μὴ πλανῶ, used parenthetically.	p. 336. 18. μὴ πλανῶ, used parenthetically.
p. 5, c. 2. Description of Ancient Prophecy; also p. 16, cap. 31.	p. 337. 46. Description of Ancient Prophecy.
p. 5, c. 3. Λόγος ὁ τοῦ Θεοῦ Παῖς.	p. 336. 44. Λόγος ὁ Θεοῦ, ὁ πρωτόγονος Πατρὸς Παῖς.
p. 6, c. 3. εἷς ὁ τοῦ Θεοῦ Παῖς.	

[6] Compare p. 25, c. 50, on the name of the Beast in the Apocalypse, with Irenæus v. 30.

to Millenarian tenets, favoured in some degree by his predecessor and teacher, St. Irenæus. Indeed, he inculcates doctrines wholly at variance with Millenarian notions[7]. What has been already said[8] with regard to the Author of the Treatise on the Universe, in this respect is applicable here.

This Treatise was not a public address, but was transmitted privately to a certain Theophilus, and was accompanied with expressions of reverential fear[9], and with a strict charge of secrecy, reserving and limiting it to the use of holy and faithful men, and prohibiting any communication of it to Unbelievers.

One reason for such caution appears to have been as follows. The Author identifies the Fourth Monarchy of Daniel with the Roman Empire[1]; and he also identifies the Babylon of the Apocalypse with the City of Rome[2]. And, since the Prophecies of Daniel and the Apocalypse, as he interprets them, describe the utter destruction of the Fourth Monarchy, and portend the total extinction of the mystical Babylon, his expositions would have been very

[7] See particularly cap. 44—46, on the Two Advents of Christ, and cap. 64, on the Second Advent, represented as contemporaneous with the General Resurrection, and Judgment, and Conflagration of the Earth.

[8] Above, p. 157.

[9] c. 29, ταῦτά σοι μετὰ φόβου μεταδίδομεν.

[1] P. 14, c. 25; p. 16, c. 32. θηρίον τέταρτον—τίνες οὗτοι ἀλλ' ἢ Ῥωμαῖοι, ὅπερ ἐστὶν ὁ σιδηρὸς, ἡ νῦν ἑστῶσα βασιλεία;

P. 16, c. 34. ἤδη κρατεῖ σιδηρός.

[2] P. 18, c. 36.

obnoxious to such Roman readers as did not look with pious hope beyond the subversion of the Roman Empire, and the fall of the Roman City, to the full and final victory of Christ[3].

Photius, in his Comment[4] on this Treatise of St. Hippolytus on Antichrist, remarks that it re-

[3] Thus incidentally the author explains St. Paul's reserve in 2 Thess. ii. 6.

[4] Photius, Cod. 203, prefers the exposition of Theodoret to that of Hippolytus; from whom, however, Theodoret appears to have derived benefit. Such persons as may be disposed to renounce the exposition of Time for the exposition of the Fathers, with regard to prophecies *unfulfilled* in *their* age, and who would thus elevate the Fathers into Prophets, may be invited to reflect on the judicious observations of Photius, contained in his article on this Treatise of Hippolytus. And such persons as may be tempted to imagine that they can form a harmonious system of interpretation from the works of the Fathers with respect to such Prophecies as had *not* been fulfilled in their age, may read with benefit the article in Photius (Cod. 203), on the Exposition of Daniel by Theodoret, as contrasted with that of St. Hippolytus. "Many are the *discrepancies* between them," says Photius. No "*School* of prophetic interpretation" can be formed from such elements as these. And they who appeal to the Fathers for guidance in such matters, do much to invalidate the authority of the Fathers in regard to prophecies which *had been fulfilled* in their age, and also in matters of Christian *doctrine*, where their authority is of great weight. They thus also forfeit the privilege which Providence has given them of living in a later age, and of reading prophecy by the light of history.

In order to be consistent, ought not such expositors of prophecy to interpret the prophecies of the *Old* Testament concerning Christ, not by the facts of the Gospel, but by the opinions of learned Jews, who lived *before Christ?*

sembled the Exposition by the same Author of the Book of Daniel[5], and that both writings evinced somewhat of a fervid and confident spirit, in the speculative attempts there made to determine *how* and *when* the *unfulfilled* prophecies of Scripture *would be* fulfilled. But as far as this Treatise records the judgment of the Church concerning the true interpretation of prophecies which *had been fulfilled* in that age, it is of very great value, particularly if it be supposed, which appears to be most probable, to have come from the pen of Hippolytus,

[5] Cod. 202. Fabricius appears to have been led in one instance to mistake the one for the other. He quotes St. Germanus, Archbishop of Constantinople, asserting that Hippolytus supposed that Antichrist would appear in the five hundredth year after Christ*: and he imagines that St. Germanus is quoting from the Treatise on Antichrist. No such assertion, however, occurs in that Treatise. But this assertion was contained in the Exposition on Daniel by Hippolytus, as appears from Photius, Cod. 202, who adds that Hippolytus reckoned 5500 from the Creation to Christ.

M. Bunsen infers that Hippolytus wrote the Treatise in a time of *peace*, *because* he placed the appearance of Antichrist at about 300 years *after* his own time.

But this reasoning is fallacious. Hippolytus placed the appearance of Antichrist at A.D. 500, because he supposed with many of the Fathers, that the world would last for *six* millenary periods (cf. ad S. Iren. v. 28), which, according to his chronological calculations, would have expired then.

* The MS. of St. Germanus has ἐξακισχιλιοστῷ πεντακοσίῳ ἔτει: but the true reading, I conceive, is ἐκ χριστοῦ πεντακοσίῳ ἔτει. The reason of this will appear from what is said in the note above.

the scholar of Irenæus, and a Bishop of the Roman Church. If this is a work of Hippolytus, then this Treatise is also of importance to Sacred Philology. For it cites a large portion of the Apocalypse. In these citations we have perhaps[6] the readings of the manuscript used by Hippolytus, the third in order from St. John[7].

It is also an important witness of primitive doctrine.

It teaches, in the most explicit manner, the Divinity and Humanity of Christ, the Word of God[8], by Whom we, says the Author, have received the Regeneration effected through the Holy Ghost[9]. It represents the Church as a ship tossed on the waves of this world, agitated by storms, but never wrecked, having CHRIST as her Pilot, and the cross of Christ as her mast, and the Word of God as her rudder, and the precepts of Christ as her anchor, and the laver of regeneration with her, and above her the Divine Author of these blessed privileges, the Holy Spirit, breathing as the wind upon her sails, and

[6] "Perhaps,"—because the reading in Hippolytus *may* have been altered to suit a text of the Apocalypse.

[7] In Rev. xvii. 8 this MS. had *καὶ παρέσται*, and Rev. xviii. *ἐκολλήθησαν*. Both these readings have disappeared from most recent MSS., and from many editions; but they are preserved in the Alexandrine MS., and appear to be the true readings, and have been restored by Scholz and others as such.

[8] c. 61. *χριστὸν, παῖδα Θεοῦ, Θεὸν καὶ ἄνθρωπον καταγγελλόμενον.*

[9] c. 3.

wafting the Vessel in its course to the harbour of eternal peace[1].

V. Another Work ascribed to St. Hippolytus is a Homily on "the [2] THEOPHANIA," or Baptism of our Blessed Lord. This is a Sermon addressed to Catechumens, inviting them to Baptism. It represents to them, in glowing language, the privileges to which they would be introduced through that Holy Sacrament, and the blessings to which they would be led by the Divine Love, if they lived a life corresponding to their baptismal obligations. This interesting and beautiful Homily has some points of resemblance to the exhortation at the close of the newly-discovered Treatise. But there is, in one respect, a wide difference between them. The Homily was addressed to those who had been previously trained under Christian Instruction. But the peroration of the Treatise on Heresy was addressed to those who had had no such previous training.

The former is to Catechumens: the latter to Heathens. This difference of occasion has necessarily produced a difference of treatment of the subject in these two compositions respectively; as is sufficiently evident from the fact that in the two last pages of the Homily there are *twenty-five* direct

[1] See the notes on this passage below, pt. ii. near the end.

[2] M. Bunsen translates this title "a (baptismal) Sermon *on Epiphany*," p. 276, which conveys an incorrect idea. On the word θεοφάνεια, see Casaubon, Exc. Baron. ii. sect. xi.

quotations from Holy Scripture, but in the peroration to the Treatise on Heresy there is not *one*. The reader, therefore, will not expect to find in *that* peroration an exposition of Christian Doctrine.

It has, however, been called by some "the Confession of Faith" of St. Hippolytus.

But this is a very unhappy appellation. It might rather be termed his "Apology." We should fall into a great error, and do much injustice to St. Hippolytus and his cause, if we were to judge him and his Creed from a speech made to Idolaters[3].

This Homily on the Theophania was supplied to Fabricius, for his edition, by Roger Gale, from a MS. in the valuable library of his father, Thomas Gale, and is the only contribution of that kind which was made by the libraries of this country[4].

[3] It is to be regretted that M. Bunsen has not attended to these considerations. M. Bunsen's Fourth Letter, from p. 139 to p. 195, treats of this peroration to the Heathen, and bears the following title: "*Hippolytus' own Confession.*"

It is also to be deplored that M. Bunsen, in framing a "Confession of Faith" for St. Hippolytus, has paid little or no regard to the various heresies which Hippolytus refutes in his Treatise on Heresy. From the many-sided opposition of Hippolytus to the different forms in which heterodoxy showed itself in the Heresies before and in his own times (*e. g.* in the Heresies of Cerinthus, Ebion, Theodotus, Apelles, Noetus, and Callistus), his own orthodoxy comes forth in a very precise and definite form.

[4] It is now among the Gale MSS. in the Library of Trin. Coll., Cambridge, where it is marked O. 5. 36. Cf. Fabric. Hippol. i. p. 261.

It is ascribed in that MS. to St. Hippolytus, and this ascription appears to be confirmed by the internal evidence, particularly by its similarity in thought and diction to our Treatise [5]. Thus it may be regarded as supplementary to that other address, and may aid us in ascertaining from St. Hippolytus what he himself would have recognized as his own "Confession of Faith."

In corroboration of this assertion, let me adduce some paragraphs from the conclusion of this Homily.

Perhaps there is no document extant, among the Patristic remains of the Antenicene age, which states in a shorter compass and clearer terms the doctrine of the primitive Church concerning the Sacrament of Baptism.

The Author is speaking to the candidates for Baptism, and thus expresses himself. "Give me your attention, I beseech you, with earnestness, for I desire to recur to the fount of life, and to see the well-spring of healing flowing forth. The Father of Immortality sent forth his Immortal SON and WORD into the World. He came to wash man with Water and the Holy Ghost, and having regenerated him to incorruption of soul and body, breathed into us the breath of life, having clothed us with the armour of immortality. If then man has become immortal, he will

[5] Some evidences of this may be seen in the Notes to the Translation at the close of this Volume.

also be divinized[6]; and if he is divinized through water and the Holy Spirit after the Regeneration of the baptismal font, he will also be fellow-heir with Christ after the Resurrection from the dead....

"Come, therefore, and be born again to the adoption of God."

He then warns his hearers not to delude themselves by imagining that these baptismal privileges can be enjoyed otherwise than by a renunciation of sin, and by holiness of life. "Come to the adoption of sonship to God.... And how? you may ask. ... As follows—If you do not commit adultery, or murder, or idolatry[7]. If you are not the slave of pleasure, if pride is not master over you, if you wipe off the stain of impurity, and cast off the burden of iniquity. If you put off the armour of Satan and put on the breastplate of Faith, as saith Isaiah[8],

[6] ἔσται καὶ Θεός, εἰ δὲ Θεὸς δι' ὕδατος καὶ πνεύματος ἁγίου μετὰ τὴν τῆς κολυμβήθρας ἀναγέννησιν γίγνεται, καὶ συγκληρόνομος χριστοῦ εὑρίσκεται. See Philosoph. p. 239. γέγονας γὰρ Θεὸς . . . σοῦ πτωχεύει Θεὸς, καὶ σὲ Θεὸν ποιήσας εἰς δόξαν αὐτοῦ.

[7] A negative argument against *Infant* Baptism has been derived by some from the silence of St. Hippolytus in respect to it. But it must be remembered, St. Hippolytus had to deal mainly with adult idolaters. Nothing can be clearer than that he dates the origin of spiritual life from Baptism; and therefore, according to his teaching, they who have the charge of infants and children are bound to bring them to Baptism, if they would not have the blood of their souls required of themselves by Him Who instituted Baptism as the laver of the new Birth.

[8] Is. i. 16.

Wash ye and seek judgment, relieve the oppressed, judge the fatherless, plead for the widow. Come now, let us reason together, saith the Lord: though your sins be as scarlet, they shall be as white as snow; though they be red as crimson, they shall be as wool; if ye be willing and obedient, ye shall eat the good of the land.

"You see, beloved, how the Prophet foretold the purifying efficacy of Baptism. For he who descends with faith into the laver of Regeneration renounces the Devil, and dedicates himself to Christ, he rejects the Enemy, and confesses that CHRIST is GOD. He puts off slavery, and puts on sonship. He comes forth from Baptism bright as the sun, and shedding forth the rays of righteousness, and, what is most of all, he comes forth a son of God, and fellow-heir with CHRIST, To HIM be Glory and Power, with His all holy and good and life-giving SPIRIT, now and ever. *Amen.*"

VI. Another very important document for ascertaining the Doctrine of its Author is *found in* the Homily against Noetianism, contained in the works of St. Hippolytus. This Homily is ascribed to him in the ancient Vatican MS., from which it was transcribed by Montfaucon, and first printed by Fabricius[9]. It has generally been received as his, and the points of resemblance in thought and language, between that Homily and the Ninth Book of our Treatise, are so numerous and so striking, that

[9] S. Hippol. Opera, ii. 5—20.

they greatly strengthen the proof, that they are from the same person,—and that this person is Hippolytus[1].

The whole of this Homily is so valuable and instructive, as a witness of Christian teaching in the beginning of the third century, that it would be difficult to make extracts from it. But as it has been alleged that our Author has not spoken clearly on the doctrine of the Blessed Trinity[2], and as it has been thence inferred that this doctrine was not taught in the Christian Church in his age, it may not be amiss to indicate one or two passages relevant to that subject.

Having stated that Christ is the Word by Whom all things were made[3], and having quoted the beginning of St. John's Gospel in proof of this assertion, he proceeds to say, that we "behold the Word Incarnate in Him; we understand the Father by Him; we believe the Son; we worship the Holy Ghost." He then encounters the argument of the Noetians, who charged the orthodox with belief in two Gods, because they maintained that the Father is God, and the Son God,—He replies, "I will not say two Gods[4],

[1] Portions of this Homily have been adopted by Epiphanius in his article on Noetus. Hæres. lvii. pp. 479—489. It does not appear that Epiphanius had read the article on Noetus and Callistus in our Treatise, or he could hardly have said (p. 479) that Noetus arose about 130 years before his time; which would bring Noetus down as low as A.D. 245.

[2] M. Bunsen, i. pp. 302—304.

[3] S. Hippol. in Noet. c. 12, ed. Fabric. ii. p. 14.

[4] c. 14.

but one God, and two Persons. For the Father is one; but there are two Persons, because there is also the Son, and the third Person is the Holy Ghost[5]. The Father is over all things; the Son through all things; the Holy Ghost in all things. We cannot otherwise acknowledge one God, except we believe really in the Father, and in the Son, and in the Holy Ghost." And he adds that "the Word of God, Christ, having risen from the dead, gave therefore this charge to His disciples[6], *Go and teach all Nations, baptizing them in the name of the Father, and of the Son, and of the Holy Ghost,* showing that whosoever omits one of these, does not fully glorify God. For through this TRINITY the Father is glorified. The Father willed, the Son wrought, the Holy Ghost manifested. All the Scriptures proclaim this." And having described the human acts and sufferings, as well as the divine miracles, of Christ, he concludes with saying[7], This is He "Who ascended on a cloud into heaven, and sits on the right hand of the Father, and will come again to judge the quick and dead. This is He Who is

[5] Compare also ibid. cap. 9: "Whatsoever the Holy Scriptures declare, let us learn; and as the Father wills to be believed, let us believe; and as He wills the Son to be glorified, so let us glorify Him; and as He wills to give the Holy Spirit, so let us receive." Yet M. Bunsen (p. 297) quotes with approval the following statement, which he has translated from the German original: "Hippolytus decidedly ascribes no personality to the Holy Spirit."

[6] Matt. xxviii. 19.

[7] c. 18.

God, and Who was made Man for our sakes, to whom the Father subjected all things. To HIM be Glory and Power with the FATHER and the HOLY SPIRIT, in the Holy Church, now and for ever. *Amen.*"

Sufficient has now been said to show the value of the newly-discovered Treatise, with regard to those other Works ascribed to St. Hippolytus [8]. The

[8] It has not been the design of this Chapter to notice all the works assigned to Hippolytus; particularly the work "De Consummatione Mundi," printed by Fabricius in an Appendix to the First Volume among "Dubia et Supposititia," is not mentioned here. It appears to have been attributed to Hippolytus, because it is formed in a great measure from his work on Antichrist; but it contains many evidences of a different hand and a later age. See the authorities in Ceillier, ii. p. 368. Lumper, viii. 109.

St. Hippolytus is recorded to have been among the earliest expositors of Holy Scripture. On his Statue are inscribed the words *ᾠδαὶ εἰς πάσας τὰς γραφάς·* M. Bunsen, p. 281, conjectures that *ᾠδαὶ*, which he says "is absurd," is an abbreviation of *ὁμιλίαι*. This is a bold conjecture. It is probable that *ᾠδαὶ* is correct; and that it is a title of an integral work, and that Hippolytus wrote ᾨΔΑΙ, such as he himself describes, ap. Euseb. v. 28, *ψαλμοὶ δὲ ὅσοι καὶ* ᾨΔΑΙ *ἀδελφῶν ἀπ' ἀρχῆς ὑπὸ πιστῶν γραφεῖσαι τὸν Λόγον τοῦ Θεοῦ τὸν χριστὸν ὑμνοῦσι θεολογοῦντες.* Then "*εἰς πάσας τὰς γραφὰς*" is another distinct title, *i. e.* "In omnes Scripturas," "On all the Scriptures," according to the common mode of expression for designating expositions of Scripture by means of the preposition *εἰς*. See instances in Nicephor. Callist. iv. 31, in his account of Hippolytus, *e. g.* *εἰς τὸ Ἆισμα τῶν ᾀσμάτων—εἰς μέρη τοῦ Ἰεζεκιήλ.*

In his Exposition on the Psalms, published by Mai (Script.

learned World has been hitherto divided and in doubt concerning the genuineness of those Works. Henceforth these doubts may be considered as at an end. If the newly-discovered Treatise is generally received as the work of Hippolytus (as there is little doubt it will be), then it will also be allowed that those other works were rightly ascribed to him. And the independent ascription of those other works to him strengthens the conviction that this Treatise is his.

The recent discovery, therefore, is not only valuable in itself, but it adds to our former possessions. It is an accession of a new treasure, and a recovery of what was old. It does, in a considerable degree, for Hippolytus, what was done for his fabulous namesake, who, after he had been torn in pieces, was again brought to light and life [9]. It restores him to himself [10].

Thus, also, a gain has accrued to the cause of Christianity. Henceforth we may appeal to these works with confidence, as authentic witnesses of the Doctrine and Discipline of the Christian Church, in the earlier part of the Third Century after Christ.

Vat. ii. 439—448), Hippolytus describes the difference between *ψαλμοὶ* and *ᾠδαί.*

[9] Virg. vii. 761.

[10] It is to be hoped that a new and complete Edition of the remains of St. Hippolytus may now be undertaken; and that it may be accompanied by an edition of the works of his forerunner and master, St. Irenæus, with supplements and amendments, by the aid of the Philosophumena.

CHAPTER XI.

ON THE THEORY OF DEVELOPMENT OF CHRISTIAN DOCTRINE, AS APPLIED TO THE WRITINGS OF ST. HIPPOLYTUS.

In the preceding Chapter, we were led to notice incidentally certain allegations that have been made concerning the doctrine of St. Hippolytus.

1. It has been argued by a distinguished writer[1],

[1] M. Bunsen, who says (i. p. 302): "I doubt not that some people will think it their duty to prove that Hippolytus had the correct doctrine respecting the Athanasian definition of the Three Persons. It is true he says the contrary; but that does not signify with the doctors of the old school. . . . .

"The definitions of the ancient Church are good so far as they are meant to exclude unchristian or illogical imaginations, whether really or supposed* to be against the historical and philosophical groundwork of the Christian Faith. But they are imperfect, and have been *foisted into Scripture* and into the early Fathers by means of *supposititious words and verses in the New Testament, by forgeries in Patristic Literature, and by dishonest or untenable readings and interpretations* in both." See also p. 297 as cited above, p. 176. See also M. Bunsen, i. p. 176, who says that "as he prefers St. John's and St. Paul's speculative doctrines to those of the Fathers of the 2nd and 3rd centuries," so he prefers the doctrines of those Fathers to the Nicene Creed.

* Can "*illogical* imaginations" be otherwise than inconsistent with the groundwork of the Christian Faith?

that St. Hippolytus had no clear view of the doctrine of the Holy Trinity as now taught in the Church Universal, and especially as defined in the Athanasian Creed; and that he ascribes no distinct Personality to the Holy Spirit.

2. It has also been affirmed by another eminent person[2], of a different character, that St. Hippolytus "makes the generation of Christ *temporary;*" and it is implied, that he did not believe in the existence of the Son, as the Son, from eternity; and he is even charged with not teaching the doctrine of His Divinity[3].

3. The inference which is derived from these allegations, is, that the system of Christian Doctrine, now taught in the Church, has been of gradual growth, and that it did not exist in its present form in the primitive ages of Christendom.

[2] Dr. Newman, in his "Essay on the Development of Christian Doctrine," p. 13. "St. Hippolytus speaks as if he were ignorant of our Lord's Eternal Sonship."

[3] Dr. Newman says, ibid. p. 14, "If we limit our views of the teaching of the Fathers by what they expressly state, St. Hippolytus is a *Photinian.*" The doctrine of *Photinus* is thus described by St. Augustine (Hæres. 44, 45): "Christum non semper fuisse dicunt sed Ejus initium ex quo de Mariâ natus est asseverant, nec Eum aliquid amplius quam hominem putant; ista hæresis aliquando cujusdam *Artemonis* fuit." And therefore, in fact, Hippolytus, whom Dr. Newman calls a Photinian, and who, in his "Little Labyrinth," had contended against the *Artemonites,* had, by anticipation, taken up arms *against* the heresy of *Photinus.* See above, p. 162.

4. It would follow as a corollary from this proposition, that the body of Christian Doctrine has an elastic quality, and is capable of indefinite expansion, and that, whatever may now be held to be true, may be augmented by additional articles of faith, propounded at a future time.

5. It is affirmed by the former [4] of these two parties, that this process of evolution has been effected by what he terms "the Universal Conscience," which, when analyzed, appears to be only another name for the spirit of each individual claiming supremacy—if not infallibility—for himself [5].

6. The other party [6] to whom we have referred does not allow this, but maintains that the office of guiding and regulating "the Development of Christian Doctrine," is a prerogative appertaining to one per-

[4] M. Bunsen, p. 172. "The Universal Conscience is God's highest Interpreter." See also p. 175.

[5] If this is not the true meaning of the term "Universal Conscience," and if it be affirmed that this "Universal Conscience" is a spirit pervading and animating a well-organized body, let us be permitted to enquire, Where are its corporate acts? Where are its confessions? Has it ever promulgated a symbol, or even a single article, of Faith? Has it ever *received* any? Till it has performed these elementary functions, and has articulated the language of a body, we must be permitted to doubt whether it is a corporate principle, and must believe that it is only another name for that self-sufficient individualism, which resolves men into units, who can coalesce only in negations.

[6] Dr. Newman's Essay, chap. ii. sect. ii., "On a developing Authority in Christianity."

son in the Church, who is regarded by this party as her supreme and infallible Head on earth—the Bishop of Rome.

The first of these theories is that of M. Bunsen.
The second, that of Dr. Newman.

M. Bunsen's high position entitles him to consideration. His character, abilities, and influence, commend his statements to respectful attention, which doubtless they will receive, and have already received, from a large number of persons. His assertions refer to matters of paramount importance. Therefore it is indispensable, for the sake of truth, that they should be carefully examined, and that, if they are not well grounded, their inaccuracies should be made manifest, and the world be cautioned against them. And M. Bunsen himself, as a lover of Truth, will be among the first to desire that this should be the case.

Let me, therefore, observe, with feelings of deferential respect to M. Bunsen's station and office, that he has not dealt fairly with St. Hippolytus. He has imagined his address to Heathens to be "a Confession of Faith." He asserts, that the Scriptures and the Works of the Fathers have been interpolated with "supposititious words and verses foisted into them," in order to make them speak the language of ecclesiastical definitions. He affirms, that the Sacred Text of the New Testament has been adulterated with "dishonest or untenable readings and interpretations." He has allowed this charge to stand, in vague and dark generality, to overawe the ignorant and alarm the credulous. And, having brought these heavy accusations against the text of Holy Writ [7],—accusations the more formidable because they are indefinite, and cannot therefore be fairly met, and encountered face to face,—he has proceeded to treat St. Hippolytus as he charges others with having treated Holy Scripture. Sometimes he has corrupted the text of Hippolytus with untenable readings. Sometimes he has disfigured his sense by erroneous interpretations. He has charged others with the heinous sin of tampering with the Scriptures, in order to make them square with preconcerted definitions. Far be it from us to impute any such motives to M. Bunsen, in his dealings with Hippolytus. But the fact is, in some cases he has made St. Hippolytus appear to be heretical.

In the speech which he puts into the mouth of St.

[7] By verses "foisted in" for a particular purpose, and on which certain definitions of the ancient Church have been founded, it is probable that M. Bunsen means 1 John v. 7. Did M. Bunsen ever read Bentley's Letter on that subject? (Correspondence, ii. 529.) His general insinuation of "supposititious verses" and "dishonest readings," and consequently of uncertainty in the Sacred Text, is a repetition of the charge made by Antony Collins, in another form, against the integrity of the text of the Gospels as altered, "tanquam ab Idiotis Evangelistis composita," which was refuted so triumphantly by the same writer, Dr. Bentley, "On Free-thinking," p. 112. Cambridge, 1743.

Hippolytus, and which he supposes him to deliver at the time of the "Great Exhibition of the Industry of all Nations," in the character (it may be supposed) of "Bishop of the Nations," with which M. Bunsen has invested him,—he makes St. Hippolytus say that the Second Epistle of St. Peter was not written by that Apostle, and was not even known to the ancient Church[8]. And, since the Author of that Epistle claims to *be* St. Peter himself[9], and since the Church receives the Epistle as his, M. Bunsen, in so doing, has ventured on an act of irreverence and injustice. He has suborned St. Hippolytus as an accuser of the Christian Church, and charges her through him with reading, as Canonical Scripture, a work composed by an Impostor[1]!

In the same imaginary harangue, M. Bunsen represents St. Hippolytus as regarding with complacency the theory of a recent German writer, affirming that the Book of Daniel was composed in the times of Antiochus Epiphanes[2], and that, therefore, while it professes to be a Prophecy, it was fabricated *after* the events which it pretends to predict; and

[8] iv. 33. [9] 2 Pet. i. 17; iii. 1.

[1] M. Bunsen says, iv. p. 34: "The ancient Churches did not know such a letter." This is not true. Origen, a contemporary of St. Hippolytus, says (in libr. Jesu Nave, Hom. 8), "Petrus *duabus* Epistolarum personat tubis." Other ancient authorities, to the same effect, may be seen in the Appendix to the Writer's Lectures on the Canon of Scripture.

[2] iv. pp. 38, 39.

thus he has brought St. Hippolytus from his grave to connive at a revival of the exploded notion of the infidel Porphyry, which has been treated as it deserves by St. Jerome[3].

Other evidence of the manner in which St. Hippolytus has been treated by M. Bunsen has been already adduced, and more will be found in the following pages[4]. The task of collecting it has been a painful one. But respect for Hippolytus and the Truth required that it should not be declined.

Whether St. Hippolytus held the doctrine of the Personality of the Holy Spirit, and acknowledged the three Divine Persons of the Blessed Trinity, is a question which has been already examined[5]. Proofs have already been brought to show his doctrine in these respects[6].

[3] St. Jerome (Præfat. in Daniel.). Contra Prophetam Danielem scripsit Porphyrius, nolens eum ab ipso cujus inscriptus est nomine esse compositum, sed a quodam qui temporibus *Antiochi* qui appellatus est *Epiphanes* fuerit in Judæa, et *non tam Danielem ventura dixisse, quàm narrâsse præterita.* See also in cap. IV. and cap. XI. Hæc ideo prolixius exposui ut Porphyrii ostendam *calumniam* qui hæc omnia ignoravit, aut nescire se finxit.

[4] Especially in the Notes in the latter portion of this Volume.

[5] Above, pp. 174—177.

[6] How different from M. Bunsen's judgment concerning the theology of St. Hippolytus is that of another German Theologian who had examined his works with care. "*Castigatissimè* loquitur sanctus Hippolytus de mysterio Sanctissimæ *Trinitatis* apertèque declarat fidem circà unitatem Naturæ et distinctionem Personarum. . . . Sanè nemo posset hisce temporibus magis accuratè loqui de Mysterio Trinitatis. . . . Pari præcisione loquitur sanc-

With regard to Dr. Newman's allegation, that the Eternal Generation of the Son is not taught by Hippolytus, this has been fully discussed in another place, and it would be superfluous to say more on that subject here [7]. To prove that Hippolytus was not a Photinian is happily as needless [8].

But for the sake of some readers it may be desirable to offer some remarks on the Theory of M. Bunsen and Dr. Newman as applied to St. Hippolytus, and to others of his age [9].

1. First then, let it even be supposed, for argument's sake, that St. Hippolytus and other ancient Fathers of the Church *had* spoken ambiguously or inadequately, or even erroneously, concerning certain Articles of the Faith, now received by the Church, and embodied in her Creeds.

tus ille Episcopus de Divinitate ac consubstantialitate Verbi." P. Gottf. Lumper, Histor. Theol. Critica, viii. 123—131. It may here be observed also, that the venerable President of St. Mary Magdalene College, Oxford, Dr. Routh, has made choice of the Homily of St. Hippolytus against Noetus for a sound Exposition of the Catholic doctrine concerning the Nature of Christ. Script. Eccl. Opuscula, Pref. iii. Oxon. 1832.

[7] Letters to M. Gondon, Letter viii. pp. 210—214, ed. 3. See also below, Notes to Pt. II. near the end.

[8] See above, p. 180, note.

[9] I call it the theory of *both*, for though the developing Authority is different in the two systems, yet each asserts the principle of Development.

It would not therefore follow that the Christian Faith did not exist, or did not exist in perfect symmetry and fulness, in their age; or that they imagined this to be the case; or that they did not acknowledge *that* Faith, and acknowledge it as *complete;* or that a single iota has been added to it since their age.

For (2) let it be remembered that the SCRIPTURES of the OLD and NEW TESTAMENT existed in their time.

3. St. Hippolytus, and the other Catholic Fathers acknowledged the Holy SCRIPTURES to be Divinely inspired, and to be the sole and all-sufficient Rule of the Christian Faith. They acknowledged and affirmed, that the true Faith, *whole* and *complete,* is contained in those Scriptures. Nothing can be more explicit than the testimony of St. Hippolytus, and of his master St. Irenæus, and of other ancient Fathers to this effect [10].

[10] See, for example, S. Hippol. c. Noet. § 9. εἷς Θεὸς, ὃν οὐκ ἄλλοθεν ἐπιγιγνώσκομεν, ἢ ἐκ τῶν ἁγίων γραφῶν . . . ὅσοι θεοσέβειαν ἀσκεῖν βουλόμεθα οὐκ ἄλλοθεν ἀσκήσομεν ἢ ἐκ τῶν λογίων τοῦ Θεοῦ. Ὅσα τοίνυν κηρύσσουσιν αἱ θεῖαι γραφαὶ, ἴδωμεν, καὶ ὅσα διδάσκουσιν ἐπίγνωμεν, . . . μὴ κατ' ἰδίαν προαίρεσιν μηδὲ κατ' ἴδιον νοῦν, μηδὲ βιαζόμενοι τὰ ὑπὸ τοῦ Θεοῦ διδόμενα, ἀλλ' ὃν τρόπον αὐτὸς ἐβουλήθη διὰ τῶν ἁγίων γραφῶν δεῖξαι, οὕτως ἴδωμεν. See also S. Hippol. ap. Euseb. v. 28, concerning heretics, γραφὰς θείας ῥεραδιουργήκασι . . . καταλιπόντες τὰς ἁγίας τοῦ Θεοῦ γραφὰς, γεωμετρίαν ἐπιτηδεύουσιν ἢ οὐ πιστεύουσιν Ἁγίῳ Πνεύματι λελέχθαι τὰς θείας γραφάς, καί εἰσιν ἄπιστοι ἢ ἑαυτοὺς ἡγοῦνται σοφωτέρους τοῦ Ἁγίου Πνεύματος ὑπάρχειν. The

Next (4) let it not be forgotten that Articles of *Faith* are confessedly mysterious; and that a careful consideration, collation, and comparison of various texts of Holy Scripture is requisite for the avoidance of error, and for the declaration of truth in perfect plenitude and harmonious proportion; and that such consideration, collation, and comparison, is a work of time.

statements of St. Irenæus on this subject are also very forcible and clear. See S. Iren. ii. 46, where he describes the doctrines received by the true Christian as *ὅσα φανερῶς καὶ ἀναμφιβόλως ἐν ταῖς θείαις γραφαῖς λέλεκται.* See the whole of that eloquent chapter, and particularly iii. 11, where he calls the written Gospel *στῦλον καὶ στήριγμα τῆς Ἐκκλησίας.* Other testimonies to the same effect are the following:—

Scriptor Anon. ap. Euseb. v. 16, against the Montanist heresy, *δεδιὼς μή πη δόξω τισὶν ἐπισυγγράφειν ἢ ἐπιδιατάττεσθαι τῷ τῆς τοῦ εὐαγγελίου καινῆς διαθήκης λόγῳ, ᾧ μήτε προσθεῖναι μήτ᾽ ἀφελεῖν δυνατόν.* S. Athanas. c. Gentes, i. 1, *αὐταρκεῖς αἱ ἁγίαι καὶ θεόπνευστοι γραφαὶ πρὸς τῆς ἀληθείας ἀπαγγελίαν.* Festal. Epist. 39, *ἐν τούτοις βιβλίοις μόνον τὸ τῆς εὐσεβείας διδασκαλεῖον εὐαγγελίζεται· μηδεὶς τούτοις ἐπιβαλλέτω μηδὲ τούτων ἀφαιρέσθω.* S. Basil. de Fide, c. 2, *φανερὰ ἔκπτωσις πίστεως ἢ ἀθετεῖν τι τῶν γεγραμμένων, ἢ ἐπεισάγειν τῶν μὴ γεγραμμένων.* So that Hooker had good cause to say, Eccl. Pol. ii. v. 4, "To urge any thing upon the Church, requiring thereunto that religious assent of Christian belief wherewith the words of the Holy Prophets are received,—to urge any thing as part of that supernatural and celestially revealed truth which God hath taught, and *not to show it in* SCRIPTURE, *this did the ancient Fathers evermore think unlawful, impious, execrable.*" See also the authorities quoted in the seasonable publication of the Christian Advocate, The Rev. J. A. Frere, Cambridge, 1852, pp. 110—135.

5. Let it be observed, that men are prone to dwell on specific truths, to the neglect of others equally important. In dealing with Holy Scripture, they are wont to forget the Apostolic precept, to *compare* Spiritual things with Spiritual; and are apt to fix their eyes on particular texts of Scripture detached from the context; and are often blind to other passages of Scripture, which ought to be viewed in juxtaposition with them; and thus they disturb the balance and mar the proportion of faith.

6. The Catholic Fathers protest against this partiality—and no one more forcibly than St. Hippolytus[1].

7. The tendency of the human mind is to be driven by an excess of reaction from one error to its opposite extreme. Thus in the primitive ages of the Church, when Idolatry was yet dominant at Rome, the fear of Polytheism tended to produce Monarchianism, and so acted as an obstacle, in certain quarters, to the reception of the doctrine of the Holy Trinity, misconceived to be Tritheism. This fear of abandoning the doctrine of the Divine Unity engendered Sabellianism on one side, and Photini-

[1] See, for example, c. Noetum, § 3, where he rebukes the Noetians for quoting the Scriptures *μονόκωλα*, *i. e.* piecemeal, —single texts, broken off from the context,—and refutes their false reasoning deduced from isolated texts, by reference to Scripture as a *whole*, ὁλοκλήρως, § 4. ὁπόταν θελήσωσι πανουργεύεσθαι περικόπτουσι τὰς γραφάς· ὁλοκλήρως δὲ εἰπάτω. So Tertullian c. Praxean. c. 20: *Tribus* capitulis *totum* volunt Instrumentum cedere. Proprium hoc est omnium hæreticorum.

anism on the other. So in later times, the dread of Sabellianism drove some into Arianism, and Nestorianism begat Eutychianism.

8. Thus Heresies arose, and propagated one another.

But, under the all-wise and overruling Providence of Almighty God, Heresies were made subservient to the advancement of Truth. They excited the vigilance of orthodox Christian Teachers, and stimulated them to examine with greater diligence what was the teaching of HOLY SCRIPTURE in those particular matters, which "Heresy went about to deprave." Thus the True Faith was seen more clearly, and was expressed more definitely; it was embodied in Confessions, and stereotyped in the Creeds of the Church[2].

[2] This has been admirably stated by the Fathers themselves. *e.g.* Origen, Hom. ix. in Num. "Si doctrina ecclesiastica nullis intrinsecus hæreticorum dogmatum assertionibus cingeretur, non poterat tam clara et tam examinata videri fides nostra. Sed idcirco doctrinam catholicam contradicentium obsidet oppugnatio ut Fides nostra non otio torpescat sed exercitiis elimetur." "Illorum error nobis profuit," says St. Ambrose, in De Incarn. i. 6. So St. August. iii. 2056. "Hæretici abundant, et cœperunt fluctuare corda fidelium; jam tam necessitas facta est spiritualibus viris qui aliquid secundum Divinitatem Domini Nostri Jesu Christi non solum legerant in *Evangelio*, sed intellexerant, ut contra arma Diaboli Christi arma proferrent." Hence he says, iv. p. 730, "Ex hæreticis asserta est Catholica." See also, iii. 102. 2055; iv. 730. 978; vii. 661; viii. 33. Hence, in the words of the venerable Hooker, v. xlii., "though those contentions (with hereticks) were cause of much evil, yet some good the

But it must not be imagined, that the Truth was *made* by being *elucidated.* No; not a single article of it was so formed. It had *existed,* and had existed in its perfect plenitude, even *from the beginning,* in the pages of HOLY WRIT.

The process here described is similar to what takes place in the World of Nature. The rays of the Sun are often veiled from our sight by Clouds. But the Sun is shining behind them. And, when the clouds break and are dissolved, not a single new ray of the sun is created; but it is *seen* by us more clearly, and then "Nube solet pulsâ clarior ire dies."

So, when the clouds of Heresy were dispersed, no new article of Faith was made; no new beam of Divine Revelation radiated forth; but the winds of Controversy had blown away the mists of Heresy,—the Storm had cleared the sky and purified the air, and the Orb of Truth was seen more clearly by the eye of the Church, as that Orb had shone from the first, in the firmament of Holy Writ.

9. The question now is—

How was this process of elucidation performed?

By "the Universal Conscience;" Or by a Pope?

By neither.

Doubtless St. Hippolytus and the other Catholic Fathers admitted and affirmed, that every one is

Church hath reaped by them, in that they occasioned the learned and sound in faith to explain such things as Heresy went about to deprave."

bound to exercise all the faculties which God has given him. But they did not imagine that any one might interpret Scripture as he pleased, or that whatever *seems* to be truth to any man, *is* truth to him. The "Refutation of all Heresy" by St. Hippolytus is a protest against such a notion as that.

Again, St. Hippolytus did not acknowledge the existence of any "developing authority" inherent in the Bishop of Rome, and as an *apanage* of that See. *If* there had been such a power and privilege in that Church in the third century, the Church of Christ would have become Noetian. She would have denied the proper personality of her Divine Head. The struggle of St. Hippolytus against Zephyrinus and Callistus, proves that in his view the Bishops of Rome might become heretics, and must not be followed when they fall into heresy. And the Church Universal, by professing his doctrine as true, and proscribing theirs as heretical, has pronounced him to have been right.

How, then, was it to be determined, what the *true* doctrine of Scripture is?

By the aid of sound Reason, disciplined and informed by Learning, and exercised with caution, industry, and humility, and enlightened by Divine Grace given to earnest prayer, and controlled and regulated by the judgment and guidance of the Church Universal, to whom Christ has promised His Presence, and the Light of the Holy Spirit to guide her into all truth.

This was the doctrine of St. Hippolytus[3], and the other Catholic Fathers.

10. Whatever, therefore, has been received by the Church Universal as the true Exposition of Scripture, that *is* the true sense of Scripture. And the *true sense* of Scripture,—that, and that alone, *is* Scripture. And, since the Creeds have been so received, we believe them to contain the True Faith as propounded in Scripture. And since the Personality of the Holy Spirit and the Divine Trinity in Unity are taught in the Creeds, we believe that those doctrines are contained in Holy Scripture,—and that they *have been in Scripture from the beginning.*

11. Therefore, even if it could be shown that St. Hippolytus, or any other among the ancient Fathers of the Church, had exaggerated a truth through fear of its opposite error; or if, not being gifted with prescience, they did not guard their language against possible misconstruction, in regard to some heresies which did not arise in the Church till many years after they were laid in their graves; or did not fully put forth such transcendental truths as the eternal generation of the Son of God, before those truths had been impugned,—What is all this to us? What is it to the question before us? They received the Holy Scriptures. They received them as the Rule of Faith. They received therefore *all* that is in the Scriptures.

[3] See above, pp. 88—91.

They received all that the Church Universal, the Body and Spouse of Christ—to whom He has committed the Scriptures, and whom He has commissioned to guard and interpret them—could *show to be in those Scriptures.* They received, therefore, by implication, and by anticipation, the Three Creeds, promulgated lawfully, and generally received by the Church.

We have the Holy Scriptures; we have the blessing of Catholic teaching, and enjoy the benefits which Almighty God in His mercy has elicited from Heresies, for the victorious vindication and clearer manifestation of His Truth. We have the Creeds. We do not see any *new* sun, or any single *new ray* of the sun, in them. But by their means we see the Orb of divine light shining more brightly. By means of the Creeds, the Church Universal,—acting under the governance of her Divine Head, and under the guidance of the Holy Spirit—has rendered a greater service to the whole World than that which, in that celebrated speech, the noblest orator of Antiquity[4] said had been effected by one of his decrees for his own State. The Church, by means of the Creeds, has made the dangers of Heresy, which from time to time have hung over her, to pass away,—like a cloud.

[4] Demosth. de Coronâ, c. 56. § 4, *τοῦτο τὸ ψήφισμα τὸν τότε τῇ πόλει περιστάντα κίνδυνον παρελθεῖν ἐποίησεν, ὥσπερ νέφος.* Longinus, de Sublim. c. 39.

CHAPTER XII.

APPEAL TO ST. HIPPOLYTUS ON THE PRESENT CLAIMS OF THE ROMAN CHURCH TO SUPREMACY.

THE main question on which the controversy between the Church of Rome and the other Churches of Christendom hinges, is that of Papal Supremacy. "What is the point at issue," says Cardinal Bellarmine, "when we argue concerning the Primacy of the Roman Pontiff?" "It is," he replies, "the sum of Christianity [1]."

1. Among the arguments adduced by our Romanist brethren, in behalf of the Papal claim to Supremacy, none appears to be urged with greater frequency or more confidence than that which they derive from a well-known passage of St. Irenæus [2].

That great Bishop and Doctor of the Church, who was the disciple of St. Polycarp, Bishop of Smyrna, employs, they say, the following words in his Treatise on Heresy;

[1] Bellarmin. de Pontifice, vol. i. p. 189, ed. 1615. De quâ re agitur cùm de primatu Pontificis agitur? Brevissimè dicam, *De summâ rei Christianitatis.*

[2] S. Iren. iii. 3.

He is describing "the Church of Rome, as founded by the two most glorious Apostles, St. Peter and St. Paul," and he then says, "Ad *hanc Ecclesiam*, propter potentiorem principalitatem, *necesse est omnem convenire Ecclesiam*—hoc est, eos qui sunt *undique* fideles,—in quâ semper ab his, qui sunt undique, conservata est ea quæ est ab Apostolis traditio [3]."

Here, it is affirmed by Romanist Theologians, is a declaration from St. Irenæus, one of the most eminent Bishops of the Church in the second century after Christ, that every Church "*must conform* to the Church of Rome, on account of its more powerful principality."

Therefore here is an acknowledgment, they say, of her Supremacy; and an assertion that it is the duty of all Christians and of all Churches, to submit to the Church of Rome. And, since the Bishop of Rome is the head of that Church, therefore all, they affirm, are bound to pay dutiful homage and filial obedience to him.

2. This passage, it will shortly be seen, may form an introduction to an Appeal on this important question to the authority of St. Hippolytus.

But more on this shortly. In the mean time, let us examine the context and scope of the words of St. Irenæus.

He is arguing against Heretics. Having first refuted them by reference to Holy Scripture [4], he next [5],

[3] S. Iren. iii. 3. [4] iii. 2.

[5] As was usual with the primitive Catholic writers in his age.

proceeds to encounter them by the testimony of the Catholic Church.

3. How was this testimony to be obtained? "It would be very tedious[6]," he tells them, to cite, as it were, *all* the Churches of Christendom as witnesses. He will therefore be content with *one* Church. His argument is—ab *unâ* disce *omnes*. He will, we say, be satisfied with one. And since he is writing in the West, the Church, which he will select, shall be a Western Church; it shall be the Church generally acknowledged to have been planted by Apostolic hands in the West—it shall be a Church founded by the two most glorious Apostles, Peter and Paul—one whose succession of Bishops was well authenticated and generally known—the CHURCH of ROME[7].

St. Irenæus then introduced the passage to which

Bp. Pearson, Dissert. i. cap. 3, says, "ab Episcoporum successione argumentari solebant secundi tertiique seculi Patres adversus sui temporis Hæreticos."

[6] Valdè longum esset omnium Ecclesiarum enumerare successiones.

[7] The reader may compare the very similar argument of a contemporary of St. Irenæus, Tertullian, De Præscr. Hæreticor. c. 21. Constat omnem doctrinam quæ cum illis Ecclesiis Apostolicis *matricibus* et *originalibus* fidei conspirat veritati deputandam. C. 36: Percurre Ecclesias Apostolicas apud quas ipsæ *adhuc* cathedræ Apostolorum suis locis præsident, apud quas authenticæ literæ eorum recitantur, sonantes vocem et repræsentantes faciem uniuscujusque.

It is observable that Tertullian dwells on nearness of *time* to the Apostles, as well as identity of place, as a ground for this

we have already adverted. Unhappily that passage is known to *us* only through the medium of an old *Latin* Translation. The original Greek words of Irenæus are lost. The Latin version of them is as follows :—

"*Ad hanc* Ecclesiam (sc. Romanam), propter potentiorem principalitatem, *necesse est omnem convenire* Ecclesiam, hoc est, eos qui sunt undique fideles, in quâ semper ab his, qui sunt undique, conservata est ea quæ est ab Apostolis traditio."

4. The divines of the Church of Rome interpret these words to mean, that it "is necessary for *every* Church to conform to *this* Church, *i. e.* to the Church of Rome;" and thus they deduce a moral obligation on all men to submit to her.

Are these inferences justified by the words of Irenæus?

It does not appear that they are.

For (1) they are at variance with the drift of the

appeal, so that the appeal would lose its force in course of time, and would ultimately be inapplicable, as now.

"Proxima est tibi Achaia? Habes Corinthum; Si potes in Asiam tendere, habes Ephesum."

What, we may ask, would the Roman Church say to such an appeal *now* to the Churches of Ephesus and Corinth, whom she charges with heresy and schism? But if the appeal to Rome is valid, so is that to Ephesus and Corinth.

"Si autem Italiæ adjaces, habes Romam, unde nobis quoque auctoritas præsto est."

argument. St. Irenæus is refuting Heretics, by an appeal to the witness of the Church Universal. He has selected *one* Church as an exponent of that testimony. The Church so selected is the Church of Rome. His argument leads him to add that the selection is a fair one; and that, in appealing to one Church, the Church of Rome, he has virtually collected the witness of all.

And how does he show this? By reminding them, that the Church of Rome had been founded by the two most glorious Apostles, Peter and Paul, whom they knew to have suffered at Rome only about a century before, and from whom they could trace the succession of Bishops, whose names were well known to them, and which he himself enumerates from the first Bishop of Rome, Linus, to whose charge (he says) those two blessed Apostles committed the Roman Church, down to the then presiding Bishop of Rome, the twelfth in order, Eleutherus.

2. What then would he next say? What does he say in the words "ad hanc Ecclesiam *necesse est* omnem convenire Ecclesiam hoc est omnes qui sunt undique fideles?"

Not, that every one, then and for ever *after*, must submit to the Church of Rome. No. *If* that had been true, then he would never have said, that, "*because* it *would be tedious* to appeal to *all* Churches," he would therefore appeal to *one* Church—the Church of Rome. Such a statement would have been absurd, *if* Rome had been supreme over *all* Churches, and if *all* Churches were bound to conform to *her*.

No one would say, It would be a tedious process to ascertain the opinions of *all* the *Peers* of the Realm—we will *therefore* appeal to the *Crown*. What, then, do his words mean? They signify this: That, on account of the *greater antiquity* of Rome—for such is the meaning of the words "potentior principalitas[8]"—it may be taken for granted, that every Church coincides with Rome, and is represented by her; that is, all believers, who exist in all places[1], agree with her; or, in other words, every Church (he says) in which the tradition from the Apostles has been preserved by those who exist every where, *i. e.* by true Catholics, as opposed to heretics, who existed only in particular places. Hence, then, he means to

[8] *Principalitas*, in the old Latin version of Irenæus (as Stieren has shown), is used in the same sense as in Tertullian, for priority of time (see S. Iren. v. 14. v. 21), and is opposed to *posterioritas*. The argument may be illustrated by Tertullian's reference (see above, p. 197, note) to Ecclesiæ *originales* et *matrices*. The original words used by Irenæus were probably *ἱκανωτέραν ἀρχαιότητα*. In this same chapter the Latin Translator has rendered *ἱκανωτάτη* by *potentissima*. The Church of Rome was the only Church in the West that was *known to have been founded by Apostles*. It had therefore a potentior principalitas, "a more august primitiveness."

[1] The word *undique*, as is well observed by Thiersch on this passage, is used in this old Latin Version of Irenæus for *ubique*.

say, his reference to Rome is a just one; and by appealing to *that* Church he has appealed to all Churches, whose testimony may be supposed to be embodied and involved in hers.

3. Let it be observed, further, that St. Irenæus, so far from countenancing in this passage the doctrine of Papal Supremacy, as taught by Romish Divines, does in fact, by implication, overthrow the foundation on which they make it rest.

They base that doctrine on the words of our Blessed Lord to St. Peter [2]; whom they affirm to be the Rock on which the Church is built. And they then proceed to say, that the Bishop of Rome is the Rock of the Church, by virtue of his succession to St. Peter.

This is their assertion.

But what is the language of St. Irenæus?

He refers to the Church of Rome, as founded by the *two* most glorious Apostles, St. Peter and St. Paul. He appeals to the Bishop of Rome as succeeding Linus, who, he says, was placed in that see by the same *two* Apostles. And thus he shows, in a striking manner, that he knew nothing of the Romish theory which claims infallibility and supremacy for *St. Peter alone,* as Head of the Church, and also claims the same prerogatives for the Bishops of Rome, *as successors of St. Peter.*

[2] Matth. xvi. 18, " On this Rock I will build My Church."

Such then appears to be the true meaning of the words of St. Irenæus.

4. In confirmation of this interpretation, let us revert to the fact, that the words quoted by our Romanist brethren as from St. Irenæus are *not* his *own words*, but are only a Latin Version of them.

This is necessary to be borne in mind.

Since this Old Latin Version is a literal one (as is evident by comparison of it with the Greek in those passages where the Greek has been preserved), it is probable, and almost certain, that where we now read in the Latin "*necesse est*," St. Irenæus wrote ἀνάγκη.

The word ἀνάγκη, it is well known, often implies a reasonable inference,—not a moral obligation. Such an use is common to all Greek Writers in prose and verse; πολλή γ' ἀνάγκη—πᾶσ' ἐστ' ἀνάγκη—in the Greek dramatic writers, and in the Dialogues of Plato, signify simply, "*By all means*," or, "*it follows, of course, that it is so*, or *will be so*." The same is the case in Ecclesiastical Writers. Thus when Theodoret says[3], ἀνθρώπους ἀνάγκη προσπταίειν ὄντας, he certainly does not intend to assert that it is a moral duty for a man to err—no; but that "humanum est errare," and that no one is free from error. When St. Chrysostom says[4], ἀνάγκη τὸν ὁμι-

[3] Eccl. Hist. iv. 5.

[4] These words are quoted from St. Chrysostom in "HELE's Select Offices of PRIVATE DEVOTION," published by the "Society

λοῦντα θεῷ κρείττονα γενέσθαι θανάτου, καὶ πάσης διαφθορᾶς, he does not mean to affirm that it is *a moral duty* for a man who converses with God to conquer Death and Destruction. This would be a very presumptuous speech. But he means, that a man who holds habitual intercourse with God by prayer and meditation, does by *natural consequence become* superior to Dissolution. So again, when St. Hippolytus says[5], in his description of the lower world, φωτὸς τοίνυν ἐν τούτῳ τῷ χωρίῳ μὴ καταλάμποντος, ἀνάγκη σκότος διηνεκῶς τυγχάνειν, he certainly cannot mean to assert any moral necessity for darkness, but, that, light not being admitted, darkness is the natural result[6].

Such then is the signification of the word ἀνάγκη, which Irenæus appears to have used, and which is represented by *necesse est* in the passage before us. And we may observe, in confirmation of what has now been said on that point, that the word ἀνάγκη is used in this sense by Plato in his Timæus, and is translated "necesse est" by Cicero[7].

for Promoting Christian Knowledge," and form the appropriate motto of that admirable Manual.

[5] De Universo, p. 220, ed. Fabr.

[6] Several examples of a similar use of ἀνάγκη may be seen in the fragment of Maximus, who appears to have been contemporary with St. Irenæus, in Routh's Reliquæ, i. p. 432.

[7] The words of Plato are*, τὸν νοῦ καὶ ἐπιστήμης ἐραστὴν ἀνάγκη τὰς τῆς ἔμφρονος φύσεως αἰτίας πρώτας μεταδιώκειν, which Cicero renders, "Illum qui intelligentiæ sapientiæque se amato-

* Plato Timæus, 46. D. vol. vii. p. 32. Stallbaum, Leips. 1824, cp. Cicero, vii. p. 942, ed. Ernesti, Oxon. 1810.

This, then, appears to be evident, that St. Irenæus did not mean to affirm any moral obligation constraining all men to submit to the Church of Rome.

He knew the Church of Rome well. He knew her to have been founded in the *preceding* century by St. Peter and St. Paul; he knew that her first Bishop was placed there by them. He knew her to be an orthodox Church. But he does not state it to be the *duty* of any other Church to *submit* to her, even as she then was. Much less, not knowing, as he could not know, what she would *become* in future ages, does he lay upon all Churches in coming generations the responsibility of accommodating themselves to her opinions, whatever they might be. And yet this is the doctrine which the Divines of Rome now impute to the great Bishop of Lyons, and which they derive from this passage, and which they would make to pass current in the world under his venerable name!

5. Let us now advance a step further.

We (as was before observed) do *not* possess the original *Greek* of St. Irenæus, in this passage. It is lost. We have only the old Latin Version of it.

But the original Greek *was* extant in the third century; it was in the hands of St. HIPPOLYTUS. He was a Scholar of St. Irenæus, and has made frequent

rem profitetur *necesse est* intelligentis sapientisque naturæ primas causas conquirere."

use of that Original in the Treatise on Heresy before us.

St. Hippolytus had this passage before him in the original *Greek. He* had the advantage of personal intercourse with St. Irenæus; he was his pupil, had heard his lectures, and gave an abstract of them to the world. He was formed in his school.

How then did St. Hippolytus understand this passage of St. Irenæus? How did he show that he understood it, by *his own practice?*

This becomes an interesting topic, not merely as bearing on the passage itself, but as of far more extensive import. For it aids us in deciding aright a question on which the whole controversy turns between the Church of Rome and the other Churches of Christendom; viz.—

1. Whether the claim put forth by the Bishop of Rome to Spiritual Supremacy is an equitable claim? Was it acknowledged as such by the primitive Church?

2. Whether the Papal claim to Infallibility is a just claim or not? Was it admitted—was it even known—in primitive times?

An answer to these enquiries is contained in the newly-discovered Volume before us.

1. It exhibits the condition of the Church of Rome, and displays the conduct and teaching of two Bishops of Rome in succession, Zephyrinus and Callistus, in the writer's own age, the beginning of the third century, that is, just *after* the *decease* of

St. Irenæus, not more than a hundred years after the death of the last surviving Apostle.

The person who wrote this history, was a scholar of St. Irenæus; he was a Suffragan Bishop of the Roman Church; one who passed his life at or near Rome; one who was honoured in his day, and has ever since been honoured, as among the most eminent Teachers of the Church; one, whom the Church of Rome herself now venerates as a Martyr, and commemorates as a Saint, in her Breviary; one, whose Statue she has received with honourable marks of distinction within the doors of the Vatican, and has placed in the Pontifical Library, where it now is —St. Hippolytus.

2. What then, let us enquire, is *his* testimony with respect to the Bishop of Rome? Did he regard him as Supreme Head of the Church Universal? Did he think it the duty of all men, did he think it his own duty, to submit to him as such? Did he venerate him as infallible? Does he give any intimation that the Bishops of Rome were looked upon as Supreme or Infallible by others, or even by themselves? Had the Bishops of Rome put forth any claims to Supremacy or Infallibility in that age?

3. In replying to these questions, let us make all such allowances as Charity suggests. Let us take into consideration the circumstances in which the two successive Bishops of Rome, Zephyrinus and Callistus, were placed. They lived in a heathen

city. The clergy and laity of the Roman Church do not appear to have been gifted with endowments of Learning [8]. The Latin Church had few eminent Teachers at that time. In controverted questions of Theology, they had not the benefit of clear dogmatic decisions, such as we possess in the Creeds. From their errors we may learn to appreciate our own blessings. They were liable to be swayed by the eager partisanship of heretical teachers, resorting to Rome from Asia [9], and bringing with them the restless spirit and dialectic shrewdness of the East [1], and bearing down upon them with an array of Scriptural texts torn from their context, and not interpreted by reference to the general scope of Scripture, but by subtle syllogistic processes, derived from the schools of human Philosophy, and inapplicable to the mysteries of Faith. The Bishops

[8] Bp. Pearson, Diss. 1. c. 13, contrasts the *Roman* Christians of that age with the *Easterns* in that respect, "ipsi alumni in eâ urbe nati et educati Christiani (*i. e.* Romani) qui eo tempore propter fidem celebres, propter *doctrinam aut literarum scientiam* non adeò præclarum testimonium nacti sunt."

[9] Simon Magus, Valentinus, Marcion, Praxeas, and Sabellius, all came in person to Rome.

[1] What Juvenal says of Greek and Asiatic Vices, Philosophical Systems and Superstitions finding their way to Rome and flowing into it as a common reservoir,

> "Jam pridem Syrus in Tiberim defluxit Orontes"—iii. 62, &c.

is remarkably true of all heresies discharging their streams from the same countries into the same basin. Indeed, his picture of Rome in those respects is very descriptive of her religious condition.

of Rome, in that age, were not a match for such disputants. They had also a dread—a reasonable one—of Polytheism. The City in which they dwelt was crowded with false deities. Wherever they turned their eyes, they witnessed the vicious and debasing effects of Idolatry. They heard the terrible denunciations sounding in Scripture against it. The Unity of the True God must be maintained at any rate against the manifold pretensions of the Roman Pantheon. Hence there naturally existed at Rome a predisposition to what is commonly called the Monarchian System of Theology.

And here let us remark, that, *if* the *Trinitarian* doctrine is not *true*, its existence in the primitive Church is *unaccountable*. All antecedent probability was against it. The doctrine of Three Persons, each of them Divine, could never have risen spontaneously in a Church whose prevailing spirit was a dread of Polytheism [2]. There was much in the Church at that time to stifle the doctrine of the Trinity. Nothing to produce it. The predisposition to Monarchianism showed itself in two opposite forms. One was the heresy of Theodotus and Artemon [3], which

[2] The common question with which the Sabellians accosted the orthodox, especially of the simpler sort, when they met them was, ὦ οὗτοι, ἕνα Θεὸν ἔχομεν ἢ τρεῖς θεούς; Well, my friends, have we one God or three? Epiphan. Hæres. 62, a question which supplies evidence of what the faith of the Church was, and gives an answer to M. Bunsen's allegation that the doctrine of the Divine Personality of the *Holy Spirit* was not developed because St. Hippolytus was only accused of being a *Ditheist*. (p. 297.)

[3] On the doctrine of Theodotus, see Philosophumena, p. 257.

denied the Divinity of Christ; the other, the heresy of Noetus, which did not acknowledge the Son of God to be the Word[4], and denied the distinct proper Personality of the Son, and affirmed that the Son is the same as the Father, under a different name[5].

4. Between this Scylla and Charybdis of two Heresies the Church steered her course. To adopt another illustration, of a Scriptural character, supplied by an ancient writer, who combated both these heresies, the Blessed Son of God was crucified afresh between two Malefactors[6]. The one acknowledged Him to be Man, but would not worship Him as

Epiphan. c. Hæres. xxxiv., sive liv. p. 462, ed. Petavii, Colon. 1682.

[4] The Noetian argument was, that it was a new thing to call the Son the Word, ξένον μοι φέρεις, λόγον λέγων υἱόν, S. Hippol. c. Noet. xv. According to the Noetian and Sabellian theology, the man Jesus *became* the Son of God by communication of the Word, which it did not regard as a Person, but as a property of the Divine Nature. See Marcellus ap. Euseb. de Eccl. Th. ii. c. 8. To which St. Hippolytus replies from the Apocalypse, xix. 11, "that the Word of God is *He* Who was from the beginning, and has now been *sent* into the World."—c. Noet. xv. *τὸν Λόγον τοῦ Θεοῦ τοῦτον ὄντα ἀπ' ἀρχῆς καὶ νῦν ἀπεσταλμένον.*

[5] On the Heresy of Noetus, see Epiphanius, xxxvii. sive lvii. p. 479. The Article of Epiphanius on Noetus is derived in a great measure from the Homily of St. Hippolytus (ed. Fabr. ii. 5—20), but without any mention of his name. Epiphanius, p. 481, contrasts the heresy of Noetus with that of Theodotus, and shows that they owed their origin to similar causes.

[6] Novatian de Trin. § 30.

God; the other confessed Him to be God and Man, but would not acknowledge His Divine Personality.

5. Each of these Heresies was coupled with a Truth; each struggled against the other, by means of the Truth it possessed. The Artemonite rightly maintained against the Noetian, that the Son is not the Father; the Noetian rightly affirmed against the Artemonite, that the Son is God. Between the Artemonite and the Noetian, the Church held her place. She retained the truth, and rejected the error, of each. She affirmed that the Son is God, as well as Man; and that the Son, Who is God, is a distinct Person from God the Father.

This was the position of the Church; this was the doctrine of St. Hippolytus.

6. Now, it does not appear that any Roman Bishop was betrayed into the opinion, which taught heretically, that Christ is a mere man, in whom the Godhead dwelt in an eminent degree.

7. But it is too clear from the recital contained in the Ninth Book of the recently-discovered Treatise on Heresy, that two Bishops of Rome in succession, Zephyrinus and Callistus, fell into the opposite heresy—that of Noetus.

It is not necessary to dwell on the motives of this apostasy, or on the practices with which it was accompanied, or on the results by which it was followed. But it *is* requisite to state the fact. These two Bishops of Rome lapsed into heresy, in a primary article of the Christian Faith, and in opposition to the exhortations of Orthodox Teachers. They strenuously maintained that heresy, and propagated it by their official authority, as Bishops of Rome[7].

They tenaciously maintained, and they promulgated publicly, a doctrine, which the Church of Rome herself, with all other Churches of Christendom, now declares to be heretical.

They also denounced those who held the true faith. Zephyrinus and Callistus charged St. Hippolytus with Heresy.

8. Hence it is apparent, that the Bishops of Rome may err, and have erred,—they may err and have erred, as Bishops of Rome—in matters of Faith.

[7] And yet, as has been shown above, Zephyrinus and Callistus are canonized as Martyrs in the Breviarium Romanum (see p. 114). How painful must it be to a religious mind to discover that those whom it has been taught to venerate and invoke as Saints, were in fact Heretics, and that it has been deceived by fables inserted in the public Liturgy of the Church. What a shock must such a discovery give to its faith! How can it place any confidence in other records of the Breviary, or join with heartiness in the prayers tendered there for its use? Thus Superstition leads to Scepticism, and pious frauds (as they are sometimes called) prepare the way for Infidelity. And yet one of the so-called Reforms for which the Church of Rome is now contending is to make all Churches (even those of France) surrender their own Liturgies, and conform to the Roman Breviary! How much reason for thankfulness have the members of the Church of England, not only for what the Anglican Liturgy supplies, but also for what (as compared with some other Liturgies) it does *not* contain!

Therefore the Bishop of Rome is not Infallible.

9. Next with regard to Supremacy.

When Zephyrinus and Callistus fell into heresy, in the beginning of the third century, and when they endeavoured to disseminate their false doctrine, they were resisted by St. Hippolytus.

He does not appear to have imagined that he was bound to conform to them in their doctrine. On the contrary, he stood forth boldly and rebuked them. He has thus given a practical reply to the question, which has been raised concerning the sense of St. Irenæus, his master, in the passage recited above. Hippolytus certainly had never learnt that every Church, and every Christian, must submit to the Bishop of Rome.

Let it not be said, that he merely resisted Zephyrinus and Callistus from a transient impulse of passion, and swayed by the feelings of a moment. His resistance was deliberate; it was a resistance of years. Not only when Zephyrinus and Callistus were alive, did he think it his duty to contend against them and their heresy; but when they were in their graves, he sate down and committed to writing the History of their Heresy, and of his own opposition to it. And he published that History to the World, in order that none might be deluded by the false doctrine which those Roman Bishops had propagated, and which was disseminated after their death by some who had been deceived by them.

He published that History after the death of Callistus, and probably in the time of his successor Urbanus. He affirms that he wrote his Treatise in the discharge of his duty as a Bishop of the Church [8]. He therefore remained a Bishop—a Roman Suffragan,—although he had resisted two Bishops of Rome. As we know from Prudentius and others, he was Bishop of Portus even to his death. Nothing occurs in the whole course of the Ten Books to suggest any surmise that he had encountered any Ecclesiastical censure, on the ground of his having opposed Zephyrinus and Callistus; or that, by this publication, he contravened the just authority of the Bishop of Rome at the time when he published his work. Nothing exists in it to excite any suspicion, that, however the Church of Rome might regret the facts which his treatise related, she made any remonstrance against the publication, or regarded it as a breach of order and discipline. On the contrary, he promises himself the gratitude of the world for it [9]. And he seems to have not been disappointed. The veneration in which his memory was held at Rome indicates this.

Such was the conduct of St. Hippolytus. Such is his commentary—the commentary of his life—on the teaching of his master, Irenæus, concerning the Church of Rome.

[8] See above, p. 21; Lib. i. p. 3.

[9] See Lib. i. p. 3, and Lib. ix. p. 309.

10. It may be hoped that our Romanist brethren will no longer urge against us the authority of St. Irenæus. We may rather trust that they will examine the teaching of St. Irenæus, as illustrated by the acts of St. Hippolytus.

It does not appear from the narrative before us, that the Bishops of Rome themselves, in the third century, entertained any idea that they were Supreme Heads of the Church, or that Christians and Churches were bound to submit to them as such.

St. Hippolytus *was* indeed charged by Zephyrinus and Callistus with being a *Ditheist*, because he would not say with them that the Father and the Son are one Divine Being under two different names. But we can discover no intimation that they put forth any claim to Supremacy, and much less to Infallibility [1], or that he was accused of heresy as one who resisted the Divine Head of the Church, and rebelled against the Vicegerent of Christ on earth, because he opposed the Bishop of Rome.

Let not therefore the Divines of Rome censure us as innovators, because we do not acknowledge the Bishop of Rome as Supreme Head of the Church.

We tread in the ancient paths, which we should be deserting for new and devious ways, if we ad-

[1] Indeed, as we have seen above (p. 121) from the "Liber Diurnus" of the Popes themselves, they had no notion that they were infallible, in the eighth century.

mitted claims—claims urged as of Divine Right and in the name of Christ—but unknown to the primitive Church.

11. But, on the other hand, the Bishops of Rome, by putting forth such claims in Christ's name, and by endeavouring to enforce those claims on all men and on all Churches, as terms of Church-communion, are chargeable with innovation,—and with such an innovation as is contrary to Christian Charity, and has rent the Church asunder, and is therefore of such a nature, that no gifts or graces can compensate for it [2].

12. If the claims which are put forth by the Bishops of Rome to Infallibility and Universal Supremacy are *not* just, then there is no alternative, they are nothing short of Blasphemy. For they are claims to participation in the attributes of God Himself. And if He does not authorize these claims, they are usurpations of His Divine prerogatives. They therefore who abet those claims are fighting against Him. They are defying Him, Who "is a jealous God, and will not give His honour to another," and Who is "a consuming fire [3]." May they therefore take heed in time, lest they incur His malediction! And since they affirm that their system of Christianity *rests* on the basis of Papal Supremacy, may they be led to consider whether, instead of being founded on a Rock,

[2] 1 Cor. xiii. 1—3.

[3] Exod. xx. 5. Heb. xii. 29.

they are not building on the Sand? Are they not tempting others to do so? Are they not beguiling them to place their hopes on a false foundation, and so leading them on to everlasting destruction? If this is so, then their house will fall, and "great will be the fall thereof[4]."

13. St. Hippolytus, Bishop of Portus, resisted the errors of the Bishops of Rome. His resistance to error, and maintenance of the truth, appear to have been signally blessed by the Divine Head of the Church.

In due time, the Heresy, patronized by Zephyrinus and Callistus, was suppressed. In due time, the Truth, maintained by St. Hippolytus, prevailed at Rome. His memory was blessed,—and so much the more, we may believe, because he, a Suffragan of Rome, had rescued the Roman Church from a deadly Heresy, patronized by two Roman Bishops; and because, in defiance of their threats, he held firmly the true faith, though reviled by them as a heretic.

A marble Statue was erected in his honour[5];

[4] Matth. vii. 27.

[5] Cardinal Mai thus speaks of St. Hippolytus and his Statue (Scriptorum Veterum Nova Collectio Vatican. Rom. 1825). Proleg. p. xxxv. "Hippolyti commentariorum in Danielis Vaticinium, in Vaticanis codicibus pars adhuc mediocris erat inedita quam libenter propter *tanti Doctoris et Martyris reverentiam* luce impertivi. Statuam ejus cum paschali cyclo operumque

having been buried for many centuries, it was brought to light three hundred years ago, and was restored by the reverent care of a Cardinal and a Pope. And the opponent of two Bishops of Rome, the Historian of their Heresy, the deliverer of the Church of Rome from the error of her own two Chief Pastors, Zephyrinus and Callistus, is now revered by Prelates, Cardinals, and Pontiffs, and sits enshrined in the Vatican.

14. In this newly-discovered Volume, a solemn caution has been given to the Church, and to the world, at this critical juncture, fraught with great results. We need not hesitate to say, that the warning is from Heaven. The hand of God Himself is visible in it. Three centuries ago the Statue, to which we have referred, was dug up near Rome; it bore no name; but it had a Greek inscription engraven upon it, containing the titles of an Author's Works. By a comparison of these titles with notices in ancient Writers, this Statue was recognized to be a Statue of ST. HIPPOLYTUS, and as such, it was received into the Papal Library at Rome. It was restored to its pristine form under the auspices of *that* Pope, Pius the Fourth, who promulgated the Trent Creed, in which the Doctrine of Papal Supremacy is set forth

Catalogo inscripto prope Urbem in agro Verano Marcelli Card. Cervini auspiciis effossam, deinde a Pio IV. in Bibliothecâ Vaticanâ, ubi adhuc asservatur, positam, in fronte libri mei incidendam curavi."

as an Article of Faith. Three hundred years passed away. And now in our own age,—another Discovery has been made—in a very different quarter. An ancient Manuscript has been brought to light, from a monastic cloister of Mount Athos. On examination, it is found to state that its Author wrote a Work bearing one of the titles mentioned on the Statue—a Work "On the Universe." Thus the disinterred Statue, now in the Papal Library of the Vatican, furnished the first clue for the discovery of the Author of the MS. found three centuries afterwards in the cloistral Library of Mount Athos. Other evidences have accrued; and it appears to be now established, that the Author of the Treatise is St. Hippolytus.

The Treatise was printed before this evidence was produced. The book bore the name of Origen. May it not be said, that it owed its preservation in some degree to these circumstances? We know too well, that many passages of the ancient Fathers have been placed in the Roman Index, and proscribed by the Roman Church, as contravening the tenets of Rome. Is it not therefore probable, that this Treatise of St. Hippolytus might have been stifled, if it had been known to those who direct the affairs of the Roman Censorship[6]? Hippolytus was concealed under

[6] The argument of the Jesuit writer, James Gretser, in his ingenious treatise "on the Right of prohibiting Books," Ingoldstadt, 1603, affords a remarkable illustration of these statements.

the name of Origen. The Roman Narrative escaped notice from its position in the Ninth Book. And who would expect to find a History of the Roman Church, in a work on Heathen Philosophy?

When, also, we consider the eight long years, during which, after its discovery, this Manuscript reposed quietly, in one of the greatest Cities of the World, before it was printed, are we presumptuous in saying that it had a second providential deliverance, and that it was again restored, almost by a miracle, from the dead, when it first saw the light in England?

15. Great reason have all persons, of whatever nation, for gratitude to Almighty God, that He has

He pleads that the Pope in prohibiting or expurgating any works *whatever*, does an act of mercy, "opus misericordiæ," to the writer; and that *all* Catholic Writers, and consequently the Ancient Fathers, as dutiful children of the Church, owe filial reverence to the *Bishop* of *Rome*, and that, by anticipation, they submitted all their writings to his judgment, and that they would feel greatly obliged to him for undertaking the labour of correcting their works. His words are as follows: "Adjeci, hunc in Ecclesiâ Catholicâ esse morem ut *omnes Scriptores Catholici* pro animi sui modestiâ et submissione, ac in Ecclesiam summumque Pontificem reverentiâ, scripta sua omnia subjiciant Ecclesiæ vel summo Pontifici vel expressè vel tacitè, ita ut *velint corrigi*, sive vivant adhuc, sive post mortem. Quo posito, quis tam stupidus est, qui non videat Ecclesiam aut summum Pontificem dum *filiorum suorum* lucubrationes revidet, et ubi opus est, corrigit, *gratum ipsis auctoribus præstare* obsequium, et utilem operam posteritati, atque adeo tunc exhibere *filiis suis opus misericordiæ?*"

thus watched over the work of His faithful soldier and servant, the blessed Martyr, Hippolytus.

We of the Church of England may recognize in this Treatise a Catholic and Apostolic, yes, and a Roman, Vindication, of our own Reformation. Here a Roman Bishop, Saint and Martyr, supplies us with a defence of our own religious position with respect to Rome. In his " Refutation of all Heresies," we see a practical Refutation of that great Heresy of our own day—the Heresy, which either directly or indirectly, is at the root of many prevalent Heresies —a Refutation of the Heresy of Papal Supremacy, and of Papal Infallibility.

Whenever then *we* are charged by Romish Divines with Heresy, and Schism, for not acknowledging the Bishop of Rome as Supreme Head of the Church, and Infallible Arbiter of the Faith, we may henceforth refer them to the marble Statue in the Vatican, and bid them consult St. Hippolytus.

16. Thankful, however, as *we* ought to be for this recent discovery, perhaps they who have cause to be most grateful, are the Clergy and Laity of Rome. Truth is to be prized above all things, especially in matters of Faith. Arguments from *adversaries*, real or supposed, and especially from contemporaneous adversaries, are often regarded with suspicion, and rejected with scorn. But here the members of the Church of Rome may read a Treatise, written by one whose name they love and venerate,

one who has no interests to serve, no passions to gratify; a Bishop, Doctor, Saint, and Martyr, of their own Church.

"He being dead yet speaketh [7]."

He speaks to them from the grave, he speaks to them from primitive times—from the third century. He sits on his marble chair in the Pontifical Library at Rome, and teaches them there.

May it not be supposed, that Roman Prelates and Cardinals, passing along those ancient galleries, may pause for a while, and contemplate his venerable form, and hearken to the words of Truth which proceed from his lips? May it not be believed, that Divines of Rome, proceeding to or from that rich Library, may muse on the precepts of wisdom delivered to them by St. Hippolytus? May we not cherish the hope, that Clergy and Laity of the Roman Church, whether residing at Rome, or coming thither from afar, may not quit the courts of the Vatican, without listening to the solemn warnings and exhortations on Church Polity and Christian Doctrine, which are suggested by that Statue, and are inculcated in the History of him whom it represents, and whom they venerate as a Saint?

May it please the same merciful Providence, which has awakened the voice of Hippolytus from its silence of sixteen centuries, to bless its accents to

[7] Heb. xi. 4.

their souls' health! May it be so blessed from on high, that it may promote the peace of Nations, and the cause of Truth, and the Unity of the Church, and the Glory of Almighty God, now and for evermore!

PHILOSOPHUMENA;

SIVE,

REFUTATIO HÆRESIUM.

NONNULLA EX LIBRIS IX ET X EXCERPTA.

*** PRELIMINARY NOTE.—*The Paging on the left hand Margin refers to M. Miller's Edition. Any variations from his Text that may appear requisite to the present Editor of this portion of the Work will be specified in the notes beneath the Text, but none have been introduced into the Text itself.*

The figures prefixed to the present Editor's notes refer to the Lines of the English Translation.

The readings of the Paris Manuscript, when not followed in the Text, are indicated in the collation immediately under the Greek Text.

ΤΟΥ ΚΑΤΑ ΠΑΣΩΝ ΑΙΡΕΣΕΩΝ ΕΛΕΓΧΟΥ

ΒΙΒΛΙΟΝ Θ'.

P.278 ΤΑΔΕ ἔνεστιν ἐν τῇ ἐννάτῃ τοῦ κατὰ πασῶν αἱρέσεων Ἐλέγχου.

Τίς ἡ Νοητοῦ βλάσφημος ἀφροσύνη, καὶ ὅτι δόγμασιν Ἡρακλείτου τοῦ Σκοτεινοῦ προσέσχεν, οὐ τοῖς Χριστοῦ.

Καὶ πῶς Κάλλιστος μίξας τὴν Κλεομένους μαθητοῦ Νοητοῦ καὶ Θεοδότου αἵρεσιν, ἑτέραν καινοτέραν αἵρεσιν συνέστησε, καὶ τίς ὁ τούτου βίος.

Τίς ἡ κενὴ ἐπιδημία τοῦ ξένου δαίμονος Ἠλχασαΐ καὶ ὅτι σκέπη τῶν ἰδίων σφαλμάτων τὸ δοκεῖν προσέχειν νόμῳ τῷ δέοντι, γνωστικοῖς δόγμασιν ἢ καὶ ἀστρολογικοῖς καὶ μαγείαις πρόσκειται.

2. Cod. ἐλλέγχου. 13. Cod. μαγίαις.

---

1. Similia præmisit Sanctus Irenæus, Lugdunensis Episcopus, Sancti Hippolyti magister, Libris suis adversus Hæreses. Vide ante Libros IV. et V. ad quorum exemplar sua composuisse videtur noster.

4. τοῦ Σκοτεινοῦ. De hoc Heracliti, Philosophi Ephesii, epitheto, propter scriptorum obscuritatem indito, vide, si placet, Clem. Alex. Potter, ii. 676, not. Non illibenter recordabere graves Lucretii versus, i. 636 :

"Quapropter qui materiem rerum esse putarunt
Ignem, atque ex igni summam consistere solo,

PHILOSOPHUMENA; OR, REFUTATION OF HERESY.—BOOK THE NINTH.

THE following are the Contents of the NINTH BOOK of the REFUTATION of ALL HERESIES. P.278

What was the impious infatuation of NOETUS, and that he clave to the doctrines of Heraclitus the Obscure, and not to those of Christ.

How CALLISTUS blended the Heresy of Cleomenes, the disciple of Noetus, with that of Theodotus, and constituted another stranger Heresy; and what was his manner of life.

What was the strange sojourn at Rome of the portentous spirit of Elchasai; and how a semblance of reverence for the Law (of Moses) was made by him a cloke for his errors; whereas, in fact, he adheres to Gnostic or even to Astrological Theories, and to Magic.

Magnopere a verâ lapsi ratione videntur.
HERACLITUS init quorum dux prœlia primus,
Clarus ob *obscuram* linguam magis inter inanes,
Quamde graveis inter Graios qui vera requirunt.
Omnia enim stolidi magis admirantur amantque,
Inversis quæ sub verbis latitantia cernunt,
Veraque constituunt, quæ belle tangere possunt
Aureis, et lepido quæ sunt fucata sonore."

7. S. Hippol. c. Noët. § 3. Θεόδοτος τὸν Χριστὸν ἄνθρωπον συνιστᾶν ψιλὸν βουλόμενος.

10. κενῇ ita M.S. Sed legendum καινῇ quivis viderit.

13. τὸ δοκεῖν προσέχειν νόμῳ τῷ δεόντι, γνωστικοῖς δογμάσιν . . . πρόσκειται. Ita ex codice MS. unico Millerus. Sed interpungendum post νόμῳ, deinde legendum, vocibus disjunctis, ΤΩι ΔΕ ΟΝΤΙ γνωστικοῖς δ. π. i. e. "*Simulat* se Legi Mosaicæ inhæ-

Τίνα τὰ Ἰουδαίοις ἔθη, καὶ πόσαι τούτων διαφοραί.

Πολλοῦ *τοίνυν τοῦ περὶ πασῶν αἱρέσεων γενομένου ἡμῖν ἀγῶνος, μηθέν τε ἀνεξέλεγκτον καταλιποῦσι, περιλείπεται νῦν ὁ μέγιστος ἀγὼν, ἐκδιηγήσασθαι καὶ διελέγξαι τὰς ἐφ' ἡμῖν ἐπ-*
P.279 *αναστάσας αἱρέσεις, δι' ὧν τινὲς ἀμαθεῖς καὶ τολμηροὶ διασκεδαννύειν ἐπεχείρησαν τὴν* Ἐκκλη*σίαν, μέγιστον τάραχον κατὰ πάντα τὸν κόσμον ἐν πᾶσι τοῖς πιστοῖς ἐμβάλλοντες.* Δο*κεῖ γὰρ ἐπὶ τὴν ἀρχηγὸν τῶν κακῶν γενομένην γνώμην ὁρμήσαντας διελέγξαι τίνες αἱ ταύτης ἀρχαὶ, ὅπως εὔγνωστοι αἱ ἐκφυάδες αὐτῆς ἅπασι γενόμεναι καταφρονηθῶσι.*

Γ*εγένηταί τις ὀνόματι* Ν*οητὸς, τῷ γένει* Σ*μυρναῖος.* Ο*ὗτος εἰσηγήσατο αἵρεσιν ἐκ τῶν* Ἡ*ρακλείτου δογμάτων, οὗ διάκονος καὶ μαθητὴς γίνεται* Ἐ*πίγονός τις τοὔνομα, ὃς τῇ* Ῥ*ώμῃ ἐπιδημήσας ἐπέσπειρε τὴν ἄθεον γνώμην.* Ὧ*ι μαθητεύσας* Κ*λεομένης καὶ βίῳ καὶ τρόπῳ ἀλλότριος τῆς* Ἐ*κκλησίας, ἐκράτυνε τὸ δόγμα, κατ'*

17. In cod. titulus: *Φιλοσοφουμένων ἔννατον. Νοητός.* ib. Cod. *πολλοὶ τοίνυν.* 2. Cod. *διασκεδανοίην.* 4. Cod. *πᾶσῖς πιστοῖς.* 12. Cod. *τῇ Ῥώμην.*

---

rere, *τῷ δὲ ὄντι*, sed *de facto* gnosticis deliriis se mancipavit," vide inf. p. 293. 22.

10. Vide inf. p. 329. 34—60. Hippol. c. Noët. § 1, ed. Fabr. ii. 5. *Νοήτου ὃς τῷ μὲν γένει ἦν*

What are the customs of the Jews, and how many their differences.

We have performed a laborious work with regard to all (former) heresies, and have left none unrefuted; but there remains now the hardest toil of all; to give a complete description and refutation of those P.279
Heresies which have arisen in our own age, by means of which some unlearned and bold men have undertaken to distract the Church, and have produced very great confusion throughout the world among all the faithful. For it appears requisite to revert to the dogma which was the primary source of the evil, and to expose its origin, so that its offshoots may be manifest to all, and may be contemned.

There was a certain NOETUS, of Smyrna. He introduced a heresy from the tenets of Heraclitus. One Epigonus was his agent and scholar, who, coming to Rome, disseminated his impious doctrine. Cleomenes his disciple, an alien from the Church in life and disposition, fortified that doctrine. At that time

---

Σμυρναῖος οὐ πρὸ πολλοῦ χρόνου γενόμενος. Ephesium vocat Epiphanius, Hæres. lvii. Vide et Joann. Damascen. de Hæres. c. 57. Cæterum in tono vocis fluctuant Codices, aliis *Νοητὸς*, aliis *Νόητος* exhibentibus.

13. Vide Nostrum, lib. x. p. 329. 34. *Νοητὸς εἰσηγήσατο τοιάνδε αἵρεσιν ἐξ Ἐπιγόνου τινὸς εἰς Κλεομένην χωρήσασαν*, unde sua hausisse videtur Theodoretus, iii. 3. *Νοητὸς ἀνενεώσατο τὴν αἵρεσιν, ἣν Ἐπίγονος ἀπεκύησε πρῶτος, Κλεομένης δὲ παραλαβὼν ἐβεβαίωσε*. Hinc, opinor, suspicari licet Theodoretum libro Decimo, compendiario illo, usum esse, non autem Nostri opus integrum præ manibus habuisse, idque ei in hoc loco fraudi fuisse. Vide suprà p. 148, infrà Append. ii.

ἐκεῖνο καιροῦ Ζεφυρίνου διέπειν νομίζοντος τὴν ἐκκλησίαν, ἀνδρὸς ἰδιώτου καὶ αἰσχροκερδοῦς· [ὃς] τῷ κέρδει προσφερομένῳ πειθόμενος, συνεχώρει τοῖς προσιοῦσι τῷ Κλεομένει μαθητεύεσθαι, καὶ αὐτὸς ὑποσυρόμενος τῷ χρόνῳ ἐπὶ τὰ αὐτὰ ὥρμητο, συμβούλου καὶ συναγωνιστοῦ τῶν κακῶν ὄντος αὐτῷ Καλλίστου, οὗ τὸν βίον καὶ τὴν ἐφευρεθεῖσαν αἵρεσιν μετ' οὐ πολὺ ἐκθήσομαι. Τούτων κατὰ διαδοχὴν διέμεινε τὸ διδασκαλεῖον κρατυνόμενον καὶ ἐπαῦξον, διὰ τὸ συναιρεῖσθαι αὐτοῖς τὸν Ζεφυρῖνον καὶ τὸν Κάλλιστον, καίτοι ἡμῶν μηδέποτε συγχωρησάντων, ἀλλὰ πλειστάκις ἀντικαθεστώτων πρὸς αὐτοὺς, καὶ διελεγξάντων, καὶ ἄκοντας βιασαμένων τὴν ἀλήθειαν ὁμολογεῖν· οἳ πρὸς μὲν ὥραν αἰδούμενοι, καὶ ὑπὸ τῆς ἀληθείας συναγόμενοι, ὡμολόγουν, μετ' οὐ πολὺ δὲ ἐπὶ τὸν αὐτὸν βόρβορον ἀνεκυλίοντο.

18. Addidit ὃς Millerus. 19. Cod. Κλεομένῃ, cum iota subscripto. 21. Cod. συμβόλου. 28. Cod. ἀντικαθεστότων. 29. Cod. διελλεγξάντων.

---

16. Vide apud Euseb. v. 28; vi. 21. De Zephyrino hæc habet liber Pontificalis Damaso ascriptus ap. Labbé, Concil. i. p. 602. "Zephyrinus natione Romanus ex patre Abundantio sedit annos viii (xviii?), menses vii, dies x. Fuit autem temporibus Antonini et Severi a consulatu Saturnini et Gallicani, usque ad Præsentem et Strigatum consules. Hic fecit ordinationes iv per mens. Decemb. Presbyteros 13, Diaconos 7, Episcopos per loca 13. Qui sepultus est in cœmeterio suo, non longè a cœmeterio Callisti, viâ Appiâ." Dissonantia inter se tradunt auctores de annis Zephyrini, aliis ab A.D. 198, aliis ab A.D. 201 Pontificatum ejus ordi-

ZEPHYRINUS imagined that he governed the Church, an illiterate and covetous man. He being allured by offers of lucre, conceded to those who resorted to Cleomenes to become his scholars; and at length, being inveigled himself, he ran into the same errors, having, as his adviser and coadjutor in evil, CALLISTUS, whose life and whose heresy, invented by him, I will soon relate.

During their succession this school subsisted, being strengthened and aggrandized, because Zephyrinus and Callistus co-operated with them, although we never gave place, but very often resisted them, and confuted them, and compelled them reluctantly to own the truth; which they did through shame for a time, and being constrained by the force of truth; but soon afterwards they returned to wallow in the same mire.

---

entibus; quidam in A.D. 214 exitum figunt, nonnulli ad A.D. 219 continuant. Vide Clintoni Fastos ad A.D. 210. Ab A.D. 202 ad A.D. 218 sedisse statuit Jaffé, Regest. Pontif. p. 5, ed. 1851.

ib. Ζεφυρίνου νομίζοντος διέπειν τὴν ἐκκλησίαν, de hâc loquendi formulâ vide, si lubet, quæ suprà monuimus, pp. 83—90.

20. ὥρμητο sic MS. Sed legendum videtur ὡρμᾶτο.

26. συναιρεῖσθαι ita ex Codice Millerus. Sed reposueris συναίρεσθαι; vide Philosophumena, inf. 288, 89. συναράμενον, et p. 143, 77, λέγουσι Μωσέα αὐτῶν συναίρεσθαι τῷ λόγῳ.

27. Hæc et quæ sequuntur colorem orationis traxisse videntur ex Apostoli historiâ suam ipsius cum B. Petro concertationem enarrantis, ad Galat. ii. 5—13.

31. ἐπὶ τὸν αὐτὸν βόρβορον ἀνεκυλίοντο ex B. Petr. 2. ii. 22, ὗς λουσαμένη εἰς κυλισμὸν βορβόρου: quæ quidem Sancti Apostoli verba ex Græco Senario Proverbiali videntur efficta, quem sic se olim habuisse conjecerim,

εἰς ἴδιον ἐξέραμ' ἐπιστρέψας κύων,
λελουμένη θ' ὗς εἰς κύλισμα βορβόρου.

P. 280 Ἀλλ' ἐπεὶ τῆς γενεαλογίας αὐτῶν τὴν διαδοχὴν ἐπεδείξαμεν, δοκεῖ λοιπὸν καὶ τῶν δογμάτων τὴν κακοδιδασκαλίαν ἐκθέσθαι, πρότερον τὰ Ἡρακλείτῳ τῷ Σκοτεινῷ δόξαντα παραθεμένους, ἔπειτα καὶ τὰ τούτων μέρη Ἡρακλείτεια ὄντα φανερῶσαι, ἃ τυχόντες οἱ νῦν προστάται τῆς αἱρέσεως οὐκ ἴσασιν ὄντα τοῦ Σκοτεινοῦ, νομίζοντες εἶναι Χριστοῦ. Οἷς εἰ ἐνέτυχον, κἂν οὕτω δυσωπηθέντες παύσονται τῆς ἀθέου δυσφημίας. Ἀλλ' εἰ καὶ πρότερον ἔκκειται ὑφ' ἡμῶν ἐν τοῖς Φιλοσοφουμένοις ἡ δόξα Ἡρακλείτου, ἀλλά γε δοκεῖ προσαναπαραχθῆναι καὶ νῦν, ὅπως διὰ τοῦ ἐγγίονος ἐλέγχου φανερῶς διδαχθῶσιν οἱ τούτου νομίζοντες Χριστοῦ εἶναι μαθητὰς, οὐκ ὄντας, ἀλλὰ τοῦ Σκοτεινοῦ.

Ἡράκλειτος μὲν οὖν φησὶν εἶναι τὸ πᾶν διαιρετὸν, ἀδιαίρετον, γενητὸν, ἀγένητον, θνητὸν, ἀθάνατον, λόγον αἰῶνα, πατέρα υἱὸν, θεὸν δίκαιον. "Οὐκ ἐμοῦ, ἀλλὰ τοῦ δόγματος ἀκούσαντας ὁμολογεῖν σοφόν ἐστιν, ἓν πάντα

5. Cod. ἐπεὶ καὶ τά. 7. Cod. εἴσασιν. 11. Cod. φιλοσοφουμένους. Cf. lib. I. cap. 4. 12. Cod. πρὸς ἀνπαραχθῆναι. 13. Cod. ἀγγίονος ἐλλέγχου. 20. Cod. ἐστιν ἐν.

---

11. Pro κἂν οὕτω παύσονται legendum videtur παύσαιντο τι, vide Præf. p. 2. ὅπως αἰσχυνθέντες παύσωνταί τι τῆς ἀλογίστου γνώμης.

13. Lib. i. p. 10.

21. λόγος διὰ οὐσίας τοῦ παντὸς διήκων. Heraclitus vocat οὐσίαν εἱμαρμένης, vide Stob. Ecl. Phys. i. vi. 15. Galen. Hist. Phil. x. Plutarch. Placit. Phil. 28.

ib. πάντα ψυχῶν καὶ δαιμόνων

But since we have indicated the succession of P. 280
their lineage, it seems requisite now to exhibit the pravity of their doctrines. (This we will do) first by setting down the opinions of HERACLITUS the Obscure, next by displaying those portions of their system that are derived from him, which they who now promote this heresy have espoused, being not aware that those tenets are borrowed from Heraclitus; but they imagine them to be from Christ. If, however, they met with them (thus displayed), perhaps even by this means they might be shamed out of their impious language. And although the tenets of Heraclitus have been already set forth in our "Philosophumena," yet we will now also revert to them, in order that by this closer examination, those persons may be instructed, who imagine that these men are disciples of Christ, whereas they are scholars not of Him, but of Heraclitus.

Heraclitus then asserts that all things are divisible, indivisible; created, uncreated; mortal, immortal; Reason, Eternity; Father, Son; but that Deity is by chance. "It is wise," he says, "to listen, not to me, but to the doctrine, and to confess that all things

---

εἶναι πλέα statuebat Heraclitus: vide Diog. Laert. ix.

21. *θεὸν δίκαιον.* Sic Codex, etiam Bernaysio tacente, et ut videtur, probante apud Bunsen. (iv. pp. xl. xlii.) vix a me impetrare possum, ut *Δίκαιον* sanum credam. Ne te morer, pro ΔΙΚΑΙΟΝ legendum conjecerim Δ' ΕΙΚΑΙΟΝ; *εἰκαῖον* h. e. est *fortuitum*: *εἰκαῖον* cum *δίκαιον* confundi alibi monui (ad Theocr. p. 115). Quod ad sensum attinet, rem explicare videtur noster inf. 281. 77, *τοὺς μὲν θεοὺς ἔδειξε τοὺς δὲ ἀνθρώπους*, sed utrum horum, esse incertum. Quippe Providentiam abnegabat Heraclitus et omnia casui permittebat.

εἶναι," ὁ Ἡράκλειτος φησὶ, καὶ ὅτι τοῦτο οὐκ ἴσασι πάντες οὐδὲ ὁμολογοῦσιν, ἐπιμέμφεται ὧδέ πως· "Οὐ ξυνίασιν ὅκως διαφερόμενον ἑωϋτῷ ὁμολογέειν παλίντροπος ἁρμονίη ὅκως περ τόξου καὶ λύρης." Ὅτι δὲ λόγος ἐστὶν ἀεὶ τὸ πᾶν καὶ διὰ παντὸς ὢν, οὕτως λέγει· "Τοῦ δὲ λόγου τοῦ δέοντος ἀεὶ ἀξύνετοι γίνονται ἄνθρωποι, καὶ πρόσθεν ἢ ἀκοῦσαι καὶ ἀκούσαντες τὸ πρῶτον· γινομένων γὰρ πάντων
P.281 κατὰ τὸν λόγον τόνδε ἄπειροι εἰσὶν, ἐοίκασι πειρώμενοι καὶ ἐπέων καὶ ἔργων τοιουτέων ὁκοῖα ἐγὼ διηγεῦμαι, διαιρέων κατὰ φύσιν καὶ φράζων ὅκως ἔχει." Ὅτι δέ ἐστι παῖς τὸ πᾶν καὶ δι'

21. Cod. πάντα εἰδέναι. 22. Cod. εἴσασι. 23. "Pro παλίντροπος legitur παλίντονος apud Plut. de Isid. et Osirid. p. 369, A: Παλίντονος γὰρ ἁρμονίη κόσμου ὥσπερ λύρης καὶ τόξου, καθ' Ἡράκλειτον." Miller. 25. Cod. ὢν. 26. Cod. ἀεὶ ξετοί. "Correctum ex Clem. Al. Strom. V. p. 716." Miller. 28. Cod. ἀκούσαντας et γινόμενον. 1. Cod. ὁποῖα. 2. Cod. διήγευμαι, διερέων. 3. Cod. ὅπως.

---

23. ὁμολογέειν. Millerus legendum censet ὁμολογέει, sed jungenda videntur ξυνίασιν ὁμολογέειν, dixerat enim ἐπιμέμφεται ὅτι τοῦτο οὐχ ὁμολογοῦσιν.

ib. διαφερόμενον ἑωϋτῷ παλίντροπος ἁρμονίη ὅκως περ τόξου καὶ λύρης legendum puto διαφερομένου, ut sensus sit, harmonia inest inversa in re quâlibet sibi oppositâ, quemadmodum arcus inversus, sive in dorsum rejectus, fit lyra. Cæterum monente Millero hæc citat Plutarchus de Iside et Osirid., p. 369, A, παλίντονος ἁρμονίη κόσμου ὥσπερ λύρης καὶ τόξου. His adscribi meretur nobile Heracliti fragmentum quod conservavit Stobæus Eclog. Phys. i. xlii. συνάψειας οὖλον καὶ οὐχὶ οὖλον συμφερόμενον διαφερόμενον, συνᾷδον διᾷδον, ἐκ πάντων ἓν καὶ ἐξ ἑνὸς πάντα· οὕτως τὴν τῶν ὅλων σύστασιν διὰ τῆς τῶν ἐναντιωτάτων κράσεως ἀρχῶν μία διεκόσμησεν ἁρμονία, μία διὰ πάντων διήκουσα δύναμις, ἐκ τῶν ἀμίκτων καὶ ἑτεροίων τὸν σύμπαντα κόσμον δημιουργήσασα. Vide etiam quæ de Heraclito narrat Plato Sophist. § 868,

are One." And he complains that all do not know and own this, as follows. "They have not understanding to confess how in that which is opposite to itself there is an inverse harmony as in a bow and a lyre." And that Reason is always every thing and pervades all things, he thus declares, "Men do not comprehend this Reason which is ever existent; either before they hear of it, or when they first hear of it. For although every thing is produced according to this Reason, yet they resemble men who are un- P.281
acquainted with it, although they have had experience of such words and works as I expound, distinguishing them according to their nature, and declaring their mode of existence."

And that a child (a son) is every thing, and

---

p. 368, Heindorf. διαφερόμενον ἀεὶ συμφέρεται. Euseb. Præpar. Evang. xiv. 4, et Schleiermacher de Heraclito in Mus. Antiq. Stud. I. p. 408.

26. Aristot. Rhet. iii. 5. τὰ Ἡρακλείτου διαστίξαι ἔργον, φησὶ γὰρ "τοῦ λόγου τοῦδ' ἐόντος αἰεὶ ἀξύνετοι ἄνθρωποι γίγνονται·" ἄδηλον γὰρ τὸ αἰεὶ πρὸς ὁπότερον δεῖ διαστίξαι. Citat v. 26 usque ad ὅκως ἔχει Sextus Empiricus adv. Mathem. Lib. vii. p. 162, ed. Aurel. 1621.

28. Comparari possunt verba Heracliti ap. Clem. Alex. p. 156. 14, Potter. οὐ φρονέουσιν τοιαῦτα πολλοὶ ὁκοσοι ἐγκυρέουσι, οὐδὲ μαθόντες γιγνώσκουσι.

1. ἄπειροί εἰσιν ἐοίκασι πειρώμενοι καὶ ἐπέων. Sic MS. Delet εἰσι Millerus, adstipulante, ut ait Clem. Alex. Strom. v. 718, sed ibi κωφοῖς ἐοίκασι Clemens, unde pro ΑΠΕΙΡΟΙ ΕΙΣΙΝ ἐοίκασιν, legere mallem ΑΠΕΙΡΟΙΣΙΝ ἐοίκασι, i. e. *inexpertis similes sunt*, et sic reddidi.

5. Lucian. in Vitarum Auctione, i. p. 554, ed. Hemsterh. ΑΓΟΡ. τί γὰρ ὁ Αἰών ἐστι; ΗΡΑΚΛΕΙΤΟΣ. παῖς παίζων, πεσσεύων, διαφερόμενος, ubi res humanas plorat Heraclitus, ὅτι ἔμπεδον οὐδὲν, ἀλλά κως εἰς κυκεῶνα πάντα συνειλέεται καὶ ὅτι τωὐτὸ τέρψις, ἀτερψίη, γνῶσις, ἀγνωσίη, μέγα, μικρὸν, ἄνω, κάτω, περιχορεύοντα καὶ ἀμειβόμενα ἐν τῇ τοῦ αἰῶνος παιδίῃ.

ib. παῖς. Sic enim viam sibi munit Hippolytus quâ ab Hera-

αἰῶνος αἰώνιος βασιλεὺς τῶν ὅλων οὕτως λέγει· "Αἰὼν παῖς ἐστὶ παίζων, πεττεύων· παιδὸς ἡ βασιληΐη." Ὅτι δέ ἐστιν ὁ πατὴρ πάντων τῶν γεγονότων γενητῶν, ἀγένητος κτίσις δημιουργὸς, ἐκείνου λέγοντος ἀκούωμεν· "Πόλεμος πάντων μὲν πατήρ ἐστι, πάντων δὲ βασιλεὺς," καὶ τοὺς μὲν θεοὺς ἔδειξε, τοὺς δὲ ἀνθρώπους, τοὺς μὲν δούλους ἐποίησε, τοὺς δὲ ἐλευθέρους. Ὅτι δέ ἐστιν "ἁρμονίη ὅκως περ τόξου καὶ λύρης." Ὅτι δὲ [ἐστὶν] ἀφανὴς ὁ ἀόρατος ἄγνωστος ἀνθρώποις ἐν τούτοις λέγει· "Ἁρμονίη ἀφανὴς φανερῆς κρείττων." Ἐπαινεῖ καὶ προθαυμάζει πρὸ τοῦ γινωσκομένου τὸ ἄγνωστον αὐτοῦ καὶ ἀόρατον τῆς δυνάμεως. Ὅτι δέ ἐστιν ὁρατὸς ἀνθρώποις καὶ οὐκ ἀνεξεύρετος, ἐν τούτοις λέγει· "Ὅσων ὄψις, ἀκοὴ, μάθησις, ταῦτα ἐγὼ προτιμέω," φησὶ, τουτέστι τὰ ὁρατὰ τῶν ἀοράτων. Ἀπὸ τῶν τοιούτων αὐτοῦ λόγων κατανοεῖν ῥᾴδιον· ἐξηπάτηνται, φησὶν, οἱ ἄνθρωποι πρὸς τὴν γνῶσιν τῶν φανερῶν παραπλησίως Ὁμήρῳ, ὃς ἐγένετο τῶν Ἑλλήνων σοφώτερος πάντων. Ἐκεῖνόν τε γὰρ παῖδες φθεῖρας κατακτείνοντες ἐξηπάτησαν εἰ-

9. Cod. ἀκούομεν. 14. In cod. post δέ vocula verme exesa.
19. Cod. ἂν ἐξευρετός. ib. Cod. ὅσον ὄψις.

---

clito Noëtum sua sumpsisse confirmet. "Solenne enim Hippolyto Filium Dei appellare παῖδα Θεοῦ," ait Grabius ad Bull. Def. Fid. Nic. ii. 8. 5. Sed in hac re ut in aliis plerisque, Hippolyto præiverat Irenæus v. 6. Vide c. Noët. § 5. § 7, νοῦς Πατρὸς ὁ Παῖς. § 11, Λόγος Νοῦς ὃς προβὰς ἐν κόσμῳ ἐδείκνυτο Παῖς Θεοῦ. de Antichristo, c. 3.

12. Vide Heraclit. ap. Stob.

eternal king of all things through eternity, he thus declares. "A boy at his games, playing with his dice, is eternity; the kingdom is his;" And let us hear how he teaches that uncreated creature creating is the parent of all created things. "Antagonism is the parent of all things, and the ruler of all: and some it generated to be gods, and some men; some it produced slaves, and some free." And that there is a harmony, as in a bow and lyre.

And that invisible harmony is better, unseen and unknown to men, he thus says: "Harmony invisible is better than visible." He thus praises and prefers that which is unknown and invisible of its power, before that which is visible.

But that harmony visible to men and not undiscoverable is preferable, he says thus: "As many things as are subject to the sense of sight, hearing, intelligence, these I prefer," he says: that is, he prefers the visible to the invisible.

From such words as these it is easy to comprehend him. "Men," says he, "are deceived with regard to the knowledge of what is evident, as Homer was, who was wiser than all the Greeks."

Eclog. I. iii. 28. *πῦρ ἀΐδιον ἐκ τῆς ἐναντιοδρομίας δημιουργὸν τῶν ὅλων.*

20. Post *ὅτι δὲ* vocem verme exesam notat Millerus qui supplevit *ἐστίν*. Supplendum videtur *κρείττων*. Tum post *ἀφανής* delendum ʽO.

25. *κατανοεῖν ῥᾴδιον*, ironicè dictum.

28. Cætera quæ in hoc commate leguntur prudens prætereo.

πόντες, Ὅσα εἴδομεν καὶ κατελάβομεν, ταῦτα ἀπολείπομεν, ὅσα δὲ οὔτε εἴδομεν οὔτ' ἐλάβομεν, ταῦτα φέρομεν.

Οὕτως Ἡράκλειτος *ἐν ἴσῃ μοίρᾳ τίθεται καὶ τιμᾷ τὰ ἐμφανῆ τοῖς ἀφανέσιν, ὡς ἕν τι τὸ*
P.282 *ἐμφανὲς καὶ τὸ ἀφανὲς ὁμολογουμένως ὑπάρχον.* Τίς *γὰρ, φησὶν, "ἁρμονίη ἀφανὴς φανερῆς κρείττων."* Καὶ *"ὅσων ὄψις, ἀκοὴ, μάθησις (τουτέστι τὰ ὄργανα), ταῦτα, φησὶν, ἐγὼ προτιμέω," οὐ τὰ ἀφανῆ προτιμήσας.* Τοιγαροῦν *οὐδὲ σκότος οὐδὲ φῶς, οὐδὲ πονηρὸν οὐδὲ ἀγαθὸν ἕτερον φησὶν εἶναι ὁ* Ἡράκλειτος, *ἀλλὰ ἓν καὶ τὸ αὐτό.* Ἐπιτιμᾷ *γοῦν* Ἡσιόδῳ *ὅτι ἡμέραν καὶ νύκτα οἶδεν.* Ἡμέρα *γάρ, φησὶ, καὶ νὺξ ἔστιν ἕν, λέγων ὧδέ πως·* "Διδάσκαλος *δὲ πλείστων* Ἡσίοδος· *τοῦτον ἐπίστανται πλεῖστα εἰδέναι, ὅστις ἡμέρην καὶ εὐφρόνην οὐκ ἐγίνωσκεν.* Ἔστι *γὰρ ἓν καὶ ἀγαθὸν καὶ κακόν."* Οἱ *γοῦν ἰατροὶ, φησὶν ὁ* Ἡράκλειτος, *τέμνοντες, καίοντες, πάντῃ βασανίζοντες κακῶς τοὺς ἀρρωστοῦντας, ἐπαιτιῶνται μηδὲν ἄξιον μισθῶν λαμβάνειν παρὰ τῶν ἀρρωστούντων, ταῦτα ἐργαζόμενοι τὰ ἀγαθὰ καὶ τὰς νόσους.* Καὶ *εὐθὺ δὲ, φησὶ, καὶ στρεβλὸν, τὸ αὐτό ἐστι.* Γραφέων, *φησὶν, ὁδὸς εὐθεῖα καὶ*

2. Cod. ἁρμονία ἡ ἀφανής. 12. Cod. εὐφροσύνην.

---

2. Cod. *τίς γὰρ, φησὶν, ἁρμονία ἡ ἀφανής.* Pro *τίς* Millerus legendum censet *ἐστι,* deinde *ἁρμονίη ἀφανής*—Sed si sententia

Thus Heraclitus esteems and honours alike what is visible and invisible, as if the visible and the invisible were confessedly one. "For what invisible P.282 harmony," says he, "is better than visible? And as many things as are subject to vision, hearing, intelligence, that is, the organs, these I prefer"—he, who before had preferred the invisible!

Therefore, Heraclitus denies that Darkness and Light, Good and Evil, are different, and affirms that they are one and the same. Truly, at least, he rebukes Hesiod for recognizing Day and Night. For Day and Night, he says, are one; speaking as follows. "Hesiod taught many things; and men imagine that he knew many things, although he did not know (the nature) of Day and Night. For Good and Evil is one. Certainly, at least," says Heraclitus, "Physicians, when they amputate, cauterize, and cruelly torture their patients in every way, complain that they do not receive from them any adequate remuneration for their pains, although they do them these good deeds as to their diseases."

And straight and crooked, he says, are the same. The path, says he, of the lines of the machine called

---

legitur interrogativè, vitio carere videtur, nisi quod deleta ἥ, Ionicæ formæ ἁρμονίη φανερῆς restituendæ sint.

4. Pro OY legere mallem ʽO.

17. *μηδὲν ἄξιον μισθῶν* ita Cod. mendosè. Reponendum videtur *μηδέν' ἄξιον μισθόν*, vel *μηδὲν ἄξιον μίσθωμα*.

19. *ταῦτα ἐργαζόμενοι τὰ ἀγαθὰ καὶ τὰς νόσους*. Sic vitiosè MS. —Pro ΚΑΙ ΤΑΣ *νόσους* legendum

σκολιὴ ἡ τοῦ ὀργάνου τοῦ καλουμένου κοχλίου· ἐν τῷ γραφείῳ περιστροφὴ εὐθεῖα καὶ σκολιή. Ἄνω γὰρ ὁμοῦ καὶ κύκλῳ περιέχεται· μία ἐστὶ, φησὶ, καὶ ἡ αὐτὴ, καὶ τὸ ἄνω καὶ τὸ κάτω ἕν ἐστι. Καὶ τὸ αὐτὸ ὁδὸς ἄνω κάτω, μία καὶ ὡϋτὴ, καὶ τὸ μιαρόν φησι καὶ τὸ καθαρὸν ἓν καὶ ταυτὸν εἶναι, καὶ τὸ πότιμον καὶ τὸ ἄποτον, ἓν καὶ τὸ αὐτὸ εἶναι· θάλασσα, φησὶν, ὕδωρ καθαρώτατον καὶ μιαρώτατον, ἰχθύσι μὲν πότιμον καὶ σωτήριον, ἀνθρώποις δὲ ἄποτον καὶ ὀλέθριον. Λέγει δὲ ὁμολογουμένως τὸ ἀθάνατον εἶναι θνητὸν καὶ τὸ θνητὸν ἀθάνατον διὰ τῶν τοιούτων λόγων· "Ἀθάνατοι θνητοὶ, θνητοὶ ἀθάνατοι, ζῶντες τὸν ἐκείνων θάνατον, τὸν δὲ ἐκείνων
P.283 βίον τεθνεῶτες." Λέγει δὲ καὶ σαρκὸς ἀνάστασιν ταύτης φανερᾶς ἐν ᾗ γεγενήμεθα. Καὶ τὸν θεὸν οἶδε ταύτης τῆς ἀναστάσεως αἴτιον οὕτως λέγων· "Ἔνθα δ' ἐόντι ἐπανίστασθαι καὶ φύλακας γίνεσθαι ἐγερτιζόντων καὶ νεκρῶν." Λέγει δὲ καὶ τοῦ κόσμου κρίσιν καὶ πάντων τῶν ἐν αὐτῷ διὰ πυρὸς γίνεσθαι, λέγων οὕτως·

---

putaverim ΚΑΤΤΑΣ *νόσους*, *i. e.* Ionicâ Heracliti dialecto, *κατὰ τὰς νόσους.*

24. Homeric. Allegor. § 24. *ὁ γοῦν Σκοτεινὸς Ἡράκλειτος θεολογεῖ τὰ φυσικὰ, δι' ὧν φησι, Θεοὶ θνητοὶ, ἄνθρωποι ἀθάνατοι, ζῶντες τὸν ἐκείνων θάνατον, θνήσκοντες τὴν ἐκείνων ζωήν.* Huc fortasse respexerit Clem. Alex. Pædagog. iii. p. 251. *ὀρθῶς ἄρα εἶπεν Ἡράκλειτος, Ἄνθρωποι θεοί· Θεοὶ ἄνθρωποι.* Sext. Empir. iii. 24. *ὁ Ἡράκλειτός φησιν ὅτι καὶ τὸ ζῆν καὶ τὸ ἀποθανεῖν καὶ ἐν τῷ ζῆν ἡμᾶς ἐστὶ καὶ ἐν τῷ τεθνάναι· ὅτε μὲν γὰρ ἡμεῖς ζῶμεν τὰς ψυχὰς ἡμῶν τεθνάναι.* Clem. Alex. Strom. iii.

the screw is both straight and crooked; and the revolution in the graving-tool is both straight and crooked. For it goes upwards at the same time, and revolves in a circle. And ascent and descent is one.

And a road upward and downward is one and the same. And, he says, that what is impure and pure is one and the same, and what is potable and not potable is one and the same. The sea, says he, is very pure water and very impure, being potable and preservative to fish, but not potable and destructive to men. Similarly he says, that what is immortal is mortal, and what is mortal is immortal, in such language as follows: Immortals are mortal, mortals are immortal, the one living the death, but having died the life of the other.

He affirms also the Resurrection of this visible P. 283
flesh in which we were born; and recognizes God as the cause of this Resurrection, saying thus: That they arise again there [through God's aid], and become the guardians vigilantly of quick and dead.

He asserts also a Judgment of the world and all things therein by Fire. Thunder, says he, steers all

---

p. 434. *οὐχὶ καὶ Ἡράκλειτος θάνατον τὴν γένεσιν καλεῖ*; vide ad Plat. Gorg. p. 495. A.

26. Vide Heeren ad Stob. Ecl. Phys. lii. Cum omnia mutatione fieri statueret Heraclitus, hanc ipsam *μεταβολὴν ὁδὸν ἄνω καὶ κάτω* vocavit teste Diog. Laer. ix. 8.

4. *ἔνθα δ' ἐόντι ἐπανίστασθαι καὶ φύλακας γίνεσθαι ἐγερτιζόντων καὶ νεκρῶν.* Sic Cod. Locum ita constituit Bernaysius, apud Bunsenium, iv. p. xliii. *ἔνθα διὰ Θεόν τε ἐπανίστασθαι καὶ φύλακας γίνεσθαι ἐγερτὶ ζώντων καὶ νεκρῶν.* Color poëticus esse videtur, ita ut fortasse versuum hujusmodi reliquias delitescere censeam,

——— *ἔνθα δ' ἐόντας*
εἶπεν ἀνίστασθαι φύλακάς τε γενέσθαι ἐγερτὶ
ζώντων καὶ νεκρῶν.

7. De igne omnium exploratore Heraclitus ap. Clem. Al. p. 235.

"Τὰ δὲ πάντα οἰακίζει κεραυνὸς," τουτέστι κατευθύνει· κεραυνὸν τὸ πῦρ λέγων τὸ αἰώνιον. Λέγει δὲ καὶ φρόνιμον τοῦτο εἶναι τὸ πῦρ καὶ τῆς διοικήσεως τῶν ὅλων αἴτιον· καλεῖ δὲ αὐτὸ χρησμοσύνην καὶ κόρον. Χρησμοσύνη δέ ἐστιν ἡ διακόσμησις κατ' αὐτὸν, ἡ δὲ ἐκπύρωσις κόρος· "Πάντα γὰρ, φησὶ, τὸ πῦρ ἐπελθὸν κρινεῖ καὶ καταλήψεται." Ἐν δὲ τούτῳ τῷ κεφαλαίῳ "πάντα ὁμοῦ" τὸν ἴδιον νοῦν ἐξέθετο. Ἅμα δὲ καὶ τὸν τῆς Νοητοῦ αἱρέσεως δι' ὀλίγων ἐπέδειξα οὐκ ὄντα Χριστοῦ, ἀλλὰ Ἡρακλείτου μαθητήν. Τὸν γὰρ πρῶτον κόσμον αὐτὸν δημιουργὸν καὶ ποιητὴν ἑαυτοῦ γινόμενον οὕτω λέγει· "Ὁ θεὸς ἡμέρη, εὐφρόνη, χειμὼν, θέρος, πόλεμος, εἰρήνη, κόρος, λιμός." Τἀναντία ἅπαντα· οὗτος ὁ νοῦς. "Ἀλλοιοῦται δὲ ὅκως περ ὁκόταν συμμιγῇ θυώμασιν ὀνομάζεται καθ' ἡδονὴν ἑκάστου." Φανερὸν δὲ πᾶσι τοὺς νοητοὺς Νοητοῦ διαδόχους καὶ τῆς αἱρέσεως προστάτας, εἰ καὶ Ἡρακλείτου λέγοισαν ἑαυτοὺς μὴ γεγο-

11. Cod. καλεῖς. 24. ὁπόταν, sed ὅκως. 27. "Scrib. vel λελουσιν vel λέγοιεν." Miller.

---

10. οἶδεν Ἡράκλειτος διὰ πυρὸς κάθαρσιν τῶν κακῶς βεβιωκότων.

16. Ipsum sibi sufficere et omnia per seipsum explorata habuisse jactitabat Ephesius, teste Laertio ix. 4. νέος ὢν ἔφασκε μηδὲν εἰδέναι, τέλειος μέντοι γενόμενος πάντα ἐγνωκέναι, ἤκουσέ τε οὐδενὸς ἀλλ' αὐτὸν ἔφη διζήσασθαι καὶ μαθεῖν πάντα παρ' ἑαυτοῦ. Vide etiam Philosophumena, p. 10. 54. αὐτὸς μὲν ἔφασκε πάντα εἰδέναι, τοὺς δὲ ἄλλους ἀνθρώπους οὐδέν.

26. ἀλλοιοῦται δὲ, ὅκως περ ὁκόταν συμμιγῇ θυώμασιν ὀνομάζεται

things, that is, *directs:* meaning by Thunder everlasting Fire. And he asserts that this Fire is intelligent, and a cause of the administration of the Universe, and he calls it Appetite and Satiety. The (systematic) adornment (of the Universe), according to him, is Appetite, and the conflagration is Satiety. For, says he, the Fire will come and judge and consume all things. And in this summary he propounded his own mind as all things collectively. At the same time I have shown that the follower of the heresy of Noetus is not the disciple of Christ, but of Heraclitus. For Heraclitus thus affirms that the first world was itself the artificer and creator of itself; God is Day, Night; Winter, Summer; War, Peace; Satiety, Hunger. Opposites are every thing; this is the true sense. But they undergo changes, as perfumes do, when, whatever is thought agreeable to any individual, is mingled with them.

It is evident to all, that the knowing successors of Noetus, and the chief patrons of his heresy, although they may assert that they have never been disciples of Heraclitus, yet by adopting the

---

καθ' ἡδονὴν ἑκάστου. Ita ex codice Millerus. Pro *συμμιγῆ* rescripserim *συμμιγῇ misceatur*, et pro vitioso 'ΟΝΟΜΑ'ΖΕΤΑΙ legerim ὉΟ ΝΟΜΙ'ΖΕΤΑΙ, *i. e. cum misceatur odoramentis quodcumque existimetur ad genium esse cujuscunque, et gustui ejus gratificaturum.*

27. Νοητοὺς Νοητοῦ διαδόχους, idem hic lusus *παρονομαστικὸς* in voce *Noëto*, qui apud S. Hippol. c. Noët. § 3. *αἱ γραφαὶ ὀρθῶς λέγουσιν ἄλλα ἢ καὶ Νόητος νοεῖ, οὐκ ἤδη δὲ εἰ Νόητος μὴ νοεῖ παρὰ τοῦτο ἔκβλητοι αἱ γραφαί.* Vide etiam ibid. § 8. *τί πρὸς ταῦτα νοήσει Νόητος μὴ νοῶν τὴν ἀλή-*

νέναι ἀκροατὰς, ἀλλά γε [τὰ] τῷ Νοητῷ δόξαντα αἱρουμένους ἀναφανδὸν, ταῦτα ὁμολογεῖν. Λέγουσι γὰρ οὕτως ἕνα καὶ τὸν αὐτὸν θεὸν εἶναι πάντων δημιουργὸν καὶ πατέρα, εὐδοκήσαντα δὲ πεφηνέναι τοῖς ἀρχῆθεν δικαίοις ὄντα ἀόρατον. Ὅτε μὲν γὰρ οὐχ ὁρᾶται ἦν ἀόρατος, ἀχώρητος
P.284 *δὲ ὅτε μὴ χωρεῖσθαι θέλει, χωρητὸς δὲ ὅτε χωρεῖται. Οὕτως κατὰ τὸν αὐτὸν λόγον ἀκράτητος, ἀγένητος, ἀθάνατος καὶ θνητός. Πῶς οὐχ Ἡρακλείτου οἱ τοιοῦτοι δειχθήσονται μαθηταί; μὴ αὐτῇ τῇ λέξει διαφθάσας ἐφιλοσόφησεν ὁ Σκοτεινός; Ὅτι δὲ καὶ τὸν αὐτὸν υἱὸν εἶναι λέγει καὶ πατέρα οὐδεὶς ἀγνοεῖ. Λέγει δὲ οὕτως· ὅτε μὲν οὖν μὴ γεγένητο ὁ πατὴρ, δικαίως πατὴρ προσηγόρευτο. Ὅτε δὲ ηὐδόκησεν γένεσιν ὑπομεῖναι, γενηθεὶς ὁ υἱὸς ἐγένετο αὐτὸς ἑαυτοῦ, οὐχ ἑτέρου. Οὕτως γὰρ δοκεῖ μοναρχίαν συνιστᾶν, ἓν καὶ τὸ αὐτὸ φάσκων ὑπάρχειν πατέρα καὶ υἱὸν, καλούμενον οὐχ ἕτερον ἐξ ἑτέρου, ἀλλ'*

28. "Add. τά. Vel τῷ in τὰ mutandum." Miller. 32. Cod. πεφηκέναι. 2. In cod. ἀκράτητος bis scriptum. 5. Cod. μῆδε λέξει (τῇ τῇ supra). 8. Cod. μὴ γένητο.

θειαν; Hinc Callistum, Noëtianam impietatem hæresim novis quibusdam additamentis adornantem, Theodoretus tradit ἐπιθήκας τινὰς ἐπινοῆσαι τῇ δυσσεβείᾳ τοῦ δόγματος, Hæret. Fab. iii. 3. Lusus etiam ad Latinos permeavit, qui Noëtianos *insensatos* appellant, vide Philastr. Hæres. in voce.

31. ταυτα ὁμολογεῖν. Legendum ταὐτὰ pro ταυτα quivis viderit.

32. Post οὕτως interpungendum.

dogmas of Noetus, avow the same tenets with Heraclitus. For they say thus, that one and the same God is the Maker and Father of all things, and that when it pleased Him, He revealed himself to the righteous from the beginning, being invisible. For when He is not seen He was invisible, and incomprehensible when He is not willing to be com- P.284 prehended; but comprehensible when He is comprehended. Thus, according to the same argument, He is incomprehensible and comprehensible; unborn and born; immortal and mortal. How will not these persons be proved to be Scholars of Heraclitus? Has not the Obscure Metaphysician anticipated them by philosophizing in their very words? For every one knows that he, Noetus, calls the same both Son and Father. For he speaks thus; When the Father had not been born, He was rightly called Father. But when it pleased Him to undergo birth, then by birth He became the Son of Himself, and not of another. Thus he professes to establish the principle of *Monarchianism*, saying, that one and the same Essence is called by the two names, Father and Son, not one born from the other, but Himself born from

3. Cod. *ἀκράτητος, ἀκράτητος, ἀγένητος, ἀθάνατος.* Ex tenore sententiarum patet esse legendum *ἀκράτητος κρατητὸς, ἀγένητος, γενητός.*

11. *προσηγόρευτο·* Mallem *προσηγορεύετο.*

15. Tertullian. c. Praxeam, 3. "*Duos* et *tres* Deos jam jactitant a nobis prædicari quasi non et Unitas irrationaliter collecta hæresim faciat, et Trinitas rationaliter expensa veritatem constituat. *Monarchiam* (inquiunt) tenemus."

16. *πατέρα καὶ υἱὸν, καλούμενον*

αὐτὸν ἐξ ἑαυτοῦ, ὀνόματι μὲν πατέρα καὶ υἱὸν καλούμενον κατὰ χρόνων τροπήν, ἕνα δὲ εἶναι τοῦτον τὸν φανέντα, καὶ γένεσιν ἐκ παρθένου ὑπομείναντα, καὶ ἐν ἀνθρώποις ἄνθρωπον ἀναστραφέντα, υἱὸν μὲν ἑαυτὸν τοῖς ὁρῶσιν ὁμολογοῦντα διὰ τὴν γενομένην γένεσιν, πατέρα δὲ εἶναι καὶ τοῖς χωροῦσιν μὴ ἀποκρύψαντα. Τοῦτον πάθει ξύλου προσπαγέντα καὶ ἑαυτῷ τὸ πνεῦμα παραδόντα, ἀποθανόντα καὶ μὴ ἀποθανόντα, καὶ ἑαυτὸν τῇ τρίτῃ ἡμέρᾳ ἀναστήσαντα, τὸν ἐν μνημείῳ ταφέντα καὶ λόγχῃ τρωθέντα, καὶ ἥλοις καταπαγέντα, τοῦτον τὸν τῶν ὅλων θεὸν καὶ πατέρα εἶναι λέγει Κλεομένης καὶ ὁ τούτου χορός, Ἡρακλείτειον σκότος ἐπεισάγοντες πολλοῖς.

Ταύτην τὴν αἵρεσιν ἐκράτυνε Κάλλιστος, ἀνὴρ ἐν κακίᾳ πανοῦργος καὶ ποικίλος πρὸς πλάνην, θηρώμενος τὸν τῆς ἐπισκοπῆς θρόνον. Τὸν Ζεφυρῖνον, ἄνδρα ἰδιώτην καὶ ἀγράμματον καὶ ἄπειρον τῶν ἐκκλησιαστικῶν ὅρων, ὃν πείθων δόγμασι καὶ ἀπαιτήσεσιν ἀπειρημέναις ἦγεν εἰς ὃ ἐβούλετο, ὄντα δωρολήπτην καὶ φιλάργυρον,

18. Cod. ἀναστρεφέντα. 30. ποικῖλος et θηρόμενος. 35. Cod. ὁ βούλετο.

οὐχ ἕτερον ἐξ ἑτέρου. Ita Millerus, sed interpunctione mutatâ legendum π. κ. υἱὸν καλούμενον,—. Vide Theodoret. Hær. Fab. iii.

3. τοῦτον καὶ υἱὸν ὀνομάζουσι καὶ πατέρα πρὸς τὰς χρείας τοῦτο κἀκεῖνο καλούμενον.

26. τοῦτον πάθει ξύλου προσ-

Himself, and called by the name of Father or Son, according to the change of times, but that He is one, He who was manifested to the world, and who deigned to undergo birth of a Virgin, and conversed as man with man, and who to those that beheld Him confessed Himself to be a Son, on account of His birth, but who also did not conceal that He was a Father from those Who received Him. That He suffered, having been nailed to the Cross, and that having commended His Spirit to Himself, and having died and not died, and having on the third day raised Himself, Who had been buried in the tomb, and wounded with the lance, and pierced with nails, that He is the God of the Universe and Father—so says Cleomenes and his school, who thus envelop many with the darkness of Heraclitus.

CALLISTUS strengthened this heresy; a man crafty in evil, and versatile in deceit, aspiring to the chair of the Episcopate. He influenced ZEPHYRINUS, who was an unlearned and illiterate person, and unskilled in Ecclesiastical Science, and whom, being a receiver of bribes and covetous, Callistus led as he pleased, persuading him by dogmas and unlawful demands; him, Callistus was ever instigating to

---

παγέντα. Ita Codex. Legere mallem *τοῦτον παθεῖν, ξύλῳ προσπαγέντα.*

35. Comparanda sunt quæ infrà de Noëto, et de Callisto, dicturus est Hippolytus in compendio sive *ἀνακεφαλαιώσει*, lib. x. pp. 329, 330.

P.285 ἔπειθεν ἀεὶ στάσεις ἐμβαλεῖν ἀναμέσον τῶν ἀδελφῶν, αὐτὸς τὰ ἀμφότερα μέρη ὕστερον κερκωπείοις λόγοις πρὸς ἑαυτοῦ φιλίαν κατασκευάζων, καὶ τοῖς μὲν ἀλήθειαν λέγων ὅμοια φρονοῦσι ποτὲ καθ' ἠδίαν τὰ ὅμοια φρονεῖν ἠπάτα· πάλιν δ' αὐτοῖς τὰ Σαβελλίου ὁμοίως, ὃν καὶ αὐτὸν ἐξέστησε δυνάμενον κατορθοῦν. Ἐν γὰρ τῷ ὑφ' ἡμῶν παραινεῖσθαι οὐκ ἐσκληρύνετο· ἡνίκα δὲ σὺν τῷ Καλλίστῳ ἐμόναζεν, ὑπ' αὐτοῦ ἀνεσείετο πρὸς τὸ δόγμα τὸ Κλεομένους ῥέπειν, φάσκοντος τὰ ὅμοια φρονεῖν. Ὁ δὲ τότε μὲν τὴν πανουργίαν αὐτοῦ οὐκ ἐνόει, αὖθις δὲ ἔγνω, ὡς διηγήσομαι μετ' οὐ πολύ. Αὐτὸν δὲ τὸν Ζεφυρῖνον προάγων δημοσίᾳ ἔπειθε λέγειν· Ἐγὼ οἶδα ἕνα θεὸν Χριστὸν Ἰησοῦν, καὶ πλὴν αὐτοῦ ἕτερον οὐδένα γενητὸν καὶ παθητόν. Ποτὲ δὲ λέγων, Οὐχ ὁ πατὴρ ἀπέθανεν, ἀλλὰ ὁ υἱός, οὕτως ἄπαυστον τὴν στάσιν ἐν τῷ λαῷ διετήρησεν, οὗ τὰ νοήματα γνόντες ἡμεῖς οὐ συνεχωροῦμεν, ἐλέγχοντες καὶ ἀντικαθιστάμενοι ὑπὲρ

1. Cod. ἀναμέσων. 3. Cod. κερκώποις. ib. Cod. ἑαυτοὺς φιλίαν. 4. Fort. τοῖς μὲν ἐν ἀληθείᾳ. Miller. ib. Fort. λέγων τὰ ὅμοια φρονεῖν ἠπάτα· πάλιν δὲ αὐτοῖς φρονοῦσι ποτὲ κατ' ἰδίαν τὰ Σαβ. Miller. 7. Leg. videtur δυνάμενος. Miller. 10. Cod. ῥαπεῖν correxit Millerus. 20. Cod. ἐλλέγχοντες.

---

3. τοῖς μὲν ἀλήθειαν λέγων ὅμοια φρονοῦσιν ποτὲ καθ' ἠδίαν τὰ ὅμοια φρονεῖν ἠπάτα· πάλιν δ' αὐτοῖς τὰ Σαβελλίου ὁμοίως. Ita MS. Pro vitioso ΚΑΘ' 'ΗΔΙ'ΑΝ legendum conjecerim ΚΑΤ' 'ΙΔΕ'ΑΝ, *i. e.* sub specie vel colore similia sentiendi. Tales hæreti-

introduce strife among the brethren; and then P.285 Callistus himself swayed both sides by wily words to incline to his own interest; and at one time speaking true doctrine to the one party, who held like sentiments (to the truth), he, under pretence of agreeing with them, deluded them; and at another time speaking with similar language (of duplicity) to those who held the doctrine of Sabellius, whom also himself he made to fall, when he was able to keep him right. For when Sabellius was exhorted by me he was not obstinate, but when he was alone with Callistus, he was instigated by him (professing to be of his opinion) to incline to the doctrine of Cleomenes. Sabellius did not then perceive his subtlety, but afterwards he discovered it, as I will shortly tell. Callistus putting Zephyrinus himself forward publicly induced him to say, "I know one God, Christ Jesus, and beside Him I know none, who was born and suffered." But he (Callistus) sometimes saying "Not the Father suffered, but the Son," thus kept alive the strife without respite among our people. But we perceiving his devices did not give place to him, confuting him and resisting him for the Truth's sake.

---

corum præstigias tangit Irenæus, iii. 17. "Similia loquentes fidelibus non solum dissimilia sapiunt sed et contraria, et per omnia plena blasphemiis per quæ interficiunt eos qui per similitudinem verborum dissimile affectionis eorum in se attrahunt venenum." Pro *αὐτοῖς* rectè Bunsenius (i. p. 132) *αὖ τοῖς*.

8. Novatian. de Trin. 12. "Quid dubitant cum Sabellii temeritate misceri qui Christum Patrem dicit?" Pro *δυνάμενον* rectè Millerus *δυνάμενος*.

τῆς ἀληθείας· ὃς εἰς ἀπόνοιαν χωρῶν διὰ τὸ πάντας αὐτοῦ τῇ ὑποκρίσει συντρέχειν, ἡμᾶς δὲ οὔ, ἀπεκάλει ἡμᾶς διθέους, ἐξεμῶν παρὰ βίαν τὸν ἐνδομυχοῦντα αὐτῷ ἰόν. Τούτου τὸν βίον δοκεῖ ἡμῖν ἀγαπητὸν ἐκθέσθαι, ἐπεὶ κατὰ τὸν αὐτὸν χρόνον ἡμῖν ἐγεγόνει, ὅπως διὰ τοῦ φανῆναι τοῦ τοιούτου τὴν ἀναστροφὴν, εὐεπίγνωστος καὶ ταχεῖα τοῖς νοῦν ἔχουσιν εὐθὴς γένηται ἡ διὰ τούτου ἐπικεχειρημένη αἵρεσις. Οὗτος ἐμαρτύρησεν ἐπὶ Φουσκιανοῦ ἐπάρχου ὄντος Ῥώμης. Ὁ δὲ τρόπος τῆς αὐτοῦ μαρτυρίας τοιόσδε ἦν.

P.286 *Οἰκέτης ἐτύγχανε Καρποφόρου τινὸς ἀνδρὸς πιστοῦ ὄντος ἐκ τῆς Καίσαρος οἰκίας. Τούτῳ ὁ Καρποφόρος, ἅτε δὴ ὡς πιστῷ, χρῆμα οὐκ ὀλίγον κατεπίστευσεν, ἐπαγγειλάμενος κέρδος προσοίσειν ἐκ πραγματείας τραπεζιτικῆς· ὃς λαβὼν τράπεζαν ἐπεχείρησεν ἐν τῇ λεγομένῃ πισκινῇ πουπλικῇ, ᾧ οὐκ ὀλίγαι παραθῆκαι τῷ χρόνῳ ἐπιστεύθησαν ὑπὸ χηρῶν καὶ ἀδελφῶν προσχή-*

23. Cod. *παραβίαν*. 24. Cod. *ἐνδομοιχοῦντα*. 29. Cod. *ἐπικεχειρημέναι.*

---

29. *ὅπως εὐεπίγνωστος καὶ ταχεῖα τοῖς νοῦν ἔχουσιν* ΕΥΘΗΣ *γένηται.* Ita MS. Millerus *εὐθὺς*, et aliud adjectivum in *ταχεῖα* latere arbitratur. Hæreticorum commenta ab Hippolyto nostro exagitantur non tantum ut odio et execratione digna, sed ut ridiculæ et aniles fabulæ ideòque ludibrio habendæ. Vide sup. 279, 7. *ὅπως καταφρονηθῶσιν*: et *αἱρέσεις καταγελάστους*, inf. 334, 35. Mihi igitur in mentem venit *καὶ* ΤΑ'ΧΑ *τοῖς νοῦν ἔχουσιν* ΕΥ'ΗΘΗ'Σ *γενῆται*, *i. e.* ut facilis cognitu sit, et fortasse fatua prudentioribus, *i. e.* eorum sententiâ.

4. *ἐπαγγειλάμενος κέρδος προσοίσειν.* Legendum potius videtur *ἐπαγγειλαμένῳ*. Cf. suprà,

Then being driven to infatuation, because all others went along with him in his hypocrisy but I did not, he used to call me a ditheist, disgorging violently the venom which was harboured within him.

This man's life it seems to me fit to narrate, since he was contemporary with me; in order, that, by the manifestation of his conversation, the Heresy which was broached by him may become easy of cognizance to those who have sense, and haply may be regarded as childish by them.

He was a martyr, when Fuscianus was Prefect of Rome. And the manner of his martyrdom was as follows;

He was servant of a certain Carpophorus, a P.286
Christian of Cæsar's household. Carpophorus entrusted him, as a Christian, with a considerable sum of money, professing that he would bring him gain from the occupation of a banker. He set up a bank in the *piscina publica*, and in course of time many deposits were entrusted to him by widows and brethren, through the influence of the name of Car-

---

Philosoph. 261. 19. ὁρᾶν ἐπαγγέλλονται τυφλώττοντες profitentur se videre, etsi cæcutiant.

6. Nondum, ut videtur, leges illæ ab Ecclesiâ fuerant latæ, quæ rem fœnerariam Christianis interdicebant, et pecuniam ex usuris conquisitam abominari jubebant. Tertullianus quidem lib. iv. c. Marcionem. "Percurre ait sequentia Ezekielis de viro justo. *Pecuniam suam fœnori non dedit*, et quod abundaverit non sumet, fœnoris scilicet redundantiam, quæ est usura." Hinc, temporis processu, primum in Clericos fœneratores, deinde etiam in laicos, pœnas irrogavit Ecclesia; Can. Nicæn. 17. Arelat. i. c. 12. Arelat. ii. c. 14. Eliberit. c. 20. Turon. i. c. 13. Vide quæ de hâc re fusè et exquisitè disseruit, sæculi nostri genio non admodum placitura, Præsul eruditissimus L. Andrewes. Lond. 1629.

ματι τοῦ Καρποφόρου. Ὁ δὲ ἐξαφανίσας τὰ πάντα ἠπόρει. Οὗ ταῦτα πράξαντος, οὐκ ἔλιπεν ὃς ἀπαγγείλῃ τῷ Καρποφόρῳ· ὁ δὲ ἔφη ἀπαιτεῖν λόγους παρ' αὐτοῦ. Ταῦτα συνιδὼν ὁ Κάλλιστος καὶ τὸν παρὰ τοῦ δεσπότου κίνδυνον ὑφορώμενος, ἀπέδρα τὴν φυγὴν κατὰ θάλασσαν ποιούμενος· ὃς εὑρὼν πλοῖον ἐν τῷ Πόρτῳ ἕτοιμον πρὸς ἀναγωγὴν, ὅπου ἐτύγχανε πλέων, ἀνέβη πλευσόμενος. Ἀλλ' οὐδὲ οὕτως λαθεῖν δεδύνηται· οὐ γὰρ ἔλιπεν ὃς ἀπαγγείλῃ τῷ Καρποφόρῳ τὸ γεγενημένον. Ὁ δὲ ἐπιστὰς κατὰ τὸν λιμένα, ἐπειρᾶτο ἐπὶ τὸ πλοῖον ὁρμᾶν κατὰ μεμηνυμένα. Τοῦτο δὲ ἦν ἑστὸς ἐν μέσῳ τῷ λιμένι, τοῦ δὲ πορθμέως βραδύνοντος, ἰδὼν πόρρωθεν ὁ Κάλλιστος τὸν δεσπότην, ὢν ἐν τῷ πλοίῳ καὶ γνοὺς ἑαυτὸν συνηλεῖφθαι, ἠφείδησε τοῦ ζῆν καὶ ἔσχατα ταῦτα λογισάμενος ἔρριψεν ἑαυτὸν εἰς τὴν θάλασσαν. Οἱ δὲ ναῦται καταπηδήσαντες εἰς τὰ σκάφη ἄκοντα αὐτὸν ἀνείλοντο. Τῶν δὲ ἀπὸ τῆς γῆς μεγάλα βοώντων, καὶ οὗτος τῷ δεσπότῃ παραδοθεὶς ἐπανήχθη εἰς

9. Cod. ἐξαφανήσας. 10. Cod. ἔλειπεν, sed ἔλιπεν bis infra lin. 18, et 21, p. 287. 21. "In μεμηνυμένα, syllabæ μην exesæ tenuia vestigia supersunt." Miller. 23. Cod. πόρροθεν.

---

11. ὁ δὲ ἔφη ἀπαιτεῖν λόγους post ἀπαιτεῖν excidisse videtur ἄν.

17. ὅπου ἐτύγχανε πλέων. Ita Cod. Lege πλέον.

18. οὐκ γὰρ ἔλιπε—In hac formulâ, ter repetitâ, salsa quædam ironia videtur inesse, quâ innuatur Callistum malo quodam genio fuisse exagitatum, qui ejus vestigiis insisteret et eum, tanquam umbra,

pophorus. But Callistus embezzled them all, and became bankrupt. And when he was in this plight, tidings did not fail to reach Carpophorus, who said that he would call him to account. When Callistus perceived this, and apprehended the danger which threatened him from his master, he ran away, taking flight toward the sea; and having found a ship at Portus ready to sail, he embarked with a purpose to sail withersoever the vessel might be bound. But not even thus could he escape: for the news did not fail to reach the ears of Carpophorus. And he, standing on the shore, endeavoured, according to the information he had received, to make for the ship, which was in the middle of the harbour. But when the boatman (who was to ferry Carpophorus) was lingering, Callistus, being in the ship, saw his master from a distance, and perceiving himself to be caught, hazarded his life, and, thinking that all was now over with him, he threw himself into the sea. But the sailors having leapt into the boats drew him out, against his will. And while those who were on the shore raised a great shout, he was delivered to his

---

semper persequeretur. Cæterùm ex hâc et similibus loquendi formulis quæ in hâc narratione passim obviæ sunt rectè statuitur, Auctoris nostri stylum etsi Græciâ vel Asiâ oriundi Latinum dicendi colorem imbibisse, eumque ipsum linguâ, ut par est credere, aliquantulum *βεβαρβαρῶσθαι, χρόνιον ὄντ᾽ ἐν βαρβάροις.*

19. Locum sic interpunge: *ἐπειρᾶτο ἐπὶ τὸ πλοῖον ὁρμᾶν κατὰ τὰ μεμηνυμένα, τοῦτο δὲ ἦν ἑστὸς ἐν μέσῳ τῷ λιμένι· τοῦ δὲ πορθμέως βραδύνοντος κ.τ.λ.*

25. Pro vitiosâ lectione Codicis *συνηλεῖφθαι* restituendum *συνειλῆφθαι*, confusio orta ex syllabarum *ὁμοφωνίᾳ*, uberrimo fonte mendarum, quibus libri scatent

τὴν Ῥώμην· ὃν ὁ δεσπότης εἰς πίστρινον κατέθετο. Χρόνου δὲ διελθόντος, ὡς συμβαίνει γίγνεσθαι, προσελθόντες ἀδελφοὶ παρεκάλουν τὸν Καρποφόρον ὅπως ἐξαγάγῃ τῆς κολάσεως τὸν δραπέτην, φάσκοντες αὐτὸν ὁμολογεῖν ἔχειν
P.287 παρά τισι χρῆμα ἀποκείμενον. Ὁ δὲ Καρποφόρος ὡς εὐλαβὴς, τοῦ μὲν ἰδίου ἔλεγεν ἀφειδεῖν, τῶν δὲ παραθηκῶν φροντίζειν· πολλοὶ γὰρ αὐτῷ ἀπεκλαίοντο λέγοντες, ὅτι τῷ αὐτοῦ προσχήματι ἐπίστευσαν τῷ Καλλίστῳ, ἃ πεπιστεύκεισαν· καὶ πεισθεὶς ἐκέλευσεν ἐξαγαγεῖν αὐτόν. Ὁ δὲ μηδὲν ἔχων ἀποδιδόναι, καὶ πάλιν ἀποδιδράσκειν μὴ δυνάμενος διὰ τὸ φρουρεῖσθαι, τέχνην θανάτου ἐπενόησε· καὶ σαββάτῳ σκηψάμενος ἀπιέναι ὡς ἐπὶ χρεώστας, ὥρμησεν ἐπὶ τὴν συναγωγὴν τῶν Ἰουδαίων συνηγμένων, καὶ στὰς κατεστασίαζεν αὐτῶν. Οἱ δὲ καταστασιασθέντες ὑπ' αὐτοῦ, ἐνυβρίσαντες αὐτὸν καὶ πληγὰς ἐμφορήσαντες, ἔσυρον ἐπὶ τὸν Φουσκιανὸν ἔπαρχον ὄντα τῆς πόλεως. Ἀπεκρίναντο δὲ τάδε· Ῥωμαῖοι συνεχώρησαν ἡμῖν τοὺς πατρῴους νόμους δημοσίᾳ ἀναγινώσκειν· οὗτος δὲ ἐπεισελθὼν ἐκώλυε καταστασιάζων ἡμῶν, φάσκων εἶναι

4. Cod. τῷ αὐτῷ. 8. Cod. φθορεῖσθαι. 9. Cod. σκεψάμενος.

præsertim recentiores, qualis hic est Codex Parisinus.

17. De Judæis Romæ patria sacra liberè colentibus Cæsareaniorum edictorum indulgentia videri potest Joseph. Antiqq.

master and brought back to Rome: where his master confined him in the pistrinum. In course of time, as is wont to be the case, certain brethren came to Carpophorus and besought him to release his runaway slave from punishment, saying that he declared that he had money vested in the hands of certain persons. Carpophorus, like a pious man, said that P.287 he did not care for his own money, but that he was anxious for the deposits; for many bewailed themselves to him, saying that it was by reason of his name that they confided to Callistus what they had entrusted to him. Being thus persuaded, he ordered him to be released. But having nothing to pay, and not being able to run away again, on account of being watched, he devised a plan for his own destruction. On a Saturday, under pretence of going to his debtors, he went to the Synagogue of the Jews, who were assembled in it; and he stood there and made an uproar against them. And they being thus disturbed abused him and beat him, and dragged him before Fuscianus, prefect of the city.

And thus they said. "The Romans have given us leave to read the Law of our Fathers in public. But this man here came in and interrupted us, say-

---

xix. 10, quæ vim obtinuisse videntur usque ad Severum Septimium, qui "Judæos fieri sub gravi pœnâ vetent," teste Spartiano, c. 17. Non tamen ille Judæis ipsis jam hereditariâ vel patriâ successione religioni suæ publicum exercitium interdicens. Post Severi dominationem Judæis favebat Elagabalus. Lamprid. c. 3, et Severus Alexander Judæis privilegia reservavit. Lamprid. c. 22.

Χριστιανός. Τοῦ δὲ Φουσκιανοῦ πρὸ βήματος τυγχάνοντος, καὶ τοῖς ὑπ' Ἰουδαίων λεγομένοις κατὰ τοῦ Καλλίστου ἀγανακτοῦντος, οὐκ ἔλιπεν ὁ ἐπαγγείλας τῷ Καρποφόρῳ τὰ πρασσόμενα. Ὁ δὲ σπεύσας ἐπὶ τὸ βῆμα τοῦ ἐπάρχου ἐβόα· Δέομαι, κύριε Φουσκιανὲ, μὴ σὺ αὐτῷ πίστευε, οὐ γάρ ἐστι Χριστιανὸς, ἀφορμὴν δὲ ζητεῖ θανάτου χρήματά μου πολλὰ ἀφανίσας, ὡς ἀποδείξω. Τῶν δὲ Ἰουδαίων ὑποβολὴν τοῦτο νομισάντων, ὡς ζητοῦντος τοῦ Καρποφόρου ταύτῃ τῇ προφάσει ἐξελέσθαι αὐτὸν, μᾶλλον ἐπιφθόνως κατεβόων τοῦ ἐπάρχου. Ὁ δὲ κινηθεὶς ὑπ' αὐτῶν, μαστιγώσας αὐτὸν, ἔδωκεν εἰς μέταλλον Σαρδονίας. Μετὰ χρόνον δὲ ἑτέρων ἐκεῖ ὄντων μαρτύρων θελήσασα ἡ Μαρκία ἔργον τι ἀγαθὸν ἐργάσασθαι, οὖσα φιλόθεος παλλακὴ Κομόδου,

19. Cod. φοσκιανοῦ. 24. Cod. μὴ ἑαυτῷ. 34. Cod. παλακή.

32. Fodinis ferri celebrem fuisse Sardiniam satis notum ex Rutilii Itinerario, lib. I. "Quæ de Sardoo cespite massa fluit." Hinc hodie "Ferraria" urbs Sardiniæ de quâ Cluverius ii. c. xi. Sardiniam pestifero aëre infamem fuisse tradit Claudianus, B. Gild. v. 514, monente Cluverio. Huc martyras fuisse deportatos, ipsumque in his (uti creditur) sanctum Hippolytum, ex Chronicis et Martyrologiis constat. Catalog. Felician. § 6. "Eodem tempore Pontianus Episcopus (Romæ) et *Hippolytus* presbyter exilio sunt deputati (deportati) ab Alexandro in *Sardiniam*, insulam Bucinam (nocivam)." Id quod Anastasius de vitis Pontif. in v. Pontiani factum fuisse tradit Severo et Quintiano Coss. h. e. A.D. 235. Maximino Thrace jam annum primum imperante, quo anno Pontianus in Sardiniâ mortem obiisse dicitur iv. Kal. Octobres.

34. De Marciâ Dio Cassius, lxxii. 4 Μαρκία τις, Κουδράτου τῶν τότε φονευθέντων ἑνὸς παλλακή, καὶ Ἔκλεκτος πρόκοιτος, ὁ

ing that he is a Christian." Fuscianus being seated on the bench, and being exasperated by what the Jews said against Callistus, tidings did not fail to come to the ears of Carpophorus. He hastened to the tribunal of the Prefect, and exclaimed, "I entreat thee, my Lord Fuscianus, do not believe him, for he is not a Christian, but seeks an occasion of death, having embezzled much money of mine, as I will show." But the Jews thought this was a subterfuge, as if Carpophorus desired to extricate him by this plea, and clamoured more vehemently in the ears of the Prefect. And he, being urged by them, scourged Callistus, and sentenced him to the mines in Sardinia.

But after a time, there being other Martyrs there, Marcia the Concubine of (the Emperor) Commodus, being a religious woman and desirous of doing a

---

μὲν καὶ τοῦ Κομμόδου πρόκοιτος ἡ δὲ (Μαρκία) παλλακὴ ἐγένετο καὶ τοῦ Ἐκλέκτου μετὰ ταῦτα γυνὴ, καὶ ἐπεῖδε καὶ ἐκείνους βιαίως ἀποθνήσκοντας· ἱστορεῖται δὲ αὕτη πολλά τε ὑπὲρ τῶν Χριστιανῶν σπουδάσαι καὶ πολλὰ αὐτοὺς εὐεργετηκέναι ἅτε καὶ παρὰ Κομμόδῳ πᾶν δυναμένη. Marciam, Commodi Imperatoris concubinam, deinde interfectricem, ab Hippolyto vocari *φιλόθεον* fortasse mireris: sed hoc, ut opinor, et uti jam docuit censor Arnoldianus, (p. 591) *εἰρωνικῶς* scripsit noster. Quo, quæris, animo? eodem fortasse quo Carpophorum pium hominem sed tamen fœneratorem, et Hyacinthum presbyterum sed tamen spadonem, dixisse videtur, ut Ecclesiæ disciplinam tum temporis nutantem tacitè notaret.

35. Cæterum hic lector meminerit quid in tali re statuerit Ecclesia, Hippolyto nostro coætanea; nisi interpolatricem manum passa sit in illo capite *παράδοσις Ἀποστολικὴ διὰ Ἱππολύτου*, p. 254, ed. Fabr. *Παλλακή τινος ἀπίστου δούλη ἐκείνῳ μόνῳ σχολάζουσα προσδεχέσθω, εἰ δὲ καὶ πρὸς ἄλλους ἀσελγαίνει, ἀποβαλλέσθω. . .*

P. 288 προσκαλεσαμένη τὸν μακάριον Οὐΐκτορα, ὄντα ἐπίσκοπον τῆς Ἐκκλησίας κατ᾽ ἐκεῖνο καιροῦ, ἐπηρώτα τίνες εἶεν ἐν Σαρδονίᾳ μάρτυρες. Ὁ δὲ πάντων ἀναδοὺς τὰ ὀνόματα, τὸ τοῦ Καλλίστου οὐκ ἔδωκεν, εἰδὼς τὰ τετολμημένα παρ᾽ αὐτοῦ. Τυχοῦσα οὖν τῆς ἀξιώσεως ἡ Μαρκία παρὰ τοῦ Κομόδου, δίδωσι τὴν ἀπολυσίμην ἐπιστολὴν Ὑακίνθῳ τινὶ σπάδοντι πρεσβυτέρῳ, ὃς λαβὼν διέπλευσεν εἰς τὴν Σαρδονίαν, καὶ ἀποδοὺς τῷ κατ᾽ ἐκεῖνο καιροῦ τῆς χώρας ἐπιτροπεύοντι, ἀπέλυσε τοὺς μάρτυρας, πλὴν τοῦ Καλλίστου. Ὁ δὲ γονυπετῶν καὶ δακρύων ἱκέτευε καὶ αὐτὸς τυχεῖν ἀπολύσεως. Δυσωπηθεὶς οὖν ὁ Ὑάκινθος ἀξιοῖ τὸν ἐπίτροπον φάσκων θρέψας εἶναι Μαρκίας, τασσόμενος αὐτῷ τὸ ἀκίνδυνον. Ὁ δὲ πεισθεὶς ἀπέλυσε καὶ τὸν Κάλλιστον· οὗ παραγενομένου ὁ Οὐΐκτωρ πάνυ ἤχθετο ἐπὶ τῷ γεγονότι· ἀλλ᾽ ἐπεὶ εὔσπλαγχνος ἦν, ἡσύχασε· φυλασσόμενος δὲ τὸν ὑπὸ πολλῶν ὄνειδον (οὐ γὰρ ἦν μακρὰν τὰ ὑπ᾽ αὐτοῦ τετολμημένα), ἔτι δὲ καὶ τοῦ Καρποφόρου ἀντιπίπτοντος, πέμπει αὐτὸν καταμένειν ἐν Ἀνθείῳ, ὁρίσας αὐτῷ μη-

5. Cod τὰ τολμημένα. 22. "Fort. Ἀντίῳ. Certe *Antium* dicere videtur." Miller.

---

8. Spadones (ἀφ᾽ ἑαυτῶν εὐνουχισθέντας) ad sacros ordines promoveri posteà vetitum Canon. Apostol. 21. Conc. Nicæn. c. 1. Arelat. ii. 7.

15. Codicis lectionem φάσκων

good work, having sent for Victor, of blessed memory, P. 288
who was then Bishop of the Church, enquired of him what martyrs were in Sardinia. He presented all their names, but did not tender the name of Callistus, knowing the crimes that had been perpetrated by him. Marcia having obtained her suit from Commodus, gives the letter of release to a certain Hyacinthus, an eunuch, a presbyter, who having received it, sailed to Sardinia, and having delivered it to the then Governor of the Island, released the martyrs,—except Callistus.

But he fell down before him, and wept and prayed that he might be released. Hyacinthus then being moved, desires the Governor to set him free, saying that he himself had brought up Marcia, and promising him indemnity. He, being persuaded, liberated Callistus also. But when he reached Rome, Victor was much distressed by what had taken place, but, being a kind-hearted man, he held his peace; but guarding against the obloquy from many, (for the crimes of Callistus were recent,) and because Carpophorus still urged his charge (against Callistus), he sent him to abide at Antium, settling on him

---

θρέψας εἶναι Μαρκίας, vitiosam censent Millerus et Bunsenius (i. p. 130), hic legendum conjectans *φάσκων ἑαυτῷ μὲν τοῦτο ἐπιτρέψαι Μαρκίαν τὸ τασσόμενον, αὐτῷ δὲ εἶναι ἀκίνδυνον*. Sed hoc tuum tentamen, vir doctissime, est librum refingentis, non corruptelam sanantis. Præterea Codicis lectio est prorsus sanissima. Participium *θρέψας Μαρκίας* dicitur pro nomine substantivo *τροφεὺς Μαρκίας*, ut *θρέψας αὐτῶν* in cippo sepulchrali apud Schaefer ad Greg. Corinth. p. 614. Vide etiam Lobeck. ad Soph. Ajac. 358, p. 277, qui exemplorum affatim dabit.

νιαῖόν τι ἐκτροφάς· μεθ' οὗ κοίμησιν Ζεφυρῖνος συναράμενον αὐτὸν σχὼν πρὸς τὴν κατάστασιν τοῦ κλήρου ἐτίμησε τῷ ἰδίῳ κακῷ, καὶ τοῦτον μεταγαγὼν ἀπὸ τοῦ 'Ανθείου εἰς τὸ κοιμητήριον κατέστησεν. Ὧι ἀεὶ συνών, καὶ καθὼς φθάσας προεῖπον ὑποκρίσει αὐτὸν θεραπεύων ἐξεφάνισε μήτε κρῖναι τὰ λεγόμενα δυνάμενον μήτε νοοῦντα τὴν τοῦ Καλλίστου ἐπιβουλήν, πάντα αὐτῷ πρὸς ἃ ἥδετο ὁμιλοῦντος. Οὕτω μετὰ τὴν τοῦ Ζεφυρίνου τελευτὴν νομίζων τετυχηκέναι οὗ ἐθηρᾶτο,
P.289 *τὸν Σαβέλλιον ἀπέωσεν ὡς μὴ φρονοῦντα ὀρθῶς,*

23. "Erat a prima m. *ἐκτροφῖ̂ς.* Corrigendum *εἰς τροφάς.*" Miller. ib. Cod. *κύμησιν.* ib. Cod. *Ζεφυρῖνον . . αράμενον,* "duabus literis "exesis, quarum prior *σ* fuisse cognoscitur : *συαράμενον.*" Miller.

---

24. *μηνιαῖον.* Auctor Parvi Labyrinthi idem qui noster Hippolytus apud Euseb. v. 28. *ἀνεπείσθη ὁ Νατάλιος ὑπ' αὐτῶν ἐπὶ σαλαρίῳ ἐπίσκοπος κληρωθῆναι ταύτης τῆς αἱρέσεως ὥστε λαμβάνειν παρ' αὐτῶν μηνιαῖα δηνάρια ἑκατὸν πεντήκοντα.*

25. *κοίμησιν,*—contrà infrà, v. 32, *Ζεφυρίνου τελευτήν,* unde satis liquet Zephyrinum non martyrio animam efflâsse, quod contrà recentiores Martyrologiorum consarcinatores monere fas sit.

26. *αὐτὸν* ad Carpophorum refert vir eruditus in Censurâ Arnoldianâ, p. 592. Sed ad Callistum potius retulerim, ut *αὐτὸν* et *αὐτῷ* duobus suprà versibus de Callisto indubiè dictum. Quod *τοῦτον μεταγαγὼν* de Callisto quoque addiderit id non sine ludibrio factum—*hunc hominem !*

27. *πρὸς τὴν* ΚΑΤΑ'ΣΤΑΣΙΝ *τοῦ* ΚΛΗ'ΡΟΥ. An legendum ΚΑΤΑΣΧΕΣΙΝ? Elementa *α* et *ε*, *τ* et *ψ* sæpe confunduntur. Dixit Irenæus (iii. 3) *τὸν τῆς ἐπισκοπῆς* ΚΑΤΕ'ΧΕΙ ΚΛΗ͂ΡΟΝ *'Ελεύθερος·* vide eundem i. 28; fortasse Noster hoc vult, Zephyrinum Callisti operâ esse usum ad sedem suam obtinendam.

29. De cœmeteriis Christianorum non tantum inhumationis causâ usitatis, sed ad divina officia peragenda, et sacros cœtus celebrandos, ideòque ad scholas habendas, vide Baronium ad A.D. 226. 258. 260. 262. De *Callisti*

a monthly allowance for his maintenance. After Victor had fallen asleep in death, Zephyrinus having had him (Callistus) as a coadjutor for the control of his Clergy, honoured him to his own damage, and, having transferred him from Antium, set him over the Cemetery. And Callistus, being always with him, and, as I said before, courting him with hypocrisy, eclipsed him being incapable of forming any judgment on the arguments used, and not perceiving the stratagem of Callistus, who accommodated all his language to his taste. Thus it came to pass, that after the death of Zephyrinus, Callistus imagining he had gained that to which he aspired, cast P.289
off Sabellius as heterodox, through fear of me, and supposing that he might thus be able to wipe off the

---

Cœmeterio in Viâ Appiâ videri potest Aringhi Roma Subterr. iii. c. xi. § 1. Ruggieri, p. 397.

31. Cod. ἐξεφάνισε, leg. ἐξηφάνισε.

1. De Callisto, Zephyrini Episcopi Romani successore, hæc leguntur in libro Damasi, p. 608, Labbé, "Callistus natione Romanus ex patre Domitio de regione urbis Ravennatum sedit annos v, mens. ii, dies x. Fuit temporibus Macrini et Heliogabali a consulatu Antonini et Alexandri. Hic martyrio coronatur. . . . Fecit cœmeterium Viâ Appiâ ubi multi sacerdotes et martyres requiescunt, quod appellatur usque in hodiernum diem *cœmeterium Callisti.*"

2. ἀπέωσεν non ἐξέωσεν, quâ voce utitur Hippol. c. Noët. § 1. τότε τοῦτον ἐλέγξαντες οἱ πρεσβύτεροι ἐξέωσαν τῆς ἐκκλησίας, quo quidem ex loco satis patet, ut id obiter notemus, jus excommunicationis, Hippolyti ætate penes fuisse Presbyterorum Collegium, —Episcopo, (dubitari nequit,) præsidente et omnia moderante. Noëtum enim a Papâ Victore damnatum ait auctor libelli Synodici a Pappo editi c. 20. a Tranquillo Episcopo Chalcedonensi, scribit Auctor Prædestinati, c. 36. Theodotum majorem τὸν σκυτέα ab Episcopo Victore ἀφωρίσθαι narrat Hippolytus. Routh. ii. 9—23.

δεδοικὼς ἐμὲ καὶ νομίζων οὕτω δύνασθαι ἀποτρίψασθαι τὴν πρὸς τὰς ἐκκλησίας κατηγορίαν, ὡς μὴ ἀλλοτρίως φρονῶν. Ἦν οὖν γόης καὶ πανοῦργος καὶ ἐπὶ χρόνῳ συνήρπασε πολλούς. Ἔχων δὲ καὶ τὸν ἰὸν ἐγκείμενον ἐν τῇ καρδίᾳ, καὶ εὐθέως μηδὲν φρονῶν, ἅμα δὲ καὶ αἰδούμενος τὰ ἀληθῆ λέγειν, διὰ τὸ δημοσίᾳ ἡμῖν ὀνειδίζοντα εἰπεῖν δίθεοί ἐστέ, ἀλλὰ καὶ διὰ τὸ ὑπὸ τοῦ Σαβελλίου συχνῶς κατηγορεῖσθαι ὡς παραβάντος τὴν πρώτην πίστιν, ἐφεῦρεν αἵρεσιν τοιάνδε, λέγων τὸν λόγον αὐτὸν εἶναι υἱόν, αὐτὸν καὶ πατέρα, ὀνόματι μὲν καλούμενον, ἓν δὲ ὄν, τὸ πνεῦμα ἀδιαίρετον· οὐκ ἄλλο εἶναι πατέρα, ἄλλο δὲ υἱόν, ἓν δὲ καὶ τὸ αὐτὸ ὑπάρχειν, καὶ τὰ πάντα γέμειν τοῦ θείου πνεύματος τά τε ἄνω καὶ κάτω, καὶ εἶναι τὸ ἐν τῇ παρθένῳ σαρκωθὲν πνεῦμα οὐχ ἕτερον παρὰ τὸν πατέρα, ἀλλὰ ἓν καὶ τὸ αὐτό. Καὶ τοῦτο εἶναι τὸ εἰρημένον "Οὐ πιστεύεις ὅτι ἐγὼ ἐν τῷ πατρί, καὶ ὁ πατὴρ ἐν ἐμοί;" Τὸ μὲν γὰρ βλεπόμενον, ὅπερ ἐστὶν

14. Cod. *οὐκ ἄλο.* 16. Cod. *γεμεῖν.* 19. Joann. xiv. 11.

---

9. Vir doctus Robertus Scott in Censurâ Arnoldianâ, ii. p. 538, legit *μηδὲν εὐθέος.*

13. *παραβάντος* Codex: mallem *παραβάντα.*

16. *ὀνόματι μὲν καλούμενον* Cod. Ante *καλούμενον* excidisse videtur *ἄλλο.*

16. *ὄντα*: sic Bunsenius rectè pro Codicis lectione *ὂν τό.*

25. Vide has Noëtianorum exceptiones recitantem Hippolytum c. Noëtum, § 7, locum huic nostro planè gemellum. *οὐ πιστεύεις ὅτι ἐγὼ ἐν τῷ Πατρὶ κ.τ.λ. καὶ θέλουσι λέγειν (οἱ Νοητιανοὶ) διὰ*

reproach to which he was exposed in the eyes of the Churches, as if he were not of unsound belief. In good truth he was a deceiver and impostor, and in course of time drew many along with him. And harbouring the venom in his bosom, and having no rectitude of mind, and at the same time being ashamed to profess sound doctrine because he had before calumniated me in public and said "You are a Ditheist," and because also he was often charged by Sabellius with having swerved from his first faith, he invented such a heresy as follows. He said that the Word is the Son and is also the Father, being called by different names, but being one indivisible Spirit; and that the Father is not one and the Son another (person), but that they both are one and the same, and that all things are full of a Divine Spirit, both things above and things beneath, and that the Spirit which was Incarnate in the Virgin was not different from the Father, but one and the same, and that this was the meaning of our Lord's words, "Believest thou not that I am in the Father, and the Father in me?" (John xiv. 10.) For that

---

τοῦτο κρατύνεσθαι τὸ δόγμα αὐτῶν. Vide etiam quæ his regerit ipse Hippolytus c. Noët. c. xiv. ed. Fabr. ii. 15, ubi τὸν Λόγον Deum prædicat, *duos autem* Deos se agnoscere disertè negat. ταύτην τὴν οἰκονομίαν παραδίδωσιν ἡμῖν καὶ ὁ μακάριος Ἰωάννης ἐν Εὐαγγελίῳ μαρτύρων, καὶ τοῦτον τὸν ΛΟ'ΓΟΝ ΘΕΟ'Ν ὁμολογεῖ οὕτως λέγων· Ἐν ἀρχῇ ἦν ὁ Λόγος καὶ ὁ Λόγος ἦν πρὸς τὸν Θεὸν, καὶ Θεὸς ἦν ὁ Λόγος. Εἰ δὲ οὖν ὁ Λόγος πρὸς τὸν Θεὸν Θεὸς ὢν, τί οὖν φήσειεν ἂν τίς δύο λέγειν Θεούς; δύο μὲν οὐκ ἐρῶ Θεοὺς, ἀλλ' ἢ ἕνα, πρόσωπα δὲ δύο, οἰκονομίαν δὲ τρίτην, τὴν χάριν τοῦ Ἁγίου Πνεύματος. Πατὴρ μὲν γὰρ εἷς, πρόσωπα δὲ δύο ὅτι καὶ ὁ υἱὸς, τὸ δὲ τρίτον τὸ

ἄνθρωπος, τοῦτο εἶναι τὸν υἱὸν, τὸ δὲ ἐν τῷ υἱῷ χωρηθὲν Πνεῦμα τοῦτο εἶναι τὸν πατέρα· οὐ γὰρ, φησὶν, ἐρῶ δύο θεοὺς, πατέρα καὶ υἱὸν, ἀλλ' ἕνα. Ὁ γὰρ ἐν αὐτῷ γενόμενος πατὴρ, προσλαβόμενος τὴν σάρκα ἐθεοποίησεν ἑνώσας ἑαυτῷ, καὶ ἐποίησεν ἕν, ὡς καλεῖσθαι πατέρα καὶ υἱὸν, ἕνα θεὸν, καὶ τοῦτο ἓν ὂν πρόσωπον μὴ δύνασθαι εἶναι δύο, καὶ οὕτως τὸν πατέρα συμπεπονθέναι τῷ υἱῷ· οὐ γὰρ θέλει λέγειν τὸν πατέρα πεπονθέναι καὶ ἓν εἶναι πρόσωπον ἐκφυγεῖν τὴν εἰς
P. 290 τὸν πατέρα βλασφημίαν ὁ ἀνόητος καὶ ποικίλος, ὁ ἄνω κάτω σχεδιάζων βλασφημίας, ἵνα μόνον κατὰ τῆς ἀληθείας λέγειν δοκῇ, ποτὲ μὲν εἰς τὸ Σαβελλίου δόγμα ἐμπίπτων, ποτὲ δὲ εἰς τὸ Θεοδότου οὐκ αἰδεῖται. Τοιαῦτα ὁ γόης τολμή-

29. Cod. συνπεπονθέναι.

῞Αγιον Πνεῦμα. Unde satis refellitur Bunsenii suspicio, ne dicam cavillatio, ex his Noëtianorum argutiis colligentis vel Meiero colligenti adstipulantis, *duorum* Deorum dogma respuentium, de *tertiâ* sacrosanctæ Trinitatis Personâ nihil adhuc innotuisse, ideoque Hippolyti ætate de Sancti Spiritûs Deitate nihil fuisse definitum. Reclamat hic ipse Hippolytus, reclamat, inquam, in sermone c. Noëtum, § 8. ἀνάγκη ὁμολογεῖν Πατέρα Θεὸν Παντοκράτορα καὶ Χριστὸν Ἰησοῦν υἱὸν Θεοῦ, Θεὸν ἄνθρωπον γενόμενον, ᾧ πάντα Πατὴρ ὑπέταξε παρεκτὸς ἑαυτοῦ καὶ Πνεύματος Ἁγίου, καὶ τούτους οὕτως εἶναι Τρία, et alio in loco c. Noët. 14. ὁ γὰρ κελεύων Πατὴρ, ὁ δὲ ὑπακούων Υἱὸς, τὸ δὲ συνετίζον Ἅγιον Πνεῦμα. Ὁ ὢν Πατὴρ ἐπὶ πάντων, ὁ δὲ Υἱὸς διὰ πάντων, τὸ δὲ Ἅγιον Πνεῦμα ἐν πᾶσιν. Ἄλλως ἕνα Θεὸν νομίσαι οὐ δυνάμεθα ἐὰν μὴ ὄντως Πατρὶ καὶ Υἱῷ καὶ Ἁγίῳ Πνεύματι πιστεύσωμεν. Adde locum c. Noët. § 9. et doxologiam in fine, p. 20, ed. Fabr. Cæterum cum his conferas quæ scripsit Tertullian. c. Prax. 13. "Duos tamen Deos et duos Dominos nunquam ex ore nostro proferimus," ubi illorum insa-

which was seen, that is man, was the Son; but the Spirit which was contained in the Son, was the Father. For, said Callistus, "I will never acknowledge two Gods, the Father and the Son, but One God. For the Father born in Him, having taken human flesh, divinized it by uniting it to Himself, and made it one, so that One God is called Father and Son; and this being One Person cannot be two." And so he said that the Father had suffered with the Son; for he does not like to say that the Father suffered and was One Person, because he shrinks from blasphemy against the Father, he (forsooth) who is so infatuated and versatile, and extempo- P. 290
rizes blasphemy hither and thither, in order only that he may appear to speak against the truth, and is not ashamed of falling at one time into the dogma of Sabellius, and at another into that of Theodotus.

This deceiver having ventured to do such things,

---

niæ quos "vanissimos Monarchianos (c. 13)" appellat, respondet. Idem argumentum tangit Novatianus, de Trin. c. 28. Vide et c. 29, qui quidem loci his Hippolyti nostri sententiis lucem affundunt.

35. Hæc sunt referentis ipsa Callisti verba vocesque in vulgus sparsas, ad se suamque ipsius hæresim tuendam.

36. ἐκφυγεῖν. Sic Cod. "Ante ἐκφυγεῖν quædam omissa esse apparet" ait Miller. . . . Legendum fortasse ΕΚ ΤΟΥ ΕΚΦΥΓΕΙΝ. De re ipsâ vide Tertullian. c. Prax. 29. "Directam blasphemiam in Patrem veriti diminui eam hoc modo sperant si Filius quidem patitur, Pater vero compatitur. . . Times Patrem dicere passibilem quem dicis (Filio) compassibilem."

5. De Theodoto Byzantio, qui ψιλὸν ἄνθρωπον χριστόν dixit, suprà 257, infrà 328. 1—13. Confer item quæ de Theodoto scripsit noster, c. Noët. § 3, et quæ scripturus est infrà, lib. x. p. 330.

σας, συνεστήσατο διδασκαλεῖον κατὰ τῆς Ἐκκλησίας οὕτως διδάξας, καὶ πρῶτος τὰ πρὸς τὰς ἡδονὰς τοῖς ἀνθρώποις συγχωρεῖν ἐπενόησε, λέγων πᾶσιν ὑπ' αὐτοῦ ἀφίεσθαι ἁμαρτίας. Ὁ γὰρ παρ' ἑτέρῳ τινὶ συναγόμενος καὶ λεγόμενος Χριστιανὸς εἴ τι ἂν ἁμάρτῃ, φασὶν, οὐ λογίζεται αὐτῷ ἡ ἁμαρτία, εἰ προσδράμοι τῇ τοῦ Καλλίστου σχολῇ· οὗ τῷ ὅρῳ ἀρεσκόμενοι πολλοὶ συνείδησιν πεπληγότες, ἅμα τε καὶ ὑπὸ πολλῶν αἱρέσεων ἀποβληθέντες, τινὲς δὲ καὶ ἐπὶ καταγνώσει ἔκβλητοι τῆς ἐκκλησίας ὑφ' ἡμῶν γενόμενοι, προσχωρήσαντες αὐτοῖς, ἐπλήθυναν τὸ διδασκαλεῖον αὐτοῦ. Οὗτος ἐδογμάτισεν ὅπως εἰ ἐπίσκοπος ἁμάρτοι τι, εἰ καὶ πρὸς θάνατον, μὴ δεῖν κατατίθεσθαι. Ἐπὶ τούτου ἤρξαντο ἐπίσκοποι καὶ πρεσβύτεροι καὶ διάκονοι δίγαμοι καὶ τρίγαμοι καθίστασθαι εἰς κλήρους. Εἰ δὲ καί

8. Cod. *συγχαρεῖν*. 11. "Leg. *ὅ τι ἄν*." Miller. 16. Cod. *ἔκκλητοι*.

---

58. de Callisto, qui dicitur *ποτὲ μὲν τῷ Νοητοῦ δόγματι περιρρηγνύμενος, ποτὲ δὲ τῷ Θεοδότου, μηδὲν ἀσφαλὲς κρατῶν*.

11. Vide locum Tertulliani infrà citandum, et quæ adnotavit doctissimus et desideratissimus Antistes, Joannes Kaye, in Tertullian. p. 239. 257.

13. Videtur esse quædam antithesis inter *Χριστὸς* et *Κάλλιστος* et inter *Χριστιανὸς* et *Καλλιστιανός*. Christiani, inquit, quantopere peccatores, peccatorum suorum reatu scilicet sunt soluti, si modo fiunt Callistiani!

22. *Ἐπὶ τούτου*, *i. e.* illo Episcopatum obtinente. Vide p. 279. 39. *τούτων κατὰ διαδοχὴν* de Zephyrino ejusque successore Callisto; et 279. 30. *Ζεφυρίνου διέπειν νομίζοντος τὴν Ἐκκλησίαν* et 284. 78. *Κάλλιστος θηρώμενος τὸν τῆς ἐπισκοπῆς θρόνον*, et 288. 96. *μετὰ τὴν τοῦ Ζεφυρίνου τελευτὴν νομίζων τετυχηκέναι οὗ ἐθη-*

set up for himself a school against the Church, teaching these doctrines; and he was the first to devise also to gratify men in their lusts, saying that all men's sins were forgiven by himself. For if any one commits any sin who is a member of another man's congregation and is called a Christian, his sin (they say) is not imputed to him if he runs off to the School of Callistus. And many persons being delighted with this decree who were wounded in their consciences, and who had also been thrown off from many Heresies, and some cast out of the Church by me after judicial sentence, flocking to them, swelled his School.

This man promulgated as a dogma, that if a Bishop should commit any sin, even if it were a sin unto death, he ought not to be deposed. In his time Bishops, Priests and Deacons, digamists and trigamists, began to be enrolled in the Clergy.

ρᾶτο quæ quidem idcirca duxi notanda, quia nonnulli videntur existimasse de alio Callisto hìc agi, quam quem in Episcopatu Ecclesiæ Romanæ Zephyrino successisse accepimus. Certè Callistum aliquem Zephyrini fuisse successorem nescire non poterat noster, et hæc quæ de Callisto scribit, nunquam fuisset scripturus, si hic, de quo scribit Callistus, alius a Callisto Zephyrini successore fuisset. Imò sedulò operam dedisset, ne quis hæc legens, Callistum hunc Noëtianum cum Callisto Episcopo Romano confundere potuisset. Sed de his satis jam suprà dictum est. Vide Dissertationis præviæ cap. vii. p. 82.

24. Tertullian. ad Uxor. c. 7, "disciplina Ecclesiæ et præscriptio Apostoli digamos non sinit præsidere." De Exhort. Cast. c. 7, "Quosdam memini Digamos loco dejectos, . . . de suis Montanistis testatur de Pudicit. c. 1. 'Digamos' (*i. e.* etiam laïcos) 'foris sistimus, *eundem* limitem liminis mœchis quoque et fornicariis figimus.' De iis autem quos ipse Psychicos pro suo arbitrio vocat, audi exclamantem de Monogam. c. 12. "Quot enim et digami præsident apud vos!" Digamorum

τις ἐν κλήρῳ ὢν γαμοίη, μένειν τὸν τοιοῦτον ἐν τῷ κλήρῳ ὡς μὴ ἡμαρτηκότα· ἐπὶ τούτῳ φάσκων εἰρῆσθαι τὸ ὑπὸ τοῦ ἀποστόλου ῥηθὲν, "Σὺ τίς εἶ ὁ κρίνων ἀλλότριον οἰκέτην;" Ἀλλὰ καὶ παραβολὴν τῶν ζιζανίων πρὸς τούτῳ ἔφη λέγεσθαι· "Ἄφετε τὰ ζιζάνια συναύξειν τῷ σίτῳ," τουτέστιν ἐν τῇ Ἐκκλησίᾳ τοὺς ἁμαρτάνοντας. Ἀλλὰ καὶ τὴν κιβωτὸν τοῦ Νῶε εἰς ὁμοίωμα Ἐκκλησίας ἔφη γεγονέναι, ἐν ᾗ καὶ κύνες καὶ λύκοι καὶ κόρακες, καὶ πάντα τὰ καθαρὰ καὶ ἀκάθαρτα· οὕτω φάσκων δεῖν εἶναι ἐν Ἐκκλησίᾳ ὁμοίως· καὶ ὅσα
P 291 *πρὸς τοῦτο δυνατὸς ἦν συνάγειν οὕτως ἡρμήνευσεν, οὗ οἱ ἀκροαταὶ ἡσθέντες τοῖς δόγμασι διαμένουσιν ἐμπαίζοντες ἑαυτοῖς τε καὶ πολλοῖς, ὧν τῷ διδασκαλείῳ συρρέουσιν ὄχλοι. Διὸ καὶ πληθύνονται γαυριώμενοι ἐπὶ ὄχλοις διὰ τὰς ἡδονὰς, ἃς οὐ συνεχώρησεν ὁ Χριστὸς, οὗ κατα-*

23. Cod. ὢν γνώμη. 25. Rom. xiv. 4. 28. Matt. xiii. 30.
3. Cod. ἐμπέζοντες. 4. Cod. διδασκαλείων.

---

quorundam exempla in nonnullis Ecclesiis ad Episcopale fastigium provectorum videas apud Bingham. iv. v. § 4.

25. Super hac re consulenda egregia doctissimi Whartoni diatribe, *De Cleri Coelibatu*, Lond. 1688.

35. Sic, uti norunt omnes, post Hippolyti ætatem, docuerunt Catholici Patres. S. Cyprian. de Unit. Eccles. p. 111, et Epist. liv. p. 99, Fell. "Etsi videntur in Ecclesiâ esse zizania, non tamen impediri debet aut fides aut caritas nostra, ut, quoniam zizania in Ecclesiâ cernimus, ipsi de Ecclesiâ recedamus. Nobis tantummodo laborandum est, ut *frumentum* esse possimus." Fulgent. de fide, ad Petrum, c. 42, et S. Aug. Epist. cv. 16. "Ecclesiam Catholicam agrum suum Dominus docet tanquam zizania inter triticum."

And if any one being in the clerical body should marry (he determined) that such a person should remain in the Clergy as not having sinned, saying that the words of the Apostle were spoken with a view to him: "Who art thou that judgest another man's servant?" (Rom. xiv. 4); and he said that the parable of the tares was spoken with reference to him: "Let the tares grow together with the wheat" (Matt. xiii. 30.), that is, let sinners remain in the Church. Besides, he said that the Ark of Noah was made for a figure of the Church, and that in it were dogs and wolves and ravens, and all clean things and unclean; affirming that it must be so in the Church.

As many passages for this purpose as he was able P.291
to collect he expounded in this manner; and his disciples being pleased with his doctrines remain, deluding themselves and others, and crowds flock to their School.

Hence they are thronged, vaunting their multitudes, on account of pleasures which Christ did not

---

S. Aug. c. Faust. lib. xii. 15. "Cuncta animalium genera in Arcâ clauduntur. Sicut in Ecclesiæ sacramentis et boni et mali versantur." Sed venia detur Hippolyto alia rigidius statuenti. Illi enim non contigit videre quæ postea deliraverunt Novatiani et 'pars Donati.' Sed "*oportebat hæreses esse, ut probati essent manifesti.*" Oportebat schismata oriri, ut disciplinæ Christianæ leges melius dispungerentur, et ut veritas "de permixtâ Ecclesiâ" a Catharis in dubium vindicata, piis Sanctorum Episcoporum, Cypriani, Optati, Augustini laboribus feliciter vindicaretur, et in perpetuum solidaretur et stabiliretur. Interea fas sit monuisse, hæc et plurima similia, quæ lector paullò attentior ipse per se animadvertet, luculenta afferre testimonia quibus hujusce libri αὐθεντία et γνησιότης corroborentur. Cæterum de his jam fusè egimus, p. 102.

φρονήσαντες οὐδὲν ἁμαρτεῖν κωλύουσι, φάσκοντες αὐτῷ ἀφιέναι τοῖς εὐδοκοῦσι· καὶ γὰρ καὶ γυναιξὶν ἐπέτρεψεν εἰ ἄνανδροι εἶεν καὶ ἡλικίᾳ τε τε καίοντα ἐναξία ἡ ἑαυτῶν ἀξίαν ἣν μὴ βούλοιντο καθαίρειν. Διὰ τοῦτο νομίμως γαμηθῆναι ἔχει ἕνα ὃν ἂν αἱρήσωνται σύγκοιτον, εἴτε οἰκέτην, εἴτε ἐλεύθερον, καὶ τοῦτον κρίνειν ἀντὶ ἀνδρὸς μὴ νόμῳ γεγαμημένην. Ἔνθεν ἤρξαντο ἐπιχειρεῖν πισταὶ λεγόμεναι ἀτοκίᾳ περιδεσμεῖσθαι καὶ φαρμάκοις, πρὸς τὸ τὰ συλλαμβανόμενα καταβάλλειν, διὰ τὸ μήτε ἐκ δούλου βούλεσθαι ἔχειν τέκνον, μήτε ἐξ εὐτελοῦς διὰ τὴν συγγένειαν καὶ ὑπέρογκον οὐσίαν. Ὁρᾶτε εἰς ὅσην ἀσέβειαν ἐχώρησεν ὁ ἄνομος μοιχείαν καὶ φόνον ἐν τῷ αὐτῷ διδάσκων, καὶ ἐπὶ τούτοις τοῖς τολμήμασιν ἑαυτοὺς οἱ ἀπηρυθριασμένοι καθολικὴν

9, 10. "Ita hæc scripta sunt in codice. Nisi gravior corruptio inest, post *ἐπέτρεψεν* supple *ἁμαρτεῖν* (scilicet assumendo *σύγκοιτον*), et scrib. *ἡλικίᾳ καίοιντο αἱ ἐν ἀξίᾳ, τὴν ἑαυτῶν ἀξίαν ἣν* (sive potius *εἰ*) *μὴ βούλοιντο καθαιρεῖν.*" Miller. 14. Cod. *ἤρξατο.* 12. Cod. *τολμήσασιν.* 22. Cod. *ἀπερυθρ.*

---

8. Cod. *αὐτῷ.* Legendum videtur *αὐτοὶ*, vide suprà p. 290. 32.

10. Sic Cod. Legit Bunsenius, i. p. 134. *καὶ γὰρ καὶ γυναιξὶν ἐν ἀξίᾳ ἐπέτρεψεν εἰ ἄνανδροι εἶεν καὶ ἡλικίᾳ γε ἐκκαίοιντο, τηρεῖν ἑαυτῶν ἀξίαν ἣν μὴ βούλοιντο καθαίρειν.* Audaciusculè. Sed in loco salebroso dandum aliquid licentiæ. Age, nos quoque symbolam afferamus. Locum integrum sic repræsentandum conjecerim, *καὶ γὰρ καὶ γυναιξὶν ἐπέτρεψεν, εἰ ἄνανδροι εἶεν, καὶ ἡλικιώτῃ καίοιντο ἀναξίῳ, ἢ ἑαυτῶν ἀξίαν μὴ βούλοιντο καθαίρειν, διὰ τοῦτο νομίμως γαμηθῆναι ἐκείνῳ ὃν ἂν αἱρήσωνται σύγκοιτον.* De *γαμηθῆναι*, *nubere*, vide Lobeck. Phryn. p. 742. Iren. v. 9. *ἡ νύμφη γαμῆσαι οὐ δύναται, γαμηθῆναι δὲ δύναται.*

16. *νόμῳ γεγαμημένην.* Con-

permit, and in despite of Him they restrain from no sin, professing that they themselves forgive sins to those who acquiesce in them.

For he also permitted women, if they had no husband, and were enamoured of a comrade unworthy of themselves, or did not wish to degrade their own dignity, therefore they might lawfully marry any one whom they chose as a consort, whether a slave or free, and that she who was not married to him lawfully might regard him in place of a husband.

Thence it was that women, called believers, began to venture to bandage themselves with ligaments to produce abortion, and to deal with drugs in order to destroy what was conceived, because they did not like to have a child from a slave or a mean person, on account of their kindred, and haughtiness of wealth.

Behold to what impiety this lawless person proceeded, teaching adultery and murder at the same time! And yet after all these enormities these men are lost to all sense of shame, and presume to call

---

feras quæ in Traditione Apostolicâ *διὰ Ἱππολύτου* statuuntur, p. 254. *πιστὸς ἐὰν ἔχῃ παλλακὴν, ἐὰν μὲν δούλην, παυσάσθω, καὶ νόμῳ γαμείτω, εἰ δὲ ἐλευθέραν, γαμείτω αὐτὴν νόμῳ.*

19. Pro *ἀτοκίᾳ* legendum videtur *ἀτόκια*, et ante *φαρμάκοις* supplendum *ἐπιχειρεῖν*.

25. De Episcopo quodam, Romanæ, ut videtur, Ecclesiæ (nomen non liquet) similia narrat Tertullianus, jam Montanista, de Pudicitiâ c. 1. "Audio Edictum esse propositum et quidem peremptorium; Pontifex scilicet Maximus, Episcopus Episcoporum, dicit, Ego et mœchiæ et fornicationis delicta pœnitentia functis dimitto."

ἐκκλησίαν ἀποκαλεῖν ἐπιχειροῦσι, καί τινες νομίζοντες εὖ πράττειν συντρέχουσιν αὐτοῖς. Ἐπὶ τούτου πρώτως τετόλμηται δεύτερον αὐτοῖς βάπτισμα. Ταῦτα μὲν οὖν ὁ θαυμασιώτατος Κάλλιστος συνεστήσατο, οὗ διαμένει τὸ διδασκαλεῖον φυλάσσον τὰ ἔθη καὶ τὴν παράδοσιν, μὴ διακρῖνον τίσι δεῖ κοινωνεῖν, πᾶσιν ἀκρίτως προσφέρων τὴν κοινωνίαν· ἀφ᾽ οὗ καὶ τὴν τοῦ ὀνόματος P.292 *μετέσχον ἐπίκλησιν καλεῖσθαι διὰ τὸν πρωτοστατήσαντα τῶν τοιούτων ἔργων Κάλλιστον, Καλλιστιανοί.*

Τούτου κατὰ πάντα τὸν κόσμον διηχηθείσης τῆς διδασκαλίας, ἐνιδὼν τὴν πραγματείαν ἀνὴρ δόλιος καὶ ἀπονοίας γέμων, Ἀλκιβιάδης τις καλούμενος, οἰκῶν ἐν Ἀπαμείᾳ τῆς Συρίας, γοργότερον ἑαυτὸν καὶ εὐφυέστερον ἐν κυβείαις κρίνας τοῦ Καλλίστου, ἐπῆλθε τῇ Ῥώμῃ φέρων βίβλον τινά, φάσκων ταύτην ἀπὸ Σηρῶν τῆς Παρθίας παρειληφέναι τινὰ ἄνδρα δίκαιον Ἠλχασαΐ, ἣν παρέδωκε τινὶ λεγομένῳ Σοβιαῒ χρηματισθεῖσαν ὑπὸ ἀγγέλου, οὗ τὸ ὕψος σχοινίων κδ̄ ὃ γίνεται μίλια ϟϛ̄· τὸ δὲ πλάτος αὐτοῦ σχοινίων δ̄, καὶ ἀπὸ ὤμου εἰς ὦμον σχοινίων ϛ̄· τὰ δὲ ἴχνη

25. Literæ *ὀλμ* in codice exesæ. ib. Cod. *βάπτησμα.* 6. Cod. *ἀλκηβιάδης.* 10. Cod. *ἀποσηρῶν.*

---

9. Vide Theodoret. Hæret. Fab. ii. 7. Epiphan. Hær. xix. c.

5. Cæterùm hanc Helcesaitarum hæresim, non adeo immuta-

themselves a Catholic Church! And some persons imagining to fare well resort to them.

In his time, first they dared to administer a second baptism.

These things this most admirable Callistus contrived, and his school still survives preserving its practices and its tradition, not making any distinction as with whom it is fit to communicate, but offering communion indiscriminately to all, from whom his scholars derived their appellation, so as to be called, P.292
on account of him who took the lead in these matters, —namely, Callistus,—Callistians.

When his teaching had been noised through the whole world, a person full of subtlety and madness, called Alcibiades, dwelling in Apamea in Syria, deeming himself a more august person, and more adroit in jugglery, than Callistus, came to Rome, bringing a Book, which he said that a certain just man, called Elchasai, had received from the Seres of Parthia, which he gave to a certain Sobiai, being delivered by an Angel.

---

tam, nostrâ ætate recoctam vidimus ab iis qui se Mormonitas appellant, et suam disciplinam a Libro quodam portentoso, divinitus dato, hausisse se profitentur.

τῶν ποδῶν αὐτοῦ ἐπὶ μῆκος σχοίνων γ̄ ἡμίσους· ἃ γίνεται μίλια δεκατέσσαρα· τὸ δὲ πλάτος σχοίνου ἑνὸς ἡμίσους, τὸ δὲ ὕψος ἡμισχοίνου. Εἶναι *δὲ σὺν αὐτῷ καὶ θήλειαν, ἧς τὰ μέτρα κατὰ τὰ προειρημένα εἶναι λέγει· καὶ τὸν μὲν ἄρσενα υἱὸν εἶναι τοῦ θεοῦ, τὴν δὲ θήλειαν καλεῖσθαι ἅγιον* Πνεῦμα. Ταῦτα *τερατολογῶν, νομίζει ταράσσειν τοὺς μωροὺς, λέγων τοῦτον εὐηγγελίσθαι τοῖς ἀνθρώποις καινὴν ἄφεσιν ἁμαρτιῶν, ἐπὶ* Τραϊανοῦ *βασιλείας τρίτῳ, καὶ βάπτισμα ὁρίζει, ὃ καὶ αὐτὸ διηγήσομαι, φάσκων τοὺς ἐν πάσῃ ἀσελγείᾳ καὶ μιασμῷ καὶ ἀνομήμασιν ἐμφυρέντας, εἰ καὶ πιστὸς εἴη, ἐπιστρέψαντα καὶ τῆς βίβλου κατακούσαντα καὶ πιστεύσαντα, ὁρίζει βαπτίσματι λαμβάνειν ἄφεσιν ἁμαρτιῶν.* Ταῦτα *δὲ ἐτόλμησε τεχνάσαι τὰ πανουργήματα ἀπὸ τοῦ προειρημένου δόγματος ἀφορμὴν λαβὼν, οὗ παρεστήσατο* Κάλλιστος. Ἡ*δομένους γὰρ*
P.293 *κατανοήσας πολλοὺς ἐπὶ τοιαύτῃ ἐπαγγελίᾳ εὐκαίρως ἐνόμισεν ἐπιχειρεῖν.* Καὶ *τούτῳ δὲ ἡμεῖς ἀντιστάντες, οὐκ εἰάσαμεν ἐπιπολὺ πλανηθῆναι, πολλοὺς ἐλέγξαντες εἶναι τοῦτο πνεύματος νόθου ἐνέργειαν καὶ ἐπίνοιαν πεφυσιωμένης καρδίας,*

23. Cod. *λέγων, λέγων. λέγων λόγον* R. Scott. 26. Cod. *αὐτῷ.* 27. Cod. *ἀσεγεία.* 28. "Vocis *πιστὸς* literæ *στο* exesæ. Addendum videtur *τις.*" Miller. ib. Cod. *ἐπιτρέψαντα.* 30. Cod. *ἄφεσιν ἄφεσιν ἁμαρτιῶν.* 2. Cod. *ἐνόμησεν.* 4. Sic codex ; sed post *πολλοὺς* distinguendum videtur. ib. Cod. *ἐλλέγξαντες.*

These artifices he ventured to contrive, having
taken occasion from the dogma aforesaid, which Cal-
listus adopted. For having perceived that many P.293
were pleased with such promises (of indulgence), he imagined that he made the attempt at a favourable opportunity. And I resisting him did not suffer the heresy to spread wide, convincing many that this was the working of a spurious spirit, and the imagi-

5. ἐπιπολὺ πλανηθῆναι. Sic ΠΛΑΤΥΝΘΗΝΑΙ, *i.e.* latè diffundi. MS. Pro ΠΛΑΝΗΘΗΝΑΙ mallem

καὶ τοῦτον λύκου δίκην ἐπεγηγερμένον πλανωμένοις προβάτοις πολλοῖς [ἃ] ἀποπλανῶν διεσκόρπισεν ὁ Κάλλιστος.

. . . . .

P.309 *Δοκεῖ μὲν ἡμῖν ἱκανῶς τὰ πάντων Ἑλλήνων τε καὶ βαρβάρων δόγματα ἐκτεθεῖσθαι, μηδὲν δὲ ἀπολελοιπέναι μήτε τῶν φιλοσοφουμένων μήτε τῶν ὑπὸ αἱρετικῶν φ[ασκο]μένων ἀναπόδεικτον. Οἷς ἐξ αὐτῶν τῶν ἐκτεθέντων φανερὸς γεγένηται ὁ ἔλεγχος ἢ κλεψιλογησάντων ἢ τινὰ ἐρανισαμένων αὐτὰ τὰ ὑπὸ Ἑλλήνων πεπονημένα παραθεμένων ὡς θεῖα. Διὰ πάντων οὖν διαδραμόντες καὶ μετὰ πολλοῦ πόνου ἐν ταῖς ἐννέα βίβλοις τὰ πάντα δόγματα ἐξειπόντες, πᾶσί τε ἀνθρώποις ἐφόδιον ἐν βίῳ μικρὸν καταλιπόντες, καὶ τοῖς παροῦσιν οὐκ ὀλίγοις χαρᾶς καὶ θυμηδίας φιλομάθειαν παρασχόντες, εὔλογον ἡγούμεθα ὥσπερ κορυφὴν τοῦ παντὸς [τὸν] περὶ ἀληθείας λόγον ἐπενέγκαι, καὶ τοῦτον ἐν μιᾷ βίβλῳ τῇ δεκάτῃ περιγράψαι, ὅπως ὁ ἐντυγχάνων μὴ μόνον ἀνατροπὴν τῶν τετολμηκότων αἱρέσεις συστήσασθαι ἐπιγνοὺς καταφρονήσῃ τῶν ματαίων, ἀλλὰ καὶ*

7. Addidi *ἅ*. 2. Cod. *ἐκτεθῆσθαι*. 3. Cod. *ἀπολελυπέναι*. Miller *ἀπολελειπέναι*. 4. " Literæ suppletæ lacunam exacte implent; supersunt vestigia literarum *α* et *κ*." Miller. 9. Cod. *τοῖς*. Vel *βιβλίοις*. 12. Cod. *θυμιδίας*. 14. " Addidi *τόν*." Miller.

---

13. *ἐφόδιον ἐν βίῳ μικρὸν καταλιπόντες*. Legendum videtur *οὐ μικρόν*. Vide suprà, Philosoph. p. 3, 57. *οὐδὲ γὰρ μικράν τινα*

nation of a proud heart, and that he had risen up like a wolf to ravage the numerous sheep whom Callistus had led astray and scattered.

. . . . . .

The dogmas of the Greeks and Barbarians ap- P.309
pear to have been now sufficiently expounded, and we seem to have left nothing undeclared, either of Philosophical systems, or of the assertions of Heretics, the Refutation of whom has been made clear from what has been propounded; since they have either plagiarized their systems, or have gathered them (like banquets made by contributions) from different quarters, and have served up what have been prepared by Heathens, as if they were divine. Having run through all these, and having with much labour displayed in Nine Books all their theories, and having bequeathed no small viaticum of life to men, and having afforded to our contemporaries a desire of learning of no slight pleasure and intellectual gratification, we deem it reasonable to add, as the sum of the whole, a discourse concerning the Truth, and to include this in one book the Tenth, so that the reader, not only recognizing a Refutation of those who have presumed to fabri-

---

βοήθειαν τῷ τῶν ἀνθρώπων βίῳ καταλείψομεν. Anne huc respexerit Nicephorus Callisti, iv. 31, de *Hippolyto* scribens, quem reliquisse memorat *σύνταγμα πρὸς πάσας τὰς αἱρέσεις βιωφελέστατον?*

15. *ὀλίγοις.* An legendum *ὀλίγης?*

τὴν τῆς ἀληθείας δύναμιν ἐπιγνοὺς, ἀξίως Θεῷ πιστεύσας σωθῆναι δυνηθῇ.

. . . . .

Lib. X. P.333 *Τούτου τοίνυν τοῦ λόγου κρατήσαντες μαθηταὶ Ἕλληνες, Αἰγύπτιοι, Χαλδαῖοι καὶ πᾶν γένος ἀνθρώπων τί τὸ Θεῖον καὶ ἡ τούτου εὔτακτος δημιουργία παρ' ἡμῶν τῶν φίλων τοῦ θεοῦ, καὶ μὴ κομπολόγῳ τοῦτο ἠσκηκότων, ἀλλ' ἢ ἀληθείας γνώσει καὶ ἀσκήσει σωφροσύνης εἰς ἀπόδειξιν αὐτοῦ λόγους ποιουμένων.*

P.334 *Θεὸς εἷς ὁ πρῶτος καὶ μόνος καὶ ἁπάντων ποιητὴς καὶ κύριος, σύγχρονον ἔσχεν οὐδὲν, οὐ χάος ἄπειρον, οὐχ ὕδωρ ἀμέτρητον ἢ γῆν στερρὰν, οὐχὶ ἀέρα πυκνὸν, οὐ πῦρ θερμὸν, οὐ πνεῦμα λεπτὸν, οὐκ οὐρανοῦ μεγάλου κυανέαν μορφήν·*

4. "Post *ἡμῶν* vel alio loco hujus periodi excidisse videtur *ἔλαβον*. 5. Fort. *κομπολόγως*." Miller. 1. Titulus rubricatus in codice: *Ὠριγένης καὶ Ὠριγένους δόξα.*

---

1. *τούτου τοῦ λόγου κρατήσαντες μαθηταὶ Ἕλληνες.* Legendum *μάθετε*, ut rectè Harius apud Bunsenium. Confer Hippolyti locum simillimum in Libro *περὶ τοῦ παντὸς*, Fabr. i. p. 221. *ἃ λελυμένα ὁρῶντες, ἀπιστεῖτε, Ἕλληνες, μάθετε μὴ ἀπιστεῖν.*

5. *ἡ τούτου εὔτακτος δημιουργία.* Vide infrà, p. 338. Sic Hippolytus, in ejusdem libri fragmento Barocciano, quod ad calcem hujusce voluminis inveniet lector, et quod cum hoc Epilogo libenter comparabit, *διὰ τῆς τοῦ εὐτάκτου νομοθεσίας.*

1. In hâc Hippolyteâ veri enarratione perlustrandâ meminerit lector eam non pro concione ad clerum, imo neque ad populum Christianum fuisse enuntiatam, sed Sancti Præsulis et Martyris orationem nunc ad *Ethnicos* converti; eam igitur *ἐξωτερικοῖς*

cate Heresies may contemn their vanities, but recognizing also the power of truth, may be saved by worthy faith in God.

. . . . . .

P.333 Making yourselves masters of this argument, learn O ye Greeks, Egyptians, Chaldæans, and all the race of men, what the Deity is and what is His well-ordered creation, from us the friends of God, not discussing this matter in sounding speeches, but uttering our words in the knowledge of truth, and in the exercise of sobriety, for the demonstration of Him.

P.334 God, One, the First and only One, and Maker and Lord of all, had nothing coeval with Himself, not infinite Chaos, nor immeasurable Water, nor solid Earth, nor thick Air, nor hot Fire, nor subtle Breath, nor the azure vault of the vast Sky. But

---

potius quàm ἐσωτερικοῖς λόγοις venerandi Doctoris esse annumerandam. Quare si qua hic desideraveris ad Christianæ religionis mysteria, et ad fidei capita disertius declaranda, ea a reliquis S. Hippolyti scriptis jam superstitibus colligas, quæ quamvis laciniosa, et tanquam divitum stragulorum fimbriæ, tamen ad omnes istiusmodi defectus supplendos abundè sunt suffectura.

2. Gemellus locus, quem vide apud Hippol. c. Noëtum, § 10, θεὸς μόνος ὑπάρχων καὶ μηδὲν ἔχων ἑαυτῷ σύγχρονον, ἐβουλήθη κόσμον κτίσαι.

5. οὐρανοῦ κυανέαν ΜΟΡΦΗΝ. Ita MS. Mallem ΟΡΟΦΗΝ, *laquear*, "the azure vault," usu loquendi Hippolyteo, qui poeticas notiones et poeticas locutiones sectari solet, ut Irenæi discipulum facile agnoscas. Sic cœlum dixit οὐράνιον δίσκον Hippolytus in Theophan. p. 261, et Theophilus Antiochenus (cujus ad Autolycum libros legisse videtur Hippolytus), τὴν ποίησιν τοῦ οὐρανοῦ τρόπον ἐπέχοντα ΟΡΟΦΗΣ. Sed hanc conjecturam jam occupavit vir eruditissimus R. Scott in Censurâ Arnoldianâ, p. 541, cujus lucubrationes post hæc exarata vidi.

ἀλλ' ἦν εἷς μόνος ἑαυτῷ, ὃς θελήσας ἐποίησε τὰ ὄντα οὐκ ὄντα πρότερον, πλὴν ὅτε ἠθέλησε ποιεῖν ὡς ἔμπειρος ὢν τῶν ἐσομένων. Πάρεστι γὰρ αὐτῷ καὶ πρόγνωσις, διαφόρους τε τοῖς ἐσομένοις ἀρχὰς πρότερον ἐδημιούργει, πῦρ καὶ πνεῦμα, ὕδωρ καὶ γῆν, ἐξ ὧν διαφόρων τὴν ἑαυτοῦ κτίσιν ἐποίει, καὶ τὰ μὲν, μονοούσια, τὰ δὲ, ἐκ δύο, τὰ δὲ, ἐκ τριῶν, τὰ δὲ, ἐκ τεσσάρων συνεδέσμει. Καὶ τὰ μὲν ἐξ ἑνὸς, ἀθάνατα ἦν· λύσις γὰρ οὐ παρακολουθεῖ. Τὸ γὰρ ἓν οὐ λυθήσεται πώποτε, τὰ δὲ ἐκ δύο, ἢ τριῶν, ἢ τεσσάρων, λυτὰ, διὸ καὶ θνητὰ ὀνομάζεται. Θάνατος γὰρ τοῦτο κέκληται, ἡ τῶν δεδεμένων λύσις. Ἱκανὸν οὖν νῦν τοῖς εὖ φρονοῦσιν ἀποκεκρίσθαι, οἳ εἰ φιλομαθήσουσι καὶ τὰς τούτων οὐσίας καὶ τὰς αἰτίας τῆς κατὰ πάντα δημιουργίας ἐπιζητήσουσιν, εἴσονται ἐντυχόντες ἡμῶν βίβλῳ περιεχούσῃ περὶ τῆς τοῦ παντὸς οὐσίας· τὸ δὲ νῦν ἱκανὸν εἶναι ἐκθέσθαι τὰς αἰτίας, ἃς οὐ γνόντες Ἕλληνες κομψῷ τῷ λόγῳ τὰ μέρη τῆς κτίσεως ἐδόξασαν τὸν κτίσαντα ἀγνοήσαντες· ὧν ἀφορμὰς σχόντες οἱ αἱρεσιάρχαι

14. Cod. ubique λῦσις. 24. Cod. γνῶντες.

---

9. Act. xv. 18.

10. Millerus post ἐσομένων plenè interpungit : quod incuriâ factum videtur. Sed rationum, quas mihi præscripsi, memor, nihil mutavi, satius ducens sententiam meam qualemcunque interpretatione et notis explicare, quàm in textum intrudere.

21. ἱκανὸν οὖν νῦν τοῖς εὖ φρονοῦσιν ἀποκεκρίσθαι. Ita MS. Vix rectè. Vel post ἀποκεκρίσθαι ad-

He was alone with Himself. He by His Will created the things that exist, which did not exist before, but when He willed to create them, as having foreknowledge of what would be. For Prescience is present with Him. He also first created divers Elements for the things that were to be, namely, Fire and Air, Water and Earth, from which divers principles He formed His own Creation; and some things He made of one element, some He compounded of two, some of three, some of four. And those things which are of one element are immortal: for they are not soluble, because what is one will never be dissolved. But those which are of two elements, or three or four, are soluble, and are therefore called mortal. For this is Death, namely, the solution of what is bound. Let then this answer now be given, which will suffice for the intelligent, who, if they are desirous of further information, and would investigate the essence of these things and the causes of the Universal Creation, may learn them by referring to my Work, containing an essay "On the Essence of the Universe." For the present it seems enough to expound the causes, which the Gentiles not knowing, with all their artificial disquisitions, glorified the parts of Creation, being ignorant of the Creator. From whom the Heresiarchs derived occa-

---

jiciendum δοκεῖ: vel pro ἀποκεκρίσθαι legendum videtur ἀποκεκρίσθω.

27. De quo vide quæ dedimus suprà, p. 154, et Fabricii Hippolytea, I. p. 220, et ἀποσμάτιον quod Fabricio nondum compertum ad finem hujus libri adjicietur.

28. Supplendum δοκεῖ vel νομίζω.

ὁμοίοις λόγοις τὰ ὑπ' ἐκείνων προειρημένα μετασχηματίσαντες, αἱρέσεις καταγελάστους συνεστήσαντο.

Οὗτος οὖν μόνος καὶ κατὰ πάντων Θεὸς, λόγον πρῶτον ἐννοηθεὶς ἀπογεννᾷ οὐ λόγον ὡς φωνὴν, ἀλλ' ἐνδιάθετον τοῦ παντὸς λογισμόν. Τοῦτον
P.335 μόνον ἐξ ὄντων ἐγέννα· τὸ γὰρ ὂν, αὐτὸς ὁ πατὴρ ἦν, ἐξ οὗ τὸ γεννηθῆναι αἴτιον τοῖς γινομένοις. Λόγος ἦν ἐν αὐτῷ φέρων τὸ θέλειν τοῦ γεγεννηκότος, οὐκ ἄπειρος τῆς τοῦ πατρὸς ἐννοίας· ἅμα γὰρ τῷ ἐκ τοῦ γεννήσαντος προελθεῖν πρωτότοκος τούτου γενόμενος, φωνὴν ἔχει ἐν ἑαυτῷ τὰς ἐν τῷ πατρικῷ ἐννοηθείσας ἰδέας, ὅθεν κελεύ-

27. Cod. τὰ ὑπέκεινα. 3. Cod. γεγενηκότος. 5. Cod. τὸ ἐκ. 6. Cod. ἔχειν ἐν.

---

32. Eâdem locutione utitur noster suprà, p. 94. 27, unde forsan hìc legendum ἀφ' ὧν. Deinde pro ὁμοίοις mallem ἀνομοίοις.

37. Theophil. Antioch. p. 129. πρὸ τοῦ τι γίγνεσθαι Πατὴρ Λόγον εἶχε σύμβουλον ἑαυτοῦ Νοῦν ὄντα, ὁπότε δὲ ἠθέλησε ὁ Θεὸς ποιῆσαι ὅσα ἐβουλεύσατο τοῦτον τὸν Λόγον ἐγέννησε προφορικὸν πρωτότοκον πάσης κτίσεως. Novatian. de Trin. 31. "Est Deus Pater omnium Institutor et Creator, solus originem nesciens, unus Deus. Ex quo quando Ipse voluit, Sermo Filius natus est, qui *non* in *sono* percussi aëris aut tono coactæ de visceribus *vocis* accipitur, sed in substantiâ prolatæ a Deo virtutis agnoscitur. Hic cum sit genitus a Patre semper est in Patre."

1. Τοῦτον μόνον ἐξ ὄντων ἐγέννα. Quæ quidem verba vertit Bunsenius, "Him alone of all things He begat," adeòque evidentissimum nostri de Filii ὁμοουσίῳ testimonium obscuravit. Quod autem dicit Hippolytus hoc est: Pater ex *nihilo cætera* fecit, VERBUM autem ex substantiâ jam existente generavit,—hoc est ex SEIPSO; velut in alio loco c. Noët. § 11. πάντα διὰ Λόγου, αὐτὸς δὲ μόνος ἐκ Πατρὸς, unde clarum lucramur testimonium contra Arianos creaturam ex nihilo factam Dei Filium somniantes. Mi-

sions for their Heresies, and having travestied their systems in similar words, have formed Heresies which are ridiculous.

This One and Supreme God generates the Word first in His own mind; He generates the Word, not as a Voice, but as the Indwelling Ratiocination of the Universe. Him alone He generates of what P.335
exists. For the essence of things is the Father Himself, from whom is the cause of generation to what is generated. The Word was in the Father: The Word, bearing the will of Him Who begat the Word, and not unconscious of His Father's cogitation. For simultaneously with His procession from Him Who begat Him, being His First-born, He had as a voice in Himself the ideas conceived in His

---

ror doleoque Bunsenium, cujus ingenii dotes suspicio, non sine amarulentâ quâdam irrisione dixisse se minimè dubitare, quin orituri sint nonnulli, qui Sanctum Hippolytum de Verbo Dei unigenito *ὀρθοδόξως* sensisse contendant, quorum quidem conatum temerarium atque adeò frustraneum fore non obscurè innuerit. Sed pace viri egregii, ipse sanctum Antistitem perversè intelligendo, ipse Sanctum Hippolytum aliquoties perperam interpretando, pænè fecit hæreticum. Sed salva res est. Non eget Hippolytus defensoribus qui ejus *ὀρθοδοξίαν* propugnent. Absint tantum pravæ interpretationes: ipse pro se loquatur: ipse se tuebitur.

7. Hippol. c. Noët. § 10. *τῶν γινομένων ἀρχηγὸν καὶ σύμβουλον καὶ ἐργάτην ἐγέννα Λόγον, ὃν Λόγον ἔχων ἐν ἑαυτῷ, ἀόρατόν τε ὄντα, τῷ κτιζομένῳ κόσμῳ ὁρατὸν ποιεῖ*, ubi *Λόγον* appellat *τοῦ Θεοῦ τὸν ἴδιον νοῦν, αὐτῷ μόνῳ πρότερον ὁρατὸν ὑπάρχοντα.*

9. *φωνὴν* EXEIN *ἐν ἑαυτῷ τὰς ἐν τῷ πατρικῷ ἐννοηθείσας ἰδέας, ὅθεν κελεύοντος Πατρὸς γίνεσθαι κόσμον τὸ κατὰ ἓν Λόγος* ΑΠΕΤΕΛΕΙΤΟ ΑΡΕΣΚΩΝ *Θεῷ*. Sic Codex, manifestâ corruptelâ. Legit Bunsenius *φωνὴ* pro *φωνὴν* et sic interpretatur, "For when He (the Word) came forth from Him, being His First-begotten Speech, He had in Himself the ideas conceived by the Father." Sed jam

οντος πατρὸς γίνεσθαι κόσμον τὸ κατὰ ἓν Λόγος ἀπετελεῖτο ἀρέσκων Θεῷ. Καὶ τὰ μὲν ἐπὶ γενέσει πληθύνοντα, ἄρσενα καὶ θήλεα εἰργάζετο· ὅσα δὲ πρὸς ὑπηρεσίαν καὶ λειτουργίαν, ἢ ἄρσενα ἢ θηλειῶν μὴ προσδεόμενα, ἢ οὔτε ἄρσενα, οὔτε θήλεα. Καὶ γὰρ αἱ τούτων πρῶται οὐσίαι ἐξ

12. "Medium ἢ delendum videtur." Miller.

---

ipse negaverat Hippolytus ΛΟΓΟΝ esse *φωνήν*. Liquet, opinor, *φωνὴν* sanum esse, deinde pro ΕΧΕΙΝ legendum duabus literulis transpositis *εἶχεν*, et pro ΑΠΕΤΕΛΕΙΤΟ 'ΑΡΕΣΚΩΝ Θεῷ reponendum 'ΑΠΕΤΕΛΕΙ ΤΟ 'ΑΡΕΣΚΟΝ Θεῷ. Non enim in his dicebant Patres *ἀποτελεῖσθαι* sed *ἀποτελεῖν*. Testis ipse Hippolytus in simillimo loco, indicio catholicæ doctrinæ evidentissimo, c. Noët. § 14. *Πατὴρ μὲν εἷς, πρόσωπα δὲ δύο, ὅτι καὶ ὁ υἱός· τὸ δὲ τρίτον τὸ ἅγιον πνεῦμα. Πατὴρ ἐντέλλεται, Λόγος* 'ΑΠΟΤΕΛΕΙ. Hinc S. Irenæi vetus interpres, ii. 47, "hic mundus factus est *apotelestos* a Deo."

Fortasse hìc dixerit quis, Hippolytum nostrum VERBI generationem facere, quod aiunt, *χρονικὴν* sive *temporariam, non* autem *sempiternam*. Quare adolescentes monitos velim, quorum præcipuè causâ hæc commentatus sum, duas Patrum Ante-nicænorum fuisse quasi familias, de hoc fidei capite specie diversa loquentes, re tamen idem sentientes; quorum alii quidem Generationem Filii manifestè prædicabant *æternam;* alii verò ut Justinus, Athenagoras, Theophilus, Tatianus, Tertullianus, inter quos etiam eminebat noster Hippolytus, quùm Deitatem *τοῦ Λόγου* declarâssent, eumque ab *æterno* extitisse in Mente Patris, *ἐνδιάθετον Πατρὸς Λόγον* docuissent, tum verò pergebant dicere Eum *in tempore* factum fuisse *προφορικὸν*, et exinde *κατ' ἐνέργειαν* et per *συγκατάβασιν προπηδῆσαι* sive *processisse* ad Patrem Seseque *manifestandum*, et ad *creanda* universa. Hanc Ejus *προέλευσιν* sive processionem ad opus Creationis exequendum, aliquoties appellabant *Generationem*, memores illius *Υἱός Μου εἶ Σὺ, Σήμερον* ΓΕΓΕΝΝΗΚΑ *Σέ* (Heb. i. 5; Ps. ii. 7). Hæc Ejus Generatio indubie fuit *temporaria*. Qui verò, ut Hippolytus noster, *τὸν Λόγον* ab æterno *extitisse* statuerant, Eum ab æterno fuisse *genitum* agnoverant, ideòque temporariam ejus generationem ad creanda universa declarantes, Generationem Ejus

Father's essence, whence, when the Father bade that the world should be created in its single species, the Word executed what was pleasing to the Father.

And some things which were to multiply by successive generation He made male and female; but whatsoever were for ministry and service, He created either male, or not needing any female, or neither male nor female. For their first elements being

---

Æternam minimè abnuebant, immò vero validissimè adstruebant. Qui enim ex Patre γεννητὸς et Patri συναΐδιος, ἀεὶ συμπαρὼν αὐτῷ καὶ σύμβουλος, Eum ab æterno genitum fuisse satis constabat. Rem optimè expressit nostri ferè æqualis Novatianus de Trin. 31. "Hic (Λόγος) cum sit genitus a Patre semper est in Patre, semper autem sic dico, ut non innatum sed natum probem. Sed qui ante omne tempus est, semper in Patre fuisse dicendus est. Nec enim tempus illi æquari potest qui ante tempus est. Semper enim in Patre, ne Pater semper non sit Pater. Hic ergo quando Pater voluit, processit ex Patre; substantia scilicet illa Divina cujus Nomen est Verbum per quod facta sunt omnia. Omnia post Ipsum sunt, quia per Ipsum sunt, et merito Ipse est ante omnia quando per Illum facta sunt omnia, qui processit ex Eo Cujus voluntate facta sunt omnia."

10. κελεύοντος Πατρός. Subordinatur enim Filius Patri tanquam sui Auctori et omnium Principio. Ut Fabricii verbis utar (Hippol. ii. p. 15) "*mandandi* et *præcipiendi* vocabulo de *Patre*, et *obediendi* de *Filio* sine ullâ offensione usos esse constat non modo *ante* Concilium Nicænum S. Irenæum, Hippolytum nostrum, Origenem, et alios; sed et *post* illud Concilium adversarios et hostes Arianæ hæreseos acerrimos, Athanasium, Basilium. Vide Petav. de Trin. ii. vii. § 7. Georgii Bull. defensionem Fidei Nicænæ," p. 133. 165. 170; iv. 2, et in Epilogo Operis, vol. v. pt. ii. p. 291. Waterland. iii. p. 319, 320. Meminerit lector hâc item uti protestatione Nostrum de *Filio* omnia Patris jussu formante contra hæreticorum illorum somnia, qui ab Angelis vel Æonibus omnia facta fuisse impiè comminiscerentur, de quibus Irenæus, ii. 55; iv. 37.

14. ἐπὶ γενέσει. Mallem unâ voce ἐπιγενέσει, *i.e. continuâ serie procreationis.*

16. *i.e.* mascula tantum *sine fœminâ;* quod propter Millerum monuerim delentem ἤ, et propter Bunsenium ejicientem ἢ ἄρσενα.

οὐκ ὄντων γενόμεναι, πῦρ καὶ πνεῦμα, ὕδωρ καὶ γῆ, οὔτε ἄρσενα οὔτε θήλεα ὑπάρχειν ἑκάστη τούτων δῦνται προελθεῖν ἄρσενα καὶ θήλεα, πλὴν εἰ βούλοιτο ὁ κελεύων Θεὸς ἵνα Λόγος ὑπουργῇ. Ἐκ πυρὸς εἶναι ἀγγέλους ὁμολογῶ, καὶ οὐ τούτοις παρεῖναι θηλείας λέγω. Ἥλιον δὲ καὶ σελήνην καὶ ἀστέρας ὁμοίως ἐκ πυρὸς καὶ πνεύματος, καὶ οὔτε ἄρσενας οὔτε θηλείας νενόμικα, ἐξ ὕδατος δὲ ζῷα νηκτὰ εἶναι θέλων καὶ πτηνὰ ἄρσενα καὶ θήλεα· οὕτω γὰρ ἐκέλευσεν ὁ θελήσας Θεὸς, γόνιμον εἶναι τὴν ὑγρὰν οὐσίαν. Ὁμοίως ἐκ γῆς ἑρπετὰ καὶ θηρία καὶ παντοδαπῶν ζῴων ἄρσενα καὶ θήλεα· οὕτως γὰρ ἐνεδέχετο ἡ τῶν γεγονότων φύσις. Ὅσα γὰρ ἠθέλησεν, ἐποίει ὁ Θεός. Ταῦτα λόγῳ ἐδημιούργει, ἑτέρως γενέσθαι μὴ δυνάμενα, ἢ ὡς ἐγένετο. Ὅτε δὲ (ἢ) ὡς ἠθέλησε καὶ ἐποίησεν, ὀνόματι καλέσας ἐσή-

15, 16. "Fort. ὑπάρχει· ἑκάστης τούτων δύναται. Aut, si malis, ὑπάρχουσιν οὔτε." Miller. 17. Cod. ὑπουργεῖ, mutatum in -ῇ. Miller. 29. "Ex præcedentibus male repetitum ἢ quod post ὅτε δὲ legitur." Miller.

---

19. οὔτε ἄρσενα οὔτε θηλέα ὑπάρχειν ἑκάστη τούτων δῦνται προελθεῖν ἄρσενα. Sic MS. mendosè. Millerus ὑπάρχει· ἑκάστης τούτων δύναται. Bunsenius ὑπάρχει. οὔτ' ἐξ ἑκάστης τούτων δύναται κ.τ.λ. Mallem ὑπ' ἀρχῇ δὲ ἑκάστῃ τούτων δύναται προελθεῖν ἄ. κ. θ.

21. Junge εἰ βούλοιτο ἵνα Λόγος ὑπουργῇ. Novatian. de Trin. 31. "Filius nihil ex arbitrio suo gerit, nec ex consilio suo facit, nec a se venit, sed imperiis paternis omnibus obedit, ut quamvis probet illum nativitas Filium, tamen morigera obedientia asserat illum paternæ voluntatis ex quo

produced of nothing, such as Fire and Air, Water and Earth, are neither male nor female, but under each principle of these may arise either male or female, provided God, Who bids, so will that the Word should minister in making it. I profess that the Angels are of Fire, and say that to them there are not females. I believe that the Sun and Moon and Stars are likewise of Fire and Breath, and are neither male nor female; believing that swimming and flying animals are of water, male and female, for so God commanded, Who willed that the moist element should be generative. In like manner from the earth are creeping things and beasts, and male and female of all kinds of creatures, for so the nature of what was born allowed. For whatsoever He willed, He made. He created by the Word these things, not having a capacity to be otherwise than as they were. But when He made them as He willed, calling them by name He marked them by signs.

---

est Ministrum, ita quamvis sit et Deus unum tamen Deum Patrem de obedientiâ suâ ostendit." Inter recentiores qui hoc argumentum tractaverunt satis erit nominasse Bull. Def. Fid. Nicæn. § iii. 5. 1, et iii. 8. 4. Waterland. vol. i. 2. p. 114. 134—140. 288; vol. iii. p. 100, 268—274. 296. ed. Van Mildert. Oxon. 1823, et p. 200, 1, de Hippolyto confitente unum Deum in tribus Personis Patre, Filio et Spiritu Sancto.

26. *ἐξ ὕδατος δὲ ζῶα νηκτὰ εἶναι θέλων*,—sic MS. Bunsenius *θέλω*, sic vertens " I conceive that from water have come swimming and flying animals, male and female." Confer sup. Philos. p. 258. 77. *τοῦτον γεγονέναι αὐτὸν θέλουσιν*, de Theodoti *placitis.*

μηνεν. Ἐπὶ τούτοις τὸν πάντων ἄρχοντα δημιουργὸν ἐκ πασῶν συνθέτων οὐσιῶν ἐσκεύασεν·
P.336 οὐ θεὸν θέλων ποιεῖν ἔσφηλεν, οὐδὲ ἄγγελον (μὴ πλανῶ), ἀλλ' ἄνθρωπον. Εἰ γὰρ θεόν σε ἠθέλησε ποιῆσαι, ἐδύνατο· ἔχεις τοῦ Λόγου τὸ παράδειγμα· ἄνθρωπον θέλων, ἄνθρωπόν σε ἐποίησεν· εἰ δὲ θέλεις καὶ θεὸς γενέσθαι, ὑπάκουε τῷ πεποιηκότι, καὶ μὴ ἀντίβαινε νῦν, ἵνα ἐπὶ τῷ μικρῷ πιστὸς εὑρεθεὶς, καὶ τὸ μέγα πιστευθῆναι δυνηθῇς. Τούτου ὁ Λόγος μόνος ἐξ αὐτοῦ· διὸ καὶ θεὸς, οὐσία ὑπάρχων Θεοῦ. Ὁ δὲ κόσμος ἐξ οὐδενός· διὸ οὐ θεός· οὗτος ἐπιδέχεται καὶ λύσιν ὅτε βούλεται ὁ κτίσας. Ὁ δὲ κτίσας Θεὸς κακὸν οὐκ ἐποίει οὐδὲ ποιεῖ καλὸν καὶ ἀγαθὸν, ἀγαθὸς γὰρ ὁ ποιῶν. Ὁ δὲ γενόμενος ἄνθρωπος,

6. Matth. xxv. 21.

38. Clem. Rom. ad Cor. i. c. 33. *ὁ δημιουργὸς ἐπὶ πᾶσι τὸ ἐξοχώτατον καὶ παμμεγεθὲς κατὰ διάνοιαν, ἄνθρωπον ταῖς ἱεραῖς καὶ ἀμώμοις χερσὶν ἔπλασεν τῆς Ἑαυτοῦ εἰκόνος χαρακτῆρα.*

ib. *δημιουργὸν* Cod. *δημιουργῶν* rectè Bunsenius.

39. Vide Phot. Bibl. Cod. 48, qui Scriptorem de Natura Universi, quem Hippolytum esse vidimus, sic disserentem proponit, *δοξάζει συγκεῖσθαι τὸν ἄνθρωπον ἐκ πυρὸς καὶ γῆς καὶ ὕδατος καὶ ἔτι ἐκ πνεύματος,* hoc est *ἐκ πασῶν σύνθετον οὐσιῶν.* Pro *συνθέτων* legit *σύνθετον* vir doctissimus R. Scott. fortasse rectè.

9. ΜΗ ΠΛΑΝΩ, eâdem loquendi formulâ utitur Scriptor Demonstrationis de Christo et Antichristo, quem ex indiciis cum extrinsecis tum intrinsecis eundem ac nostri hujusce libri Auctorem eumque Sanctum Hippolytum, Episcopum Portuensem satis, ut opinor, liquet. Vide suprà p. 165, sive § 2. vol. i. p. 5. ed. Fabric. *οὐ γὰρ ἐξ ἰδίας δυνάμεως ἐφθέγγοντο, (οἱ προφῆται)* ΜΗ ΠΛΑΝΩ.

4. *Λόγος* igitur Hippolyto Deus, isque Patri *ὁμοούσιος* idem-

Over these, when fashioning the master of all, He formed him from all essences blended together. He did not fail, desiring to make a god or an angel (be P.336
not deceived), but a man. For if He had desired to make thee a deity, He could have done so. Thou hast the example of the Word. Willing thee a man,—He made thee a man. But if thou desirest to become even a deity, hearken to Him Who made thee, and do not resist Him now, in order that having been found faithful in that which is little, thou mayest be able to be entrusted also with what is much. The Word alone is of God—of God Himself. Wherefore He is God; being the Substance of God. But the world is of nothing; wherefore it is not God: the world is liable to dissolution also, when He wills Who created it. But God Who created it neither made nor does make evil: He makes what is beautiful and good, for He Who maketh is good.

But man who was born was a creature endued

---

que *συναΐδιος*. Cæterùm de re ipsâ confer Tertullian. c. Prax. c. 5. Sibi Filium fecit Sermonem suum, c. Marcion ii. c. 27. Sermonem quem ex semet ipso *proferendo* Filium fecit.

15. Θεὸς *κακὸν οὐκ ἐποίει οὐδὲ ποιεῖ καλὸν καὶ ἀγαθὸν*, sic MS. Bunsenius, Θεὸς *κακὸν οὐκ ἐποίει· οὐδὲν ἐποίει οὐ καλὸν καὶ ἀγαθόν*. Sed leviore negotio res transigenda. Interpunge post *ποιεῖ*, deinde iterandum *ποιεῖ*. Cæterum his comparari merentur Novatianus de Trinitate, cap. 1—4, de Deo Mali non auctore, et qui expressisse Hippolytum, Hieronymo dicitur auctore, in Hexaëmero Ambrosius, c. 8. Argumentum, *πόθεν τὸ κακὸν*, in singulari libello, ut lemmata operum statuæ dorso inscripta satis docent, ipse tractavit Hippolytus.

ζῷον αὐτεξούσιον ἦν, οὐκ ἄρχον, οὐ νοῦν ἔχον, οὐκ ἐπινοίᾳ καὶ ἐξουσίᾳ καὶ δυνάμει πάντων κρατοῦν, ἀλλὰ δοῦλον καὶ πάντα ἔχον τὰ ἐναντία· ὃς τῷ αὐτεξούσιον ὑπάρχειν, τὸ κακὸν ἐπιγεννᾷ, ἐκ συμβεβηκότος ἀποτελούμενον μὲν οὐδὲν, ἐὰν μὴ ποιῇς. Ἐν γὰρ τῷ θέλειν καὶ νομίζειν τι κακὸν, τὸ κακὸν ὀνομάζεται, οὐκ ὂν ἀπ' ἀρχῆς, ἀλλ' ἐπιγινόμενον. Οὗ αὐτεξουσίου ὄντος, νόμος ὑπὸ Θεοῦ ὡρίζετο, οὐ μάτην· οὐ γὰρ μὴ εἶχεν ὁ ἄνθρωπος τὸ θέλειν καὶ τὸ μὴ θέλειν τι, καὶ νόμος ὡρίζετο. Ὁ νόμος γὰρ ἀλόγῳ ζῴῳ οὐχ ὁρισθήσεται, ἀλλὰ χαλινὸς καὶ μάστιξ, ἀνθρώπῳ δὲ ἐντολὴ καὶ πρόστιμον τοῦ ποιεῖν τὸ προστεταγμένον καὶ μὴ ποιεῖν· τούτῳ νόμος ὡρίσθη διὰ δικαίων ἀνδρῶν ἐπάνωθεν. Ἔγγιον

16. Cod. κρατῶν. ib. Cod. ἔχοντα ἐν. 21. "Vox οὗ prorsus evanida." Miller. 25. Cod. μάστιγξ.

---

18. Magistrum suum S. Irenæum hìc sequi videtur noster, adv. Hær. iv. 9. "Homo rationabilis et secundum hoc similis Deo liber in arbitrio factus et suæ potestatis ipse sibi causa est ut aliquando quidem frumentum aliquando autem palea fiat." Vide et Tertullian. c. Marcion ii. 5, 6, quem citavit Grabius.

ib. οὐκ ἄρχον οὐ νοῦν ἔχον οὐκ ἐπινοίᾳ καὶ ἐξουσίᾳ καὶ δυνάμει πάντων κρατοῦν ἀλλὰ δοῦλον καὶ πάντα ἔχον τὰ ἐναντία. Sic Codex. Bunsenius legit. οὐκ ἄρχοντα νοῦν ἔχον. Deinde καὶ πάντα ἔχον τὰ ἐναντία ita vertit "having all sorts of contraries in him." Parùm grammaticè, et contra sensum Scriptoris, qui sic videtur ratiocinari: "*Homo libero arbitrio prædictus, non tamen dominio supremo donatus est; rationem habuit divinitus inditam, non tamen vi rationis omnia potuit moderari, sed servi loco positus, et è variis elementis conflatus* (vide suprà, p. 335) *omnes contrarietates in se com-*

with free will, but not dominant; having reason, but not able to govern every thing with reason, authority, and power, but subordinate, and having all contrarieties in himself. He, in having free will, generates evil accidentally, but not in any degree taking effect, unless thou doest it. For in the volition or cogitation of evil, evil receives its name, and does not exist from the beginning, but was subsequently generated.

Man being endued with free will, a Law was given him by God; with good reason; for if man had not the faculty of volition and non-volition, wherefore was a *Law* given? For *Law* will not be given to an irrational creature; but a bit and a whip. But to *man* is given a precept and a penalty, for doing or not doing what is commanded. To him a Law was given from the first by the ministry of righteous men. In times nearer to our own, a Law full of sanctity and justice was given by the instrumentality

---

plexus est. Quare, ut brevi rem præcidam, pro οὐκ ἄρχον ΟΥ νοῦν ἔχον levissimâ mutatione corrigendum arbitror οὐκ ἄρχον ΟΝ, νοῦν ἔχον,—

22. τὸ κακὸν ἐπιγεννᾷ, ἐκ συμβεβηκότος. Ita Miller. et Bunsenius, sed jungenda videntur ἐπιγεννᾷ ἐκ συμβεβηκότος. Malum enim non directè vel ex necessitate oriri dicit, sed mediatè et quasi per accidens. Quarè sic reddidi.

26. Præclarè S. Irenæus, iv. 72, ταῦτα πάντα (*i. e.* dispositiones Dei per Legem et Prophetas) τὸ αὐτεξούσιον ἐπιδείκνυσι τοῦ ἀνθρώπου καὶ τὸ συμβουλευτικὸν τοῦ θεοῦ, ἀποτρέποντος μὲν τοῦ ἀπειθεῖν αὐτῷ ἀλλὰ μὴ βιαζομένου.

26. οὐ MS. εἰ ex conjecturâ Milleri reponendum videtur nisi malis οὗ, *ubi*.

27. θέλειν τι, καὶ νόμος ὡρίζετο. Sic Miller. Bunsen. θέλειν, τί κἂν νόμος ὁρίζοιτο; Sed manifestum videtur legi debere θέλειν, τί καὶ νόμος ὡρίζετο; et jam video virum doctissimum R. Scott. idem statuisse.

30. Vide Ps. xxxii. 9.

31. πρόστιμον vide ad Clem. Roman. c. 41.

ἡμῶν διὰ τοῦ προειρημένου Μωϋσέως, ἀνδρὸς εὐλαβοῦς καὶ θεοφιλοῦς, νόμος ὡρίζετο πλήρης σεμνότητος καὶ δικαιοσύνης. Τὰ δὲ πάντα διοικεῖ ὁ Λόγος ὁ Θεοῦ, ὁ πρωτόγονος πατρὸς παῖς, ἡ
P.337 *πρὸ ἑωσφόρου φωσφόρος φωνή· ἔπειτα δίκαιοι ἄνδρες γεγένηνται φίλοι Θεοῦ· οὗτοι προφῆται κέκληνται διὰ τὸ προφαίνειν τὰ μέλλοντα. Οἷς οὐχ ἑνὸς καιροῦ λόγος ἐγένετο, ἀλλὰ διὰ πασῶν γενεῶν αἱ τῶν προλεγομένων φωναὶ εὐαπόδεικτοι παρίσταντο· οὐκ ἐκεῖ μόνον ἡνίκα τοῖς παροῦσιν ἀπεκρίναντο, ἀλλὰ καὶ διὰ πασῶν γενεῶν τὰ ἐσόμενα προεφήναντο, ὅτι μὲν τὰ παρῳχημένα λέγοντες, ὑπεμίμνησκον τὴν ἀνθρωπότητα· τὰ δὲ ἐνεστῶτα δεικνύντες, μὴ ῥᾳθυμεῖν ἔπειθον· τὰ δὲ μέλλοντα προλέγοντες, τὸν κατὰ ἕνα ἡμῶν ὁρῶντας πρὸ πολλοῦ προειρημένα ἐμφόβους καθίστων, προσδοκῶντας καὶ τὰ μέλλοντα. Τοιαύτη ἡ καθ' ἡμᾶς πίστις, ὦ πάντες ἄνθρωποι, οὐ κενοῖς ῥήμασι πειθομένων, οὐδὲ σχεδιάσμασι καρδίας συναρπαζομένων, οὐδὲ πι-*

29. Cod. Μωϋσέος. 13. Cod. καθιστῶν.

---

37. Quemadmodum dixit noster, c. Noet. §§ 11, 12, οὗτος (ὁ Λόγος) ἔδωκεν Νόμον καὶ Προφήτας καὶ δοὺς διὰ Πνεύματος Ἁγίου ἠνάγκασεν τούτους φθέγγεσθαι ὅπως τῆς Πατρῴας δυνάμεως τὴν ἀπόπνοιαν λαβόντες τὴν βουλὴν καὶ τὸ βούλευμα τοῦ Πατρὸς καταγγείλωσιν· ἐν τούτοις τοίνυν πολιτευόμενος ὁ Λόγος ἐφθέγγετο περὶ ἑαυτοῦ, ἤδη γὰρ αὐτὸς ἑαυτοῦ Κήρυξ ἐγένετο.

39. Ex Psalmo cx. 3, ἐκ γαστρὸς πρὸ ἑωσφόρου ἐγέννησά Σε, unde citat Hippolytus c. Noët. c. 17.

of that Moses who has been already named, a devout man dear to God. But the Word of God regulates all things, the First Born Son of the Father, the Day-spring Voice before the Morning Star. Afterwards just men were born dear to God, who P.337
are called Prophets, because they predicted the Future.

To them came the Word, not of one time only; but through all generations the voices of things spoken before were manifestly present, not only in that spot when they made replies to those persons who resorted to them, but they predicted what would happen through all ages. Besides uttering what was passed they reminded mankind; and displaying the present they persuaded men not to be remiss; and foretelling the future they inspired each of us with awe, when we saw what was long since predicted, and thence expecting also the future (*which was predicted, to be fulfilled also*).

Such, O all ye men, is the faith of us who do not listen to idle words, nor are carried away by improvisations of the heart, nor bewitched by the beguile-

6. De Prophetarum veterum officio vide eodem fere dicendi tenore disserentem Hippolytum, de Antichristo, § 2, οἱ μακάριοι προφῆται ὀφθαλμοὶ ἡμῶν ἐγένοντο, οὐ μόνον τὰ παρῳχηκότα εἰπόντες, ἀλλὰ καὶ τὰ ἐνεστῶτα καὶ μέλλοντα λέγοντες, ἵνα μὴ μόνον πρόσκαιρος εἶναι ὁ προφήτης δειχθῇ, ἀλλὰ καὶ πάσαις γενεαῖς προλέγων τὰ μέλλοντα, ὡς προφήτης εἶναι νομισθῇ.

8. τοῖς παροῦσιν, *i. e.* præsentibus, qui eos consulturi adibant. Prophetas Veteres cum Oraculis Ethnicorum comparat, quæ non edebant vaticinia suâ sponte, sed responsa tantum sciscitantibus dabant. ὅτι Codex. Legerim ἔτι.

θανότητι εὐεπείας λόγων θελγομένων, ἀλλὰ δυνάμει θείᾳ λόγοις λελαλημένοις οὐκ ἀπειθούντων. Καὶ ταῦτα Θεὸς ἐκέλευε Λόγῳ. Ὁ δὲ Λόγος ἐφθέγγετο λέγων, δι' αὐτῶν ἐπιστρέφων τὸν ἄνθρωπον ἐκ παρακοῆς, οὐ βίᾳ ἀνάγκης δουλαγωγῶν, ἀλλ' ἐπ' ἐλευθερίᾳ ἑκουσίῳ, προαιρέσει καλῶν. Τοῦτον τὸν Λόγον ἐν ὑστέροις ἀπέστελλεν ὁ πατὴρ οὐκέτι διὰ προφήτου λαλεῖν, οὐ σκοτεινῶς κηρυσσόμενον ὑπονοεῖσθαι θέλων, ἀλλ' αὐτοψεὶ φανερωθῆναι τοῦτον λέγων, ἵνα κόσμος ὁρῶν δυσωπηθῇ οὐκ ἐντελλόμενον διὰ προσώπου προφητῶν, οὐδὲ δι' ἀγγέλου φοβοῦντα ψυχὴν, ἀλλ' αὐτὸν παρόντα τὸν λελαληκότα. Τοῦτον ἔγνωμεν ἐκ παρθένου σῶμα ἀνειληφότα καὶ τὸν παλαιὸν ἄνθρωπον διὰ καινῆς πλάσεως πεφορηκότα, ἐν βίῳ διὰ πάσης ἡλικίας ἐληλυθότα, ἵνα πάσῃ ἡλικίᾳ αὐτὸς νόμος γενηθῇ καὶ σκοπὸν τὸν ἴδιον ἄνθρωπον πᾶσιν ἀνθρώποις ἐπιδείξῃ

25. ἑκουσίῳ MS. ἐπ' ἐλευθερίαν ἑκουσίῳ προαιρέσει Scott. Sed legendum fortasse ἑκουσίως.

35. τὸν παλαιὸν ἄνθρωπον διὰ καινῆς πλάσεως ΠΕΦΟΡΗΚΟΤΑ. Sic Codex et Bunsen. qui sic vertit, "to have put on the old man through a new formation." Sed mendam subesse suspicor. Neque enim veterem Adamum *sumpsit et gessit* Christus sine peccato conceptus, sed veterem *refinxit et renovavit*, ut nos protinus essemus in Eo καινὴ κτίσις, vel καινὸν φύραμα. 1 Cor. v. 7; Gal. vi. 15; 2 Cor. v. 17. Vide etiam S. Iren. v. 14—16. Neque leges loquendi dicere sinunt φορεῖν διὰ πλάσεως. Quid multa? Legere mallem minimâ mutatione ΠΕΦΥΡΑΚΟΤΑ. Vide etiam quæ de hâc re dixit Hippolytus noster, c. Noët. § 17, καθ' ὃν τρόπον ἐκηρύχθη, κατὰ τοῦτον καὶ παρὼν ἐφανέρωσεν ἑαυτὸν ἐκ παρθένου καὶ ἁγίου Πνεύματος, Καινὸς ἄνθρωπος γενόμενος, τὸ μὲν οὐράνιον ἔχων τὸ πατρῷον ὡς Λόγος, τὸ δὲ ἐπίγειον ὡς ἐκ παλαιοῦ

ments of eloquent speeches, and do not disobey words spoken by divine power.

These things God gave as mandates to the Word, and the Word uttered them by His Voice, turning man thereby from transgression, not leading him captive by the force of necessity, but calling him to liberty voluntarily with free choice. This Word the Father sent in the latter days no longer to speak by a Prophet; and not willing that being obscurely preached He should only be surmised, but bidding Him be manifest face to face, in order that the world might reverence Him when it saw Him not giving His behests by the person of a Prophet, nor alarming the soul by an Angel, but beholding Him Who had spoken, present in Person.

We believe that He took a body from a Virgin, and fashioned the old man by a new creation, and that He passed through every age in life, in order that he might be a Law to every age, and by His presence might exhibit His own manhood as a pattern

---

Ἀδὰμ διὰ παρθένου σαρκούμενος. Vide etiam Scholion Hippolyti in Danielem (p. 205, Mai). *Λόγον πρωτοτόκον ἐκ Θεοῦ. . . . πρωτοτόκον ἐκ Παρθένου ἵνα τὸν πρωτόπλαστον Ἀδὰμ ἐν αὐτῷ ἀναπλάσσων δειχθῇ Λόγος ἐκ καρδίας (Πατρὸς) πρὸ πάντων γεγενημένος· ἐπιγείων βασιλεὺς ὅτι ἄνθρωπος ἐν ἀνθρώποις ἐγεννήθη ἀναπλάσσων δι' αὐτὸν τὸν Ἀδάμ.* Eadem ferè leguntur apud nostrum, de Antichristo, § 26, unde Scholium Vaticanum corrigatur, *ἀναπλάσσων δι' ἑαυτοῦ τὸν Ἀδάμ.* Cf. S. Iren. v. 6. "Glorificatur Deus in suo plasmate conforme illud et consequens suo Puero adoptans. Per manus enim Patris id est per Filium et Spiritum Sanctum fit homo secundum similitudinem Dei."

36. Hæc ab Irenæo mutuatus est ii. 39, Irenæi errorem devitans ad annum ferè quinquagesimum Christi in terris vitam prorogantis.

παρὼν, καὶ δι' αὐτοῦ ἐλέγξῃ ὅτι μηδὲν ἐποίησεν
P.338 ὁ Θεὸς πονηρόν· καὶ ὡς αὐτεξούσιος ὁ ἄνθρωπος ἔχων τὸ θέλειν καὶ τὸ μὴ θέλειν δυνατὸς ὢν ἐν ἀμφοτέροις, οὗ τὸν ἄνθρωπον εἰς μὲν τοῦ καθ' ἡμᾶς φυράματος γεγονέναι. Εἰ γὰρ μὴ ἐκ τοῦ αὐτοῦ ὑπῆρξε, μάτην νομοθετεῖ μιμεῖσθαι τὸν διδάσκαλον. Εἰ γὰρ ἐκεῖνος ὁ ἄνθρωπος ἑτέρας ἐτύγχανεν οὐσίας, τί τὰ ὅμοια κελεύει ἐμοὶ τῷ ἀσθενεῖ πεφυκότι, καὶ πῶς οὗτος ἀγαθὸς καὶ δίκαιος; ἵνα δὲ μὴ ἕτερος παρ' ἡμᾶς νομισθῇ, καὶ κάματον ὑπέμεινε, καὶ πεινῆν ἠθέλησε, καὶ διψῆν οὐκ ἠρνήσατο, καὶ ὕπνῳ ἠρέμησε, καὶ πάθει οὐκ ἀντεῖπε, καὶ θανάτῳ ὑπήκουσε, καὶ ἀνάστασιν ἐφανέρωσεν, ἀπαρξάμενος ἐν πᾶσι τούτοις τὸν ἴδιον ἄνθρωπον, ἵνα σὺ πάσχων μὴ ἀθυμῇς, ἀλλ' ἄνθρωπον σεαυτὸν ὁμολογῶν, προσδοκῶν καὶ σὺ ὃ τούτῳ παρέσχες.

10. Cod. διψεῖν.

---

4. Codex οὗ τὸν ἄνθρωπον γεγονέναι εἰς μέν. Benè Miller. τοῦτον, optimè item Bunsen. ἴσμεν pro εἰς μέν.

13. Christum, Dominum Nostrum, humanum Corpus verè sumpsisse et humanam animam, ψυχὴν λογικὴν, et splendidissima documenta dedisse τῆς ἀνθρωπότητός τε καὶ τῆς θεότητος, eloquentissimè docet Hippolytus in nobili illâ peroratione ad sermonem suum contra Noëti deliramenta, quem integrum ferè exscribere operæ pretium duxissem, nisi plerisque obvium fecisset et notis adornâsset vir sacrâ eruditione non minùs quàm annis venerabilis M. I. Routh. Eccl. Opusc. i. pp. 41—89.

20. ἀλλ' ἄνθρωπον σεαυτὸν ὁμολογῶν, προσδοκῶν σὺ ὃ τούτῳ παρέσχες. Sic MS. Corrigit Bunsen. προσδοκᾷς καὶ σὺ ὃ τούτῳ πατὴρ παρέσχεν, audaciusculâ mutatione et à tenore sententiarum

to all men, and thereby (by himself) might convince man that God made nothing evil, and that man P. 338 is endued with free will, having the power of volition or non-volition in himself, and being able to do both. Him we know to have been a man of the same nature with ourselves.

For if He was not of the same nature, He in vain commands us to imitate our Master. For if that Man was of another nature, why does He enjoin the same duties on me who am weak? And how then can He be good and just? But in order that He might be known to be not different from us, He underwent toil and consented to feel hunger, and did not decline thirst, and rested in sleep, and did not refuse His Passion, and became obedient to Death, and manifested His Resurrection, having consecrated as first fruits in all these things His own manhood, in order that when thou sufferest thou mayest not despond, acknowledging thyself a man of like nature with Christ, and thou also waiting for the appearance of what thou gavest to Him.

---

aliquantum deviâ. Consolationis fontem indicat Hippolytus in *τῇ τοῦ Λόγου ἐνσαρκώσει*. Suspice, inquit, Incarnatum jam glorificatum. Deinde teipsum aspice. Vidisti tuam ipsius carnem, quam à te assumpsit, cœlo admotam, imò in cœlo regnantem, deitate insolubiliter consociatam *διὰ παθημάτων δεδοξασμένην*. Macte, igitur, bono sis animo! Passiones tuæ terrenæ tibi viam sternunt ad gloriam cœlestem! Si compateris Christo cum Christo regnabis. Tu carnem ei dedisti. Tu carnem ab eo accipies gloriæ consortem. Vide Irenæum, v. 32, de hoc argumento disserentem. Sed quid cum *ἀλλ'* faciendum? Est enim *ἀλλ' ἄνθρωπον*, ut opinor, mendosum. Vide igitur ne pro ΑΛΛ' ΑΝΘΡΩΠΟΝ reponendum sit 'ΑΜΑΝΘΡΩΠΟΝ, *i. e.* hominem connaturalem cum Christo.

Τοιοῦτος ὁ περὶ τὸ Θεῖον ἀληθὴς λόγος, ὦ ἄνθρωποι Ἕλληνές τε καὶ βάρβαροι, Χαλδαῖοί τε καὶ Ἀσσύριοι, Αἰγύπτιοί τε καὶ Λίβυες, Ἰνδοί τε καὶ Αἰθίοπες, Κελτοί τε καὶ οἱ στρατηγοῦντες Λατῖνοι, πάντες τε οἱ τὴν Εὐρώπην Ἀσίαν τε καὶ Λιβύην κατοικοῦντες, οἷς σύμβουλος ἐγὼ γίνομαι, φιλανθρώπου Λόγου ὑπάρχων μαθητὴς καὶ φιλάνθρωπος, ὅπως προσδραμόντες διδαχθῆτε παρ' ἡμῶν τίς ὁ ὄντως Θεὸς καὶ ἡ τούτου εὔτακτος δημιουργία, μὴ προσέχοντες σοφίσμασιν ἐντέχνων λόγων, μηδὲ ματαίοις ἐπαγγελίαις κλεψιλόγων αἱρετικῶν, ἀλλ' ἀληθείας ἀκόμπου ἁπλότητι σεμνῇ, δι' ἧς ἐπιγνώσεως ἐκφεύξεσθε ἐπερχομένην πυρὸς κρίσεως ἀπειλὴν, καὶ ταρτάρου ζοφερὸν ὄμμα ἀφώτιστον, ὑπὸ Λόγου φωνῆς μὴ καταλαμφθὲν, καὶ βρασμὸν ἀεννάου
P.339 λίμνης γεννήτορος φλογὸς, καὶ ταρταρούχων ἀγγέλων κολαστῶν ὄμμα ἀεὶ μένον ἐν ἀπειλῇ,

29. Cod. ἐκφεύξεσθαι 31. Cod. ζωφερόν. 32. Cod. καταλαμφέν. 1. Cod. γεννητρος sine accentu. 2. Cod. μένων.

Quare sic interpretatus sum. Judicet lector. Commentarii vicem expleat Tertullianus de Resurr. Carnis, c. 51. "Quum sedeat Jesus ad dextram Patris, homo etsi Deus, Adam Novissimus etsi Sermo primarius, idem tamen et substantiâ et formâ quâ ascendit talis etiam descensurus. . . . Quemadmodum enim nobis arrhabonem Spiritûs reliquit, ita et *à nobis* arrhabonem *carnis accepit*, et vexit in cœlum pignus totius summæ illuc quandoque redigendæ." Vide et Apostoli cohortationes, Phil. iii. 21. Ep. Tit. ii. 13.

21. Hanc Sancti Antistitis παραίνεσιν non ad fideles esse traditam, sed ad Christianis mysteriis nondum initiatos, jam suprà monuimus. Quare ne expectet lector quæ cum ἀμυήτοις com-

Such is the true doctrine concerning the Deity, O ye Greeks and Barbarians, Chaldæans and Assyrians, Ægyptians and Africans, Indians and Æthiopians, Celts and ye army-leading Latins, and all ye that dwell in Europe, Asia, and Africa, whom I exhort, being a disciple of the man-loving Word, and a lover of men, come ye and learn from us, who is the Very God, and what is His well-ordered workmanship, not giving heed to the sophistry of artificial speeches, or the vain professions of plagiarist heretics, but to the venerable simplicity of modest Truth, by a knowledge of which ye will escape the coming malediction of the Judgment of fire, and the dark and rayless aspect of tartarus, not irradiated by the voice of the Word, and the surge of the everflowing lake, generating fire, and the eye of tartarean aveng- P.339
ing Angels ever fixed in malediction, and the worm

---

municari non licebat. Ne, inquam, requirat disertam et specialem Christianæ veritatis articulorum enarrationem. Verùm enimverò recordetur, plura in animo habere Hippolytum, quàm quæ palam ore proferat. Has igitur Præsulis venerandi sententias interpretari non aliter possit quis, quàm oculo intentè fixo in arcana Christianæ fidei mysteria. Quod ideo monendum duxi, quia quàm hic labi proclive sit, monstravit in his Anglicè reddendis (i. 185—192) vir eruditus de quo jam verba fecimus.

30. κλεψιλόγων αἱρετικῶν, "of delusive heretics," Bunsen. Sed vide sup. p. 5. 3, et p. 92, 92, ubi eandem vocem (κλεψίλογος) usurpat Noster, quâ hæreticos plagii reos agat, utpote placita sua à Philosophis Ethnicis suffuratos.

34. ταρτάρου. Hanc Ethnicis familiarem vocem quasi consecraverat Apostolus, 2 Pet. ii. 4, σειραῖς ζόφου ταρταρώσας. Præiverant LXX Interpretes, modo sana sit lectio, Hiob. xl. 15; xli. 24.

35. ἀεννάου. Lege ἀενάου.

2. ἀεὶ μένον Miller. Codex μένων.

καὶ σκώληκα σώματος ἀπουσίαν ἐπιστρεφόμενον ἐπὶ τὸ ἐκβράσαν σῶμα ὡς ἐπιστρέφων. Καὶ ταῦτα μὲν ἐκφεύξῃ, Θεὸν τὸν ὄντα διδαχθεὶς, ἕξεις δὲ ἀθάνατον τὸ σῶμα καὶ ἄφθαρτον ἅμα ψυχῇ βασιλείαν οὐρανῶν ἀπολήψῃ, ὁ ἐν γῇ βιοὺς καὶ ἐπουράνιον βασιλέα ἐπιγνοὺς, ἔσῃ δὲ ὁμιλητὴς Θεοῦ καὶ συγκληρονόμος Χριστοῦ, οὐκ ἐπιθυμίαις ἢ πάθεσι καὶ νόσοις δουλούμενος. Γέγονας γὰρ θεός· ὅσα γὰρ ὑπέμεινας πάθη ἄνθρωπος ὢν, ταῦτα δίδου ὅτι ἄνθρωπος εἶς· ὅσα δὲ παρακολουθεῖ θεῷ, ταῦτα παρέχειν ἐπήγγελται

---

4. Lectionem Codicis, quam dedi, Bunsenius ita refingit *σκώληκα ἀπαύστως ἐπιστρεφόμενον ἐπὶ τὸ ἐκβράσαν σῶμα ὡς ἐπὶ τροφὴν*, quæ sic vertit, "*the worm which winds itself without rest round the mouldering body to feed upon it;*" comparari jubens quæ scripsit S. Hippolytus noster de Universo, i. 221. 24. ed. Fabr. *σκώληξ ἀπαύστῳ ὀδύνῃ ἐκ σώματος ἐκβράσσων.* Qui hæc scripsit, (ait Bunsenius,) "non potuit *non aliter scribere*" quàm quemadmodum ipse Bunsenius scribenda pro imperio edixit. Verum hæc et similia ingenii nimiùm sibi fidentis festinantiùs ne dicam arrogantiùs effutita, aliquando, ut arbitror, ipse recogniturus est vir ingeniosissimus. Sed hæc hactenus. Quid autem de hoc loco statuendum nunc videamus. Hippolytus vermem illum *ἀτελεύτητον* humani corporis peccato obnoxii et vitiis inquinati naturalem quendam fœtum, emanationem, ebullitionem, et quasi despumationem à corrupto fonte scaturientem et gurgitantem cogitare videtur. Quarè sanissima est lectio vulgata *ἀπουσίαν*. *Ἀπουσία* enim, vox medicis non ignota, rem quamvis denotat ab ipsâ substantiâ (*ἀπὸ τῆς οὐσίας*) profluentem, *ἀποῤῥοὴν*, *ἀποσπερματισμὸν*, quo sensu utitur voce *ἀπουσία* S. Petr. Alex. ap. Routh. Rel. Sac. iv. 345. Hinc in vetusto Glossario apud Labbeum *Ἀπουσία* *Detrimentum*. Cætera proclivia sunt. Pro *ἐπιστρέφων* mallem *ἐπιτρέφον*. Simili ferè sensu *οὐσίαν* dixit Noster, —*ζώων ἐκβρασσομένη οὐσία*, p. 222, ed. Fabr. Minucius Felix, § 35, de igne gehennæ disserens: "Illic sapiens ignis membra urit et reficit, carpit et nutrit, sicut ignes

the scum of the body, turning to the Body that foamed it forth, as to that which nourisheth it.

These things you will escape, if you learn to know the true God, and you will have your body immortal and incorruptible, together with your soul; you will receive the kingdom of heaven, you who have lived on earth, and have known the King of Heaven, and you will hold converse with God, and be a coheir with Christ, not being enslaved by lust, or passion, or disease. For you have been divinized. Whatsoever sufferings you have endured these are from yourself, because you are a man, but whatsoever is pertinent to God, this God has promised to bestow

---

fulminum corpora tangunt, nec absumunt—pœnale illud incendium inexesâ corporum laceratione *nutritur*." Comparari possunt quæ in re diversâ scripsit S. Clemens Romanus, i. 25. *σηπομένης σαρκὸς σκώληξ τις γεννᾶται* (tanquam *ἀπουσία*) *ὃς ἐκ τῆς ἰκμάδος τοῦ τετελευτηκότος ζῴου ἀνατρεφόμενος πτεροφυεῖ.*

6. Vide Hippol. de Resurrectione et Incorruptione, ap. Anast. Sinait. in Hodeg. p. 356. Hippol. ed. Fabr. i. p. 244, et oratoriâ vi et pulchritudine insignem et lectu sanè dignissimam Homiliam de Baptismo in Theophaniâ, p. 264. *ὁ θεὸς ἀναγεννήσας* (*ἡμᾶς*) *πρὸς ἀφθαρσίαν ψυχῆς τε καὶ σώματος* (lavacro baptismi) *ἐνεφύσησεν ἡμῖν πνεῦμα ζωῆς.*

11. 2 Pet. i. 4.

12. Dixerant jam Apostoli, homines, Christi corpore insitos, *Θείας φύσεως εἶναι κοινωνούς.* Vide 1 Pet. i. 23; 2 Pet. i. 4; Ephes. i. 10; 1 Joh. iii. 9, et similia ex Psalmo cii. 6, traducta vero Gnostico tribuit Clemens, Strom. vi. p. 816. *δυνατὸν τὸν γνωστικὸν ἤδη γενέσθαι Θεόν.* "*Ἐγὼ εἶπα* ΘΕΟΙ ἘΣΤΕ, *καὶ υἱοὶ Ὑψίστου, τοὺς ἀναγνόντας αὐτὸν υἱοὺς ἀναγορεύει καὶ Θεούς.*" Similiter Origen. in S. Joann. t. xii. § 3. Similiter etiam S. Irenæus, iv. 75. "Non ab initio Dei facti sumus, sed primò quidem homines tunc vero Dei." Vide etiam S. Iren. v. 2.

14. *δίδου.* Sic MS. Bunsen. *ἐδίδου*, vertens "*He gave them to thee.*" Pro ΔΙΔΟΥ fortasse legendum ΔΙΑ ΣΟΥ, "*per teipsum sunt.*"

Θεὸς, ὅτε θεοποιηθῇς, ἀθάνατος γεννηθείς. Τουτέστι τὸ Γνῶθι σεαυτὸν, ἐπιγνοὺς τὸν πεποιηκότα Θεόν. Τῷ γὰρ ἐπιγνῶναι ἑαυτὸν, ἐπιγνωσθῆναι συμβέβηκε τῷ καλουμένῳ ὑπ' αὐτοῦ. Μὴ φιλεχθήσητε τοίνυν ἑαυτοῖς, ἄνθρωποι, μηδὲ τὸ παλινδρομεῖν διστάσητε· Χριστὸς γάρ ἐστιν ὁ

16. Cod. τὸ γάρ.

---

16. *ὅτε θεοποιηθῇς.* Ita Cod. Bunsenius scribit *ὅταν θεοποιηθῇς*, reddens "*when thou shalt be deified,*" sed suprà dixerat *γέγονας Θεός*. Legendum igitur videtur *ὅτι ἐθεοποιήθης*, et sic Scott.

17. *γέγονας Θεός, ἀθάνατος γενηθείς.* Ad hæc rectè intelligenda meminerit lector Hippolytum nostrum docere *πηγὴν ἀθανασίας* sive *fontem immortalitatis* esse fidelibus et obedientibus Sanctum Baptismum. Vide simillimum locum, qui commentarii instar erit, Hippol. Homil. in Theophaniâ, i. 264, ed. Fabric. *εἰ οὖν ἀθάνατος γέγονεν ἄνθρωπος, ἔσται καὶ Θεός, εἰ δὲ Θεὸς δι' ὕδατος καὶ πνεύματος ἁγίου μετὰ τὴν τῆς κολυμβήθρας* (baptisterii) *ἀναγέννησιν, εὑρίσκεται καὶ συγκληρόνομος Χριστοῦ μετὰ τὴν ἐκ νεκρῶν ἀνάστασιν.* Vide S. Iren. v. 8; v. 12.

ib. *γεννηθείς.* Sic Cod. et Bunsen., vertens "*having been born again an immortal.*" Sed Hippolyti doctrinâ de baptismo non intellectâ, non poterat non in hoc loco titubare vir ornatissimus. Lege *γενηθείς.*

21. *τοῦτ' ἐστὶ τὸ Γνῶθι σεαυτὸν ἐπιγνοὺς τὸν πεποιηκότα Θεόν· τὸ γὰρ ἐπιγνῶναι ἑαυτὸν, ἐπιγνωσθῆναι συμβέβηκε τῷ καλουμένῳ ὑπ' αὐτοῦ.* Sic MS. Pro *τὸ γὰρ ἐπιγνῶναι* Millerus *τῷ γ. ε.* Bunsenius transponit invicem clausulas *ἐπιγνοὺς—Θεὸν*, et *τοῦτ' ἐστὶ—σεαυτὸν*, totumque locum ita interpretatur, *Thou shalt be deified being born again an immortal, having known God, Who has made thee. This is the meaning of Know Thyself. For to know oneself befalls him who is called by Him in the very act of being known by Him.* Sed hæc *ἀσύστατα* videntur. Quomodo enim nosse Deum est nosse seipsum, quia nosci à Deo est nosse seipsum? Dicere videtur Noster, hominem pervenire ad notitiam sui ipsius per notitiam Dei. Quarè sana videtur codicis lectio, sed distinctione mutatâ explicanda, *τὸ γὰρ ἐπιγνῶναι ἑαυτὸν ἐπιγνωσθῆναι, συμβέβηκε τῷ κ. ὑ. α.*

22. *μὴ φιλεχθήσητε* MS. quod Græcum esse negat Bunsenius, qui *φιλεχθρήσητε* legi jubet, sed *ἔχθος*

on you, because you have been divinized, having become immortal.

This is the precept, Know thyself by knowing God Who made thee. For the knowledge of himself to have been known by God, accrues to him who is called by Him.

Do not therefore cherish enmity with one another, ye men, nor hesitate to retrace your course.

For CHRIST is the GOD Who is over all, Who

---

non minùs legitur quàm *ἔχθρα*: et *φιλεχθὴς* non minùs quàm *φίλεχθρος*, quare nihil mutaverim.

23. *μηδὲ παλινδρομεῖν διστάσητε.* Vertit Bunsenius "*Doubt not that you will exist again.*" Mira sanè interpretatio. Quod quidem viri clarissimi *παρόραμα* inter alia quibus ferè innumeris Bunsenii paginæ scatent, minimè commemorâssem, nisi eum fundamenta fidei, ut mihi quidem videtur, labefactantem, et doctissimorum virorum, et nominatim venerandorum Antistitum Cestriensis et Menevensis bonam famam deditâ operâ lædentem non sine magno dolore vidissem. Sed hoc piis eorum animabus, hoc causæ veritatis, hoc juventuti præsertim nostræ Academicæ debebatur officium, ut quanti sit facienda Bunsenii ipsius auctoritas, probè perspiciant, et ne ejus effatis commoti maximorum Angliæ theologorum nomina venerari dediscant. Sed de Nostri sensu videamus. Hippolytus, ut Portûs Romani, civitatis maritimæ et commercio deditæ, Episcopus, locutiones à re nauticâ desumptas sectari videtur; id quod in hoc loco factum vides. *Παλινδρομεῖν* enim dicitur de eo qui procellâ in mari aperto subitò deprensus, in portum, ex quo in altum imprudentiùs provectus est, se illicò recipere nititur. Hinc, "*O quid agis? fortiter occupa Portum;*" ipse sibi succinit, et "*nunc iterare cursus Cogor relictos,*" hoc est *παλινδρομεῖν*, sive ut se ipsum interpretatur noster, Philos. p. 81. *ἀφροσύνην τῶν πειθομένων κατηγορήσαντες πείσομεν παλινδρομεῖν ἐπὶ τὸν τῆς ἀληθείας εὔδιον λιμένα.* Vide etiam p. 224, 29. *ἐχρῆν τοὺς ἀκροατὰς παραπλεῖν ἐπιζητοῦντας τὸν εὔδιον λιμένα,* ubi obiter pro ΠΡΑΞΕΩΝ *θηρῶν* lege ΠΑΡΑΞΕΝΩΝ *θηρῶν*. Cf. p. 81, 6. Cæterùm *παλινδρομεῖν* simili sensu habet Theodoret., iv. 1222. *παλινδρομῆσαι πρὸς ἡσυχίαν.*

24. Hoc quoque S. Hippolyti testimonium de Christo Deo corrupit Bunsenius, legendum edicens, *Χριστὸς γὰρ ἐστὶν ᾧ ὁ κατὰ*

κατὰ πάντων Θεὸς, ὃς τὴν ἁμαρτίαν ἐξ ἀνθρώπων ἀποπλύνειν προσέταξε, νέον τὸν παλαιὸν ἄν-

---

πάντων Θεὸς τὴν ἁμαρτίαν ἐξ ἀνθρώπων ἀποπλύνειν προσέταξε, *neque* enim *dixisse potuisse* Hippolytum, ait Bunsenius, "Christus jussit homines abluere peccata." Quarè hanc esse sententiam Hippolyti statuit Bunsenius : "Christ is he whom the God of all has ordered to wash away the sins of mankind, renewing the old man." Nollem factum. Primum enim quidni dixerit Hippolytus Χριστὸν εἶναι κατὰ πάντων Θεὸν, quùm in plurimis aliis locis Christum Deum prædicaverit, et cùm id ipsum prædicantem Sanctum Paulum legerat (Rom. ix. 25)? Legerat item Hippolytus quæ de hâc re scripserat Irenæus, iii. 17. "In principio Verbum existens apud Deum, per Quem omnia facta sunt, Qui et semper aderat generi humano et Hunc in novissimis temporibus passibilem ; sic iii. 18. Ipse Deus et Dominus et Unigenitus Rex Æternus et Verbum incarnatum, prædicatur à prophetis omnibus et Apostolis." Quin et ipse dixerat Hippolytus apud Theodoret. Dialog. ii. p. 88. C. τὸ πάσχα ἡμῶν ὑπὲρ ἡμῶν ἐτύθη Χριστὸς ὁ Θεός. Deinde quidni affirmaverit Hippolytus Christum jussisse homines abluere peccata, quùm Christus Baptismum instituerit, ut esset λουτρὸν παλιγγενεσίας (Ep. Tit. iii. 5) et quùm Idem Apostolos ad baptizandas omnes nationes legatos Suos per orbem terrarum miserit, et omnes baptizari jusserit? quapropter his ipsis verbis, quæ sine dubio respexit Hippolytus, usi sunt primores Evangelii Prædicatores, quùm ad baptismum recipiendum Christi nomine invitarent, (Acta Apost. xxii. 16,) ἀναστὰς βάπτισαι καὶ ἀπόλουσαι τὰς ἁμαρτίας σου, ἐπικαλεσάμενος τὸ ὄνομα κυρίου. Quarè ipse Hippolytus alio loco sic scripsit, de Antichristo, § 3. εἷς ὁ Θεοῦ παῖς δι' οὗ καὶ ἡμεῖς τυχόντες τὴν διὰ τοῦ ἁγίου πνεύματος ἀναγέννησιν. Quod autem à Bunsenio (i. p. 340) video allegatum, Hippolytum in ἀποσπασματίῳ quodam à Cardinali Mai (Collect. Vat. i. P. ii. p. 205) nuper edito, Patrem vocare Christi δεσπότην id ab hâc re est sanè alienum, ut quod maximè. Ibi enim Hippolytus enarrans vaticinium Danielis, vii. 13, loquitur de Christo *Filio Hominis*, ut ibidem dudum monuit ipse Cardinalis Angelus Mai, minimè autem de Verbo Patris ὁμοουσίῳ. Quarè huc illa Hippolyti verba non erant violenter trahenda. De Hippolyti doctrinâ in hoc fidei articulo satis jamdudum dixerat vir eruditissimus Daniel Waterland, Vol. iii. pp. 41. 105, ed. Van Mildert, (A Second Defence of some Queries, Qu. ii.), cujus verba candido lectori attentiùs consideranda

commanded us to wash away sin from man, regenerating the old man, having called man His

---

liceat commendare. Sarta igitur et tecta manet Codicis Parisini lectio, Bunsenii rationibus inconcussa; et nobilissimum affert catholicæ veritatis contra hæreticos neotericos, sive Socini asseclæ sint, sive Baptismi efficaciam in dubium vocantes, testimonium.

Rem fortasse non injucundam lectori fecero, si alium Hippolyti locum huc apprimè facientem, mantissæ loco, subjecero. Quod quidem facio lubentiùs, quia emendatricem manum adhuc expectare videtur. Fervidioris animi ingenio fræna dans, et Asiatico more exultans, Ecclesiam Navi comparat Hippolytus, mundi, tanquam Oceani, fluctus sulcanti. Ipsum audiamus; (De Antichristo, § 59,) *θάλασσά ἐστιν ὁ Κόσμος, ἐν ᾧ ἡ* ’ΕΚΚΛΗΣΙΑ, *ὡς Ναῦς ἐν Πελάγει, χειμάζεται μὲν, ἀλλ’ οὐκ ἀπόλλυται. ἔχει μὲν γὰρ μεθ’ ἑαυτῆς τὸν ἔμπειρον κυβερνήτην* ΧΡΙΣΤΟΝ (nihil adhuc de *Petro* Ecclesiæ clavum tenente), *φέρει δὲ ἐν μέσῳ καὶ τὸ τροπαῖον κατὰ τοῦ θανάτου,* ΩΣ ΤΟΝ *σταυρὸν τοῦ Κυρίου βαστάζουσα.* Ubi pro ΩΣ ΤΟΝ legendum conjecerim ‘ΙΣΤΟΝ, *i. e. ferens Crucem Domini quasi* navis MALUM; *’Εστὶ γὰρ αὐτῆς πρῷρα μὲν ἡ ἀνατολὴ, πρύμνα δὲ ἡ δύσις, τὸ δὲ κοῖλον* (ita Gudius rectè pro *κύκλον*) *μεσημβρία.* Mallem ‘Η *μεσημβρία. Οἴακες δὲ αἱ δύο Διαθῆκαι· σχοινία δὲ περιτεταμένα ἡ ἀγάπη τοῦ Χριστοῦ σφίγγουσα τὴν ’Εκκλησίαν.* ΠΛΟΙΟΝ *δὲ ὃ φέρει μεθ’ ἑαυτῆς τὸ λουτρὸν τῆς παλιγγενεσίας ἀνανεούσης τοὺς πιστεύοντας·* ubi pro ΠΛΟΙΟΝ *δὲ* legendum literis transpositis ΛΟΙΠΟΝ *δὲ, i. e. cæterùm verò, quod portat secum inest lavacrum regenerationis, ὅθεν δὴ* (legerem *δὲ*) *ταῦτα λαμπρὰ, πάρεστιν, ὡς πνεῦμα, τὸ ἀπ’ οὐρανῶν,* (sc. *῞Αγιον Πνεῦμα*) *δι’ οὗ σφραγίζονται οἱ πιστεύοντες τῷ Θεῷ.* Ubi reponendum videtur *ὅθεν* ΔΕ *ταῦτα* ΤΑ *λαμπρὰ, et unde hæc gloriosa effunduntur munera, adest, sicuti ventus,* SPIRITUS *ille cœlestis. παρέπονται δὲ αὐτῇ καὶ ἄγκυραι σιδηραῖ, αὐταὶ τοῦ Χριστοῦ ἁγίαι ἐντολαὶ δυναταὶ ὡς σίδηρος· ἔχει δὲ καὶ ναύτας δεξιοὺς καὶ εὐωνύμους ὡς ἁγίους ἀγγέλους παρέδρους.* Legerem potiùs, voculâ transpositâ, *ἔχει δὲ,* ‘ΩΣ *ναύτας, δεξιοὺς καὶ εὐωνύμους ἁγίους ἀγγέλους παρέδρους, δι’ ὧν ἀεὶ κρατεῖται καὶ φρουρεῖται ἡ ’Εκκλησία. Κλίμαξ ἐν αὐτῇ εἰς ὕψος ἀνάγουσα ἐπὶ τὸ κέρας εἰκὼν σημείου πάθους Χριστοῦ, ἕλκουσα τοὺς πιστοὺς εἰς ἀνάβασιν οὐρανῶν·* ΨΗΦΑΡΟΙ *δὲ ἐπὶ τὸ κέρας ἐφ’ ὑψηλοῦ* ΑΙ’ΝΟΥΜΕΝΟΙ *τάξις προφητῶν μαρτύρων τε καὶ ἀποστόλων, εἰς βασιλείαν Χριστοῦ ἀναπαυομένων.* De his verò quid statuendum? In loco vexatissimo detur venia hariolanti; Lege ΨΗΦΑΡΑ *δὲ ἐπὶ τὸ κέρας ἐφ’ ὑψηλοῦ* ΑΙ’ΩΡΟΥΜΕΝΑ *τάξις προφητῶν.* Sed quid, inquies, sunt *ψη-*

θρωπον ἀποτελῶν, εἰκόνα τοῦτον καλέσας ἀπ' ἀρχῆς διὰ τύπου τὴν εἰς σὲ ἐπιδεικνύμενος στοργὴν, οὗ προστάγμασιν ὑπακούσας σεμνοῖς, καὶ ἀγαθοῦ ἀγαθὸς γενόμενος μιμητὴς, ἔσῃ ὅμοιος ὑπ' αὐτοῦ τιμηθείς. Σοῦ γὰρ πτωχεύει Θεὸς καὶ σὲ θεὸν ποιήσας εἰς δόξαν αὐτοῦ.

24. Cod. οὐ προστάγμασιν.

φαρά? Hippolytus ut apud Latinos loquens λατεινίζει, et à Latinis auctoribus explicandus. Veniat igitur Tertullianus, veniat Minucius: uterque ad eandem rem collineans. Hic ait Octav. p. 287. "Signa ipsa et vexilla castrorum, et vexilla quid aliud quàm inauratæ *Cruces* sunt et ornatæ? Signum sanè *Crucis* naturaliter visimus in navi cùm *velis* tumentibus vehitur, cùm expansis palmulis labitur, et cùm erigitur jugum, *Crucis* signum est." Sed propius ad rem Tertullianus, Apologet. cap. xvi. "In signis monilia crucum sunt; SIPHARA illa vexillorum et cantabrorum *stolæ* *Crucum* sunt." Vides nostri ψηφαρά. Similiter ad Nationes, 12. "In cantabris atque vexillis SIPHARA illa vestes crucum sunt." Memineris SIPHARA fuisse coloribus vivis picta, et formis heröum insignita, ut erat nobilissimus ille peplus Panathenaïcus. Ecclesiæ cogita SIPHARA sublime suspensa, in aërem supra navem Ecclesiæ elata, Martyribus et Apostolis, quasi ibi intertextis, insigniter decorata in regno Christi acquiescentibus. Κέρας de *mali* apice hic dici persuadent quæ suprà scripserat κλίμαξ ἐπὶ τὸ κέρας ἀνάγουσα.

Ex hoc Hippolytei ingenii scaturigine hortulos suos irrigâsse videtur Auctor non indisertus Operis Imperfecti in Matthæum, Hom. xxiii. (ap. S. Chrysost. tom. vi. p. cv. ed. Montfaucon.) "Quamvis infestatione Inimici Ecclesia vel sæculi tempestatibus laborat, quibusvis tentationum fluctibus pulsetur, naufragium facere non potest, quia FILIUM DEI habet GUBERNATOREM. Navigat enim fidei Gubernaculo, felici cursu per hujus sæculi mare, habens DEUM GUBERNATOREM, ANGELOS REMIGES, portans Choros omnium Sanctorum, erectâ in medio ipsâ salutari arbore (*i. e.* ἱστῷ, Italicè *albero*) CRUCIS, in quâ evangelicæ fidei vela suspendens, flante SPIRITU SANCTO vehitur ad portum Paradisi et securitatem quietis æternæ."

Δόξα τῷ Θεῷ.

image from the beginning, and thus showing in a figure His love to thee, and if thou hearkenest to His holy Commandment, and becomest an imitator in goodness of Him Who is good, thou wilt be like Him, being honoured by Him. For God has a longing for thee, having divinized thee also for His Glory.

APPENDIX A.

The following is from the Work of St. Hippolytus "On the Universe," and is an *addition* to the Fragment already printed by Fabricius from that Work. See above, pp. 153—158. It has been supplied from a MS. in the Bodleian Library, Baroccian MSS. No. XXVI. See "Hearne's Curious Discourses," Vol. ii. p. 394, Lond. 1773, where it was published with some conjectural emendations by Provost Langbaine. See also Routh, Rel. Sacr. ii. p. 32, ed. 1814. The present editor is indebted for a revised collation of it to Mr. Barrow and Mr. Southey, Fellows of Queen's College, Oxford. The MS. contains also the Fragment in Fabricius beginning with Ὁ ᾅδης τόπος ἐστὶν, p. 220.

Fragmentum S. Hippolyti "De Universo" ex MS. Barocc. 26.	*Idem Fragmentum conjecturali emendatione utcunque restitutum.—Voces asterisco * distinctas jam suffecerat Langbænius.*
ὁ μετὰ δικαίων ἀριθμὸς διαμένει ἀνεκλειπτος ἅμα δικαίοις ἀγγέλοις καὶ πνεύμασι Θεοῦ καὶ τοῦ τούτου Λόγου ὡς τῶν δικαίων χορὸς ἀνδρῶν τε καὶ γυναικῶν ἀγήρως καὶ ἀφθάρτως διαμένει ὑμῶν τὸν ἐπὶ ταῦτα προαγόμενον ΕΝ ΒΙΩ θεὸν διὰ τῆς τοῦ εὐτάκτου νομο-	ὁ μέγας δικαίων ἀριθμὸς διαμένει ἀνέκλειπτος, ἅμα δικαίοις ἀγγέλοις καὶ πνεύμασι Θεοῦ καὶ τῷ τούτου Λόγῳ*· ὡς ὁ τῶν δικαίων χορὸς* ἀνδρῶν τε καὶ γυναικῶν ἀγήρως καὶ ἄφθαρτος διαμένει, ὑμνῶν τὸν ἐπὶ ταῦτα προαγόμενον Θεὸν διὰ τῆς τοῦ [ΕΝ ΒΙΩ] εὐτάκτου νομοθεσίας.

θεσίας συνοις καὶ πᾶσα ἡ κτίσις ἀδιάληπτον ὕμνον ἀνοίσει[1] ἀπὸ τῆς φθορᾶς εἰς ἀφθαρσίαν διαυγῆ καὶ καθαρῶ πνεύματος δεδοξασμένη οὐκ ὑπαναγκης δεσμὸς συνχοθήσεται ἀλλὰ ἐλευθερία ζῶσα ἑκούσιον τὸν ὕμνον ἅμα τοὺς ἐλευθερωθεῖσιν πάσης δουλίας ἀγγέλοις τε καὶ πνεύμασιν καὶ ἀνθρώποις αἰνέση τὸν πεποιηκότα τούτους ἐὰν πισθέντες Ἕλλινες καταλείψεται τὴν ματαιότητα τῆς ἐπιγενους καὶ χρημάτων σπόρου σοφίας καὶ μὴ περὶ λέξεις ῥημάτων ἀσχολούμενοι τὸν νοῦν εἰς πλανησοινωητε ἀλλὰ τοῖς θεοπνεύστοις προφήταις καὶ Θεοῦ καὶ λόγοις ἐξηγηταῖς ἐνχειρίσαντες τὰς ἀκοὰς Θεοῦ πιστεύσηται ἔσεσθαι καὶ τούτων κοινωνοι καὶ τῶν μελλόντων τεύξασθαι ἀγαθῶν ἀμετρου τε οὐρανοῦ ἀνάβασιν καὶ τὴν ἐκεῖ βασιλείαν ὄψεσθαι φανερῶς γ[2] Θεὸς ἃ νῦν σεσιώπηται ἃ οὔτε ὀφθαλμὸς εἶδεν οὔτε οὖς ἤκουσεν οὔτε ἐπὶ καρδίαν ἀνθρώπου ἀνέβη ὅσα ἡτοίμασεν ὁ θεὸς τοῖς ἀγαπῶσιν αὐτόν εφ᾽ οἷς ἀνευρω ὑμᾶς επι τούτοις κρινω παρεκαστα βοατο τέλος ἅπαντων ὡς τε καὶ τω τα ευ πεποιηκότι τὸν βίον λήξαντος δε τοῦ τέλος εξοκηλαν[3] τη πρὸς κακιαν ἀνοητοι οἱ προσθεπονοι ἐπι τῇ καταστροφῇ τοῦ

Σὺν οἷς καὶ πᾶσα ἡ Κτίσις ἀδιάλειπτον ὕμνον ἀνοίσει, ἀπὸ τῆς φθορᾶς εἰς ἀφθαρσίαν διαυγῆ καὶ καθαροῦ πνεύματος δεδοξασμένη· οὐχ ὑπ᾽ ἀνάγκης δεσμοῖς συνεχθήσεται, ἀλλὰ ἐλευθεριάζουσα ἑκούσιον τὸν ὕμνον ἅμα τοῖς ἐλευθερωθεῖσιν πάσης δουλείας ἀγγέλοις τε καὶ πνεύμασιν καὶ ἀνθρώποις αἰνέσει* τὸν Πεποιηκότα. Τούτοις ἐὰν πεισθέντες Ἕλληνες καταλείψητε τὴν ματαιότητα τῆς ἐπιγείου* καὶ ῥηματοσπόρου σοφίας, καὶ μή, περὶ λέξεις ῥημάτων ἀσχολούμενοι, τὸν νοῦν εἰς πλάνησιν ἀνῆτε, ἀλλὰ τοῖς Θεοπνεύστοις Προφήταις καὶ Θεοῦ καὶ Λόγου ἐξηγηταῖς ἐγχειρίσαντες τὰς ἀκοάς, Θεῷ πιστεύσητε, ἔσεσθε καὶ τούτων κοινωνοί, καὶ τῶν μελλόντων τεύξεσθε ἀγαθῶν, ἀμέτρου τε οὐρανοῦ ἀνάβασιν καὶ τὴν ἐκεῖ βασιλείαν ὄψεσθε· φανερώσει γὰρ θεὸς ἃ νῦν σεσιώπηται, "ἃ οὔτε ὀφθαλμὸς εἶδεν οὔτε οὖς ἤκουσεν, οὔτε ἐπὶ καρδίαν ἀνθρώπου ἀνέβη, ὅσα ἡτοίμασεν ὁ Θεὸς τοῖς ἀγαπῶσιν αὐτόν·" "Ἐφ᾽ οἷς ἂν εὕρω ὑμᾶς, ἐπὶ τούτοις κρινῶ[2]," παρέκαστα βοᾷ τὸ τέλος ἁπάντων· ὥστε καὶ τῷ τὸ εὖ πεποιηκότι, τοῦ βίου δὲ λήξαντος τὸ τέλος ἐξοκείλαντι

[1] ανοιση sed corr. in ανοισει.

[2] Pro εἰ γαρ, ut videtur. φανερώσει Southeio debetur.

[3] ἐξόκειλαν· corr. in ἐξοκηλαν.

[1] 1 Cor. ii. 9.

[2] Vide Grabe, Spicileg. i. p. 14 et p. 327. Ezek. xviii. 24; xxxiii. 20.

δραματος ἐξαθλω γενόμενω τότε χειρον καὶ ἐπισεσυμένως βιώσαντι πρότερόν ἐστιν ὕστερον μετανοήσαντι πολλοῦ χρονου πολιτείαν πονηρὰν ἐκνικῆσαι τῷ μετὰ τὴν μετάνοιαν χρονῷ ἀκριβείας, δὲ δεῖται πολλῆς ὑπὲρ τῆς μακραν ασω[4] πεποιηκόσι

MEN

σώμασι διαιτης χρια καὶ προσοχης πλειονος εστιν δυνατον γὰρ ισως ἀθρόας αποκόψαι παθης τροφ[5] . . . ἀλλὰ μετὰ θεοῦ δυνάμεως καὶ ἀνθρω[6] . . . . . . καισιας καὶ ἀδελφῶν βοηθείας καὶ ειλικρινους μετανοιας καὶ συνεχης μελετης κατορθοῦται καλὸν μὲν τὸ μὴ ἁμαρτάνειν ἀγαθὸν δὲ καὶ τὸ ἁμαρτάνοντας μετανοεῖν, ὥσπερ ἄριστον τὸ ὑγιαίνειν ἀεὶ καλὸν δε καὶ τὸ ἀνασφᾶλαι μετὰ τὴν νόσον.

τῷ Θεῷ δόξα.

[4] Ὅσω, sed O in loc. raso rescript.

[5] στροφ (ut videtur).

[6] Post ἀνθρω desunt literæ sex aut septem.

πρὸς κακίαν, ἀνόνητοι* οἱ πρόσθε πόνοι, ἐπὶ τῇ καταστροφῇ τοῦ δράματος ἐξάθλῳ γενομένῳ· τῷ τε χεῖρον καὶ ἐπισεσυρμένως βιώσαντι πρότερον, ἔστιν ὕστερον μετανοήσαντι πολλοῦ χρόνου πολιτείαν πονηρὰν ἐκνικῆσαι τῷ μετὰ τὴν μετάνοιαν χρόνῳ· ἀκριβείας δὲ δεῖται πολλῆς· ὥσπερ τοῖς μακρᾷ νόσῳ* πεπονηκόσι μὲν σώμασι διαίτης χρεία καὶ προσοχῆς πλείονος· ἔστιν δυνατὸν γὰρ ἴσως ἀθρόως ἀποκόψαι πάθης στροφήν, ἀλλὰ μετὰ Θεοῦ δυνάμεως, καὶ ἀνθρώπων ἱκεσίας *, καὶ ἀδελφῶν βοηθείας καὶ εἰλικρινοῦς μετανοίας καὶ συνεχοῦς μελέτης κατορθοῦται· καλὸν μὲν τὸ μὴ ἁμαρτάνειν, ἀγαθὸν δὲ καὶ τὸ ἁμαρτάνοντα μετανοεῖν, ὥσπερ ἄριστον τὸ ὑγιαίνειν ἀεί, καλὸν δὲ καὶ τὸ ἀνασφῆλαι μετὰ τὴν νόσον.

τῷ Θεῷ δόξα.

APPENDIX B.

Philosophumena, p. 315.

Οἱ δὲ Περᾶται, [1] Ἀδέμης [2] ὁ Καρύστιος καὶ Εὐφράτης [3] ὁ Περατικὸς, λέγουσιν ἕνα εἶναι κόσμον τινὰ, οὕτως καλοῦντες τοῦτον τριχῇ διῃρημένον. Ἔστι τὲ τριχῆς [4] διαιρέσεως παρ' αὐτοῖς τὸ μὲν ἓν μέρος, οἷον ἡ μία [5] ἀρχὴ καθάπερ πηγὴ μεγάλη, εἰς ἀπείρους τομὰς τῷ λόγῳ τμηθῆναι δυναμένη. Ἡ δὲ πρώτη τομὴ καὶ προσεχεστέρα κατ' αὐτοὺς, ἐστὶν ἡ τριὰς, καὶ καλεῖται ἀγαθὸν τέλειον, μέγεθος πατρικόν. Τὸ δὲ δεύτερον μέρος τῆς τριάδος οἱονεὶ δυνάμεων ἀπείρων τι πλῆθος· τρίτον, ἰδικόν· καὶ ἔστι τὸ μὲν πρῶτον ἀγέννητον, ὅθεν διαρρήδην λέγουσι τρεῖς θεοὺς, τρεῖς λόγους, τρεῖς νοῦς, τρεῖς ἀνθρώπους. Ἑκάστῳ γὰρ μέρει τοῦ κόσμου τῆς διαιρέσεως διακεκρι-

Theodoret, Hæret. Fab. i. 17.

Ἀδέμης δὲ ὁ Καρύστιος, καὶ ὁ Περατικὸς Εὐφράτης, ἀφ' οὗ Περᾶται προσηγορεύθησαν οἱ τούτων ὁμόφρονες, ἕνα κόσμον εἶναι φασὶ τριχῇ διῃρημένον· καὶ τὸ μὲν ἓν μέρος, οἷόν τινα πηγὴν εἶναι μεγάλην, εἰς ἄπειρα διαιρεθῆναι τῷ λόγῳ δυνάμενον· τὴν δὲ πρώτην τομὴν Τριάδα προσαγορεύουσι, καὶ καλοῦσιν αὐτὴν ἀγαθὸν τέλειον, μέγεθος πατρικόν. Τὸ δὲ δεύτερον δυνάμεων ἀπείρων τὸ πλῆθος. Τὸ δὲ τρίτον καλοῦσιν ἰδικόν. Καὶ τὸ μὲν πρῶτον ἀγέννητον λέγουσι, καὶ ὀνομάζουσι τρεῖς θεοὺς, τρεῖς λόγους, τρεῖς νοῦς, τρεῖς ἀνθρώπους. Ἄνωθεν δὲ ἀπὸ τῆς ἀγεννησίας, καὶ τῆς πρώτης τοῦ κόσμου διαιρέσεως, παρ' αὐτὴν τὴν τοῦ κόσμου συντέλειαν, ἐν τοῖς Ἡρώ-

[1] Hunc parallelismum indicavit Bernays apud Bunsen. iv. p. xlv.

[2] Supra Ἀκέμβης ὁ Καρύστιος. Cod. Καροίστιος.

[3] Cod. Ἐφράτης Περατικός.

[4] Debebat δὲ τῆς τριχῇ διαιρ. Miller.

[5] Fort. οἱονεὶ μία. Miller.

μένης, διδόασι καὶ θεοὺς καὶ λόγους καὶ ἀνθρώπους καὶ τὰ λοιπά. Ἄνωθεν δὲ ἀπὸ τῆς ἀγεννησίας καὶ τῆς τοῦ κόσμου πρώτης τομῆς, ἐπὶ συντελείᾳ λοιπὸν τοῦ κόσμου καθεστηκότος, κατεληλυθέναι ἐπὶ τοῖς Ἡρώδου χρόνοις τριφυῆ[6] τινα ἄνθρωπον καὶ τρισώματον καὶ τριδύναμον, καλούμενον Χριστὸν, ἀπὸ τῶν τριῶν ἔχοντα τοῦ κόσμου μερῶν ἐν αὐτῷ πάντα τὰ τοῦ κόσμου συγκρίματα καὶ τὰς δυνάμεις. Καὶ τοῦτο εἶναι θέλουσι τὸ εἰρημένον, "Ἐν ᾧ κατοικεῖ πᾶν τὸ πλήρωμα τῆς θεότητος σώματι[7]." Κατενεχθῆναι δὲ ἀπὸ τῶν ὑπερκειμένων κόσμων δύο, τοῦ τε ἀγεννήτου καὶ τοῦ αὐτογεννήτου, εἰς τοῦτον τὸν κόσμον, ἐν ᾧ ἐσμὲν ἡμεῖς, παντοῖα δυνάμεων σπέρματα. Κατεληλυθέναι δὲ τὸν Χριστὸν ἄνωθεν ἀπὸ ἀγεννησίας, ἵνα διὰ τῆς καταβάσεως αὐτοῦ, πάντα σωθῇ[8] τὰ τριχῇ διῃρημένα. Ἃ μὲν γὰρ, φησὶν, ἔστιν ἄνωθεν κατενηνεγμένα, ἀνελεύσεται δι' αὐτοῦ, τὰ δὲ ἐπιβουλεύσαντα τοῖς κατενηνεγμένοις ἀφιεῖ εἰκῆ, καὶ κολασθέντα ἀποπέμπεται. Δύο δὲ εἶναι μέρη τὰ σωζόμενα λέγει, τὰ ὑπερκείμενα, ἀπαλλαγέντα τῆς φθορᾶς· τὸ δὲ τρίτον ἀπολλωσθαι[9], ὃν κόσμον ἴδιον καλεῖ. Ταῦτα καὶ οἱ Περᾶται.

δου χρόνοις κατεληλυθέναι τριφυῆ τινὰ ἄνθρωπον, καὶ τρίσωμον, καὶ τριδύναμον, καλούμενον Χριστόν· καὶ διελθεῖν τόν τε ἀγέννητον κόσμον, καὶ τὸν αὐτογενῆ, καὶ ἐλθεῖν εἰς τόνδε τὸν κόσμον ἐν ᾧ ἐσμέν. Κατελθὼν δὲ ὁ Χριστὸς, τὰ μὲν ἄνωθεν κατενηνεγμένα ἐπανελθεῖν ἄνω παρασκευάσει, τὰ δὲ τούτοις ἐπιβουλεύσαντα παραδώσει κολάσει. Καὶ τὸν μὲν ἀγέννητον κόσμον, καὶ τὸν αὐτογενῆ, σωθήσεσθαι λέγουσι· τοῦτον δὲ τὸν κόσμον ἀπολλύσθαι, ὃν ἰδικὸν ὀνομάζουσι.

6 Cod. *τριφυήν.* 7 Coloss. II. 9 ubi *σωματικῶς.* 8 Cod. *σωθεῖ.*
9 Cod. ἀπόλυσθαι.

Philos. p. 318.

Ὁ δὲ πάνσοφος Σίμων οὕτως λέγει· ἀπέραντον εἶναι δύναμιν, ταύτην ῥίζωμα τῶν ὅλων εἶναι. Ἔστι δὲ, φησὶν, ἡ ἀπέραντος δύναμις τὸ πῦρ καθ' αὐτὸ [1], οὐδὲν ἁπλοῦν καθάπερ οἱ πολλοὶ ἁπλᾶ λέγοντες εἶναι τὰ (δὲ) [2] τέσσαρα στοιχεῖα, καὶ τὸ πῦρ ἁπλοῦν εἶναι νενομίκασιν, ἀλλ' εἶναι τοῦ πυρὸς τὴν φύσιν διπλῆν, καὶ τῆς διπλῆς ταύτης καλεῖ τὸ μέν τι [3] κρυπτὸν, τὸ δὲ φανερὸν, κεκρύφθαι δὲ τὰ κρυπτὰ ἐν τοῖς φανεροῖς τὸ πῦρ [4], καὶ τὰ φανερὰ τοῦ πυρὸς ὑπὸ τῶν κρυπτῶν γεγονέναι· Πάντα δὲ, φησὶ, νενόμισται τὰ μέρη τοῦ πυρὸς ὁρατὰ καὶ ἀόρατα φρόνησιν ἔχειν. Γέγονεν οὖν, φασὶν, ὁ κόσμος ἀγέννητος ἀπὸ τοῦ ἀγεννήτου πύρος· Ἤρξατο δὲ, φησὶν, οὕτως γίνεσθαι· ἓξ ῥίζας τὰς πρώτας τῆς ἀρχῆς τῆς γενέσεως ὁ ἀγέννητος ἀπὸ τῆς ἀρχῆς τοῦ πυρὸς ἐκείνου λαβών· ταύτας γὰρ ῥίζας γεγονέναι κατὰ συζυγίαν ἀπὸ τοῦ πυρὸς, ἅς τινας καλεῖ νοῦν καὶ ἐπίνοιαν, φωνὴν καὶ ὄνομα [5], λογισμὸν καὶ ἐνθύμησιν.

Theodoret i. 1.

Σίμων δὲ πρῶτος, ὁ Σαμαρείτης ὁ μάγος, τῆς τούτου κακοτεχνίας ὑπουργὸς ἀνεφάνη.

Οὗτος τοῦτον μῦθον ἐγέννησεν. Ἄπειρον τινὰ ὑπέθετο δύναμιν· ταύτην δὲ ῥίζωμα τῶν ὅλων ἐκάλεσεν· Εἶναι δὲ αὐτὴν πῦρ ἔφησε, διπλῆν ἐνέργειαν ἔχον, τὴν μὲν φαινομένην, τὴν δὲ κεκρυμμένην· τὸν δὲ κόσμον γεννητὸν εἶναι, γεγενῆσθαι δὲ ἐκ τῆς φαινομένης τοῦ πυρὸς ἐνεργείας.

Πρῶτον δὲ ἐξ αὐτῆς προβληθῆναι τρεῖς συζυγίας, ἃς καὶ ῥίζας ἐκάλεσε· καὶ τὴν μὲν πρώτην προσηγόρευσε νοῦν καὶ ἐπίνοιαν, τὴν δὲ δευτέραν, φωνὴν καὶ ἔννοιαν, τὴν δὲ τρίτην λογισμὸν καὶ ἐνθύμησιν.

Philos. p. 326.

Μαρκίων δὲ ὁ Ποντικὸς καὶ Κέρδων ὁ τούτου διδάσκαλος, καὶ αὐτοὶ ὁρίζουσιν εἶναι τρεῖς τὰς

Theodoret i. 24.

Μαρκίων δὲ, καὶ Κέρδων ὁ τούτου διδάσκαλος, καὶ αὐτοὶ μὲν ἐκ τῆς Σίμωνος ἐξαπάτης

[1] Cod. καθ' αὐτόν. [2] Dele δέ, ortum ex δ'. Miller. [3] Cod. μέν τοι. [4] τοῦ πυρός. Scott. [5] An leg. ἔννοιαν?

τοῦ παντὸς[6] ἀρχὰς, ἀγαθὸν, δίκαιον, ὕλην· τινὲς δὲ τούτων μαθηταὶ προστιθέασι, λέγοντες ἀγαθὸν, δίκαιον, πονηρὸν, ὕλην. Οἱ δὲ πάντα[7], τὸν μὲν ἀγαθὸν οὐδὲν ἄλλως πεποιηκέναι, τὸν δὲ δίκαιον, οἱ μὲν τὸν πονηρὸν, οἱ δὲ μόνον δίκαιον ὀνομάζουσι, πεποιηκέναι δὲ τὰ πάντα φάσκουσιν ἐκ τῆς ὑποκειμένης ὕλης· πεποιηκέναι γὰρ οὐ καλῶς, ἀλλ' ἀλόγως. Ἀνάγκη γὰρ τὰ γενόμενα ὅμοια εἶναι τῷ πεποιηκότι· διὸ καὶ ταῖς παραβολαῖς ταῖς εὐαγγελικαῖς οὕτως χρῶνται λέγοντες· "Οὐ δύναται δένδρον καλὸν καρποὺς πονηροὺς ποιεῖν[8]," καὶ τὰ ἑξῆς, εἰς τοῦτο φάσκων εἰρῆσθαι τὰ ὑπ' αὐτοῦ κακῶς νομιζόμενα. Τὸν δὲ Χριστὸν υἱὸν εἶναι τοῦ ἀγαθοῦ καὶ ὑπ' αὐτοῦ πεπέμφθαι ἐπὶ σωτηρίᾳ τῶν ψυχῶν, ὃν ἔσω ἄνθρωπον καλεῖ, ὡς ἄνθρωπον φανέντα λέγων οὐκ ὄντα ἄνθρωπον, καὶ ὡς ἔνσαρκον οὐκ ἔνσαρκον, δοκήσει πεφηνότα, οὔτε γένεσιν ὑπομείναντα οὔτε πάθος, ἀλλὰ τῷ δοκεῖν. Σάρκα δὲ οὐ θέλει ἀνίστασθαι· Γάμον δὲ φθορὰν εἶναι λέγων κυνικωτέρῳ βίῳ προσάγων[9] τοὺς μαθητὰς, ἐν τούτοις νομίζων λυπεῖν τὸν δημιουργὸν, εἰ τῶν ὑπ' αὐτοῦ γεγονότων ἢ ὡρισμένων ἀπέχοιτο. ἔλαβον τῆς βλασφημίας τὰς ἀφορμὰς, ἀλλ' ἑτέραν ἐκαινοτόμησαν ἀσεβείας ὁδόν.

Ὁ δὲ Μαρκίων ὁ Ποντικὸς, ταῦτα παρὰ Κέρδωνος παιδευθεὶς, οὐκ ἔστερξε τὴν παραδοθεῖσαν διδασκαλίαν, ἀλλ' ηὔξησε τὴν ἀσέβειαν. Τέτταρας γὰρ ἀγεννήτους οὐσίας τῷ λόγῳ διέπλασε. Καὶ τὸν μὲν ἐκάλεσεν ἀγαθόν τε καὶ ἄγνωστον, ὃν καὶ πατέρα προσηγόρευσε τοῦ Κυρίου· τὸν δὲ δημιουργόν τε καὶ δίκαιον, ὃν καὶ πονηρὸν ὠνόμαζε. Καὶ πρὸς τούτοις τὴν ὕλην, κακήν τε οὖσαν, καὶ ὑπ' ἄλλῳ κακῷ τελοῦσαν. Τὸν δὲ δημιουργὸν περιγενόμενον τοῦ κακοῦ, τὴν ὕλην λαβεῖν τε, καὶ ἐκ ταύτης δημιουργῆσαι τὰ σύμπαντα.

[6] Cod. *τοὺς παντός.* [7] Leg. videtur *οἱ δὲ πάντες.* Miller. [8] S. Matth. vii. 18. [9] Corrig. *προσάγει.* Miller.

Philos. p. 327.

Κήρινθος δὲ ὁ ἐν τῇ Αἰγύπτῳ ἀσκηθεὶς αὐτὸς οὐχ ὑπὸ τοῦ πρώτου θεοῦ τὸν κόσμον γεγονέναι ἠθέλησεν, ἀλλ' ὑπὸ δυνάμεώς τινος ἀγγελικῆς, πολὺ κεχωρισμένης καὶ διεστώσης τῆς ὑπὲρ τὰ ὅλα αὐθεντίας, καὶ ἀγνοούσης τὸν ὑπὲρ πάντα θεόν. Τὸν δὲ Ἰησοῦν λέγει μὴ ἐκ παρθένου γεγεννῆσθαι·[1] γεγονέναι δὲ αὐτὸν ἐξ Ἰωσὴφ καὶ Μαρίας υἱὸν, ὅμοιον τοῖς λοιποῖς ἀνθρώποις, καὶ διενηνοχέναι ἐν δικαιοσύνῃ καὶ σωφροσύνῃ καὶ συνέσει ὑπὲρ πάντας τοὺς λοιπούς. Καὶ μετὰ τὸ βάπτισμα κατεληλυθέναι εἰς αὐτὸν ἐκ τῆς ὑπὲρ τὰ ὅλα αὐθεντίας τὸν Χριστὸν ἐν εἴδει περιστερᾶς, καὶ τότε κηρύξαι τὸν ἄγνωστον πατέρα καὶ δυνάμεις ἐπιτελέσαι. Πρὸς δὲ τῷ τέλει τοῦ πάθους ἀποπτῆναι τὸν Χριστὸν ἀπὸ τοῦ υἱοῦ[2]· πεπονθέναι τὸν Ἰησοῦν, τὸν δὲ Χριστὸν ἀπαθῆ μεμενηκέναι, πνεῦμα Κυρίου ὑπάρχοντα.

Theodoret i. 3.

Κατὰ δὲ τὸν αὐτὸν χρόνον καὶ Κήρινθος ἑτέρας ἦρξεν αἱρέσεως. Οὗτος ἐν Αἰγύπτῳ πλεῖστον διατρίψας χρόνον, καὶ τὰς φιλοσόφους παιδευθεὶς ἐπιστήμας, ὕστερον εἰς τὴν Ἀσίαν ἀφίκετο, καὶ τοὺς οἰκείους μαθητὰς ἐκ τῆς οἰκείας προσηγορίας ὠνόμασεν. Ἐδίδαξε δὲ οὗτος, ἕνα μὲν εἶναι τὸν τῶν ὅλων Θεὸν, οὐκ αὐτὸν δὲ εἶναι τοῦ κόσμου δημιουργὸν, ἀλλὰ δυνάμεις τινὰς κεχωρισμένας, καὶ παντελῶς αὐτὸν ἀγνοούσας. Τὸν Ἰησοῦν δὲ, τοῖς Ἑβραίοις παραπλησίως ἔφησε κατὰ φύσιν ἐξ ἀνδρὸς γεγεννῆσθαι καὶ γυναικὸς, τοῦ Ἰωσὴφ καὶ τῆς Μαρίας, σωφροσύνῃ δὲ καὶ δικαιοσύνῃ καὶ τοῖς ἄλλοις ἀγαθοῖς διαπρέψαι. Τὸν δὲ Χριστὸν ἐν εἴδει περιστερᾶς ἄνωθεν εἰς αὐτὸν κατελθεῖν, καὶ τηνικαῦτα τὸν ἀγνοούμενον κηρύξαι Θεὸν, καὶ τὰς ἀναγράπτους ἐπιτελέσαι θαυματουργίας. Κατὰ δὲ τὸν τοῦ πάθους καιρὸν, ἀποστῆναι[a] μὲν τὸν Χριστὸν, τὸ δὲ πάθος ὑπομεῖναι τὸν Ἰησοῦν.

Philos. p. 328.

Ἕτεροι δὲ καὶ ἐξ αὐτῶν πάντα τοῖς προειρημένοις λέγουσιν[3], ἓν μόνον ἐνδιαλλάξαντες ἐν τῷ τὸν Μελχισεδὲκ ὡς δύναμίν τινα ὑπειληφέναι, φάσκοντες αὐτὸν ὑπὲρ

Theodoret ii. 6.

Τοὺς δὲ Μελχισεδεκιανοὺς, τμῆμα μὲν εἶναι τούτων φασὶ, καθ' ἓν δὲ μόνον διαφωνεῖν, τὸ τὸν Μελχισεδὲκ δύναμιν τινὰ καὶ θείαν καὶ μεγίστην ὑπολαμβά-

[1] Cod. γεγενῆσθαι. [2] Ἰησοῦ. Scott. Vide not. Phil. 247, 43—9.
[3] Cod. λέγουσι. [a] An ἀποπτῆναι?

πᾶσαν δύναμιν ὑπάρχειν, οὐ[4] κατ' εἰκόνα δὲ εἶναι τὸν Χριστὸν θέλουσιν.

νειν, κατ' εἰκόνα δὲ αὐτοῦ τὸν Χριστὸν γεγενῆσθαι. Ἦρξε δὲ τῆς αἱρέσεως ταύτης ἄλλος Θεόδοτος, ἀργυραμοιβὸς τὴν τέχνην.

Philos. p. 329.

Ἕτεροι δὲ αὐτῶν[5] τῇ τῶν Νοητιανῶν αἱρέσει προσκείμενοι, τὰ μὲν περὶ τὰ γύναια καὶ[6] Μοντᾶνον ὁμοίως δοκοῦσι, τὰ δὲ περὶ τῶν ὅλων Πατέρα δυσφημοῦσιν, αὐτὸν εἶναι υἱὸν καὶ πατέρα λέγοντες, ὁρατὸν καὶ ἀόρατον, γεννητὸν καὶ ἀγέννητον, θνητὸν καὶ ἀθάνατον. Οὗτοι τὰς ἀφορμὰς ἀπὸ Νοητοῦ τινὸς λαβόντες.

Theodoret ii. 2.

Τινὲς δὲ αὐτῶν τὰς τρεῖς ὑποστάσεις τῆς θεότητος Σαβελλίῳ παραπλησίως ἠρνήσαντο, τὸν αὐτὸν εἶναι λέγοντες καὶ Πατέρα, καὶ Υἱὸν, καὶ ἅγιον Πνεῦμα, παραπλησίως τῷ Ἀσιανῷ Νοητῷ. Κατὰ τούτων συνέγραψεν Ἀπολινάριος, ὁ τῆς κατὰ Φρυγίαν ἱερᾶς πόλεως ἐπίσκοπος γεγονὼς, ἀνὴρ ἀξιέπαινος, καὶ πρὸς τῇ γνώσει τῶν θείων καὶ τὴν ἔξωθεν παιδείαν προσειληφώς. Ὡσαύτως δὲ καὶ Μιλτιάδης, καὶ Ἀπολλώνιος, καὶ ἕτεροι συγγραφεῖς. Κατὰ δὲ Πρόκλου τῆς αὐτῆς αἱρέσεως προστατεύσαντος συνέγραψε Γάϊος, οὗ καὶ πρόσθεν ἐμνήσθημεν.

Philos. p. 329.

Ὁμοίως δὲ καὶ Νοητὸς τῷ μὲν γένει ὢν Σμυρναῖος, ἀνὴρ ἀκριτόμυθος καὶ ποικίλος[7], εἰσηγήσατο τοιάνδε αἵρεσιν ἐξ Ἐπιγόνου τινὸς εἰς Κλεομένην χωρήσασαν, καὶ οὕτως ἕως νῦν ἐπὶ τοὺς διαδόχους διαμείνασαν, λέγων ἕνα τὸν Πατέρα καὶ Θεὸν τῶν ὅλων· τοῦτον πάντα πεποιηκότα, ἀφανῆ μὲν τοῖς οὖσι γεγονέναι ὅτε ἠβού-

Theodoret ii. 2.

Ὁ δὲ Νοητὸς, Σμυρναῖος μὲν ἦν τὸ γένος, ἀνενεώσατο δὲ τὴν αἵρεσιν, ἣν Ἐπίγονος μέν τις οὕτω καλούμενος ἀπεκύησε πρῶτος, Κλεομένης δὲ παραλαβὼν ἐβεβαίωσε. Ταῦτα δέ ἐστι τῆς αἱρέσεως τὰ κεφάλαια. Ἕνα φασὶν εἶναι Θεὸν καὶ Πατέρα, τῶν ὅλων δημιουργόν· ἀφανῆ μὲν ὅταν ἐθέλῃ, φαινόμενον δὲ ἡνίκα

[4] οὗ. Scott. [5] Montanistarum sc. [6] Pro καὶ fort. κατά. Miller.
[7] Cod. ποικῖλος.

λετο· φανῆναι δὲ τότε ὅτε ἠθέλησε· καὶ τοῦτον εἶναι ἀόρατον ὅτε μὴ ὁρᾶται· ὁρατὸν δὲ, ὅταν ὁρᾶται· ἀγέννητον δὲ, ὅταν μὴ γεννᾶται· γεννητὸν δὲ, ὅταν γεννᾶται ἐκ παρθένου, ἀπαθῆ καὶ ἀθάνατον, ὅταν μὴ πάσχῃ μήτε θνήσκῃ· ἐπὰν δὲ πάθῃ προσέλθῃ, πάσχειν καὶ θνήσκειν τοῦτον τὸν πατέρα· αὐτὸν υἱὸν νομίζουσι κατὰ καιροὺς καλούμενον πρὸς τὰ συμβαίνοντα. Τούτων τὴν αἵρεσιν ἐκράτυνε Κάλλιστος, οὗ τὸν βίον ἐκτεθείμεθα ἀσφαλῶς[8], ὃς καὶ αὐτὸς αἵρεσιν ἀπεγέννησεν· ἐξ ὧν ἀφορμὰς λαβὼν καὶ αὐτὸς ὁμολογῶν ἕνα εἶναι τὸν πατέρα καὶ θεὸν τοῦτον δημιουργὸν τοῦ παντὸς, τοῦτον δὲ εἶναι υἱὸν ὀνόματι μὲν λεγόμενον καὶ ὀνομαζόμενον, οὐσίᾳ δὲ [ἓν[9]] εἶναι, πνεῦμα γὰρ, φησὶν, ὁ θεὸς οὐχ ἕτερόν ἐστι παρὰ τὸν λόγον ἢ ὁ λόγος παρὰ τὸν θεόν· ἓν οὖν τοῦτο πρόσωπον ὀνόματι μὲν μεριζόμενον, οὐσίᾳ δὲ οὔ. Τοῦτον τὸν λόγον ἕνα εἶναι θεὸν ὀνομάζει καὶ σεσαρκῶσθαι λέγει. Καὶ τὸν μὲν κατὰ σάρκα ὁρώμενον καὶ κρατούμενον υἱὸν εἶναι θέλει[1], τὸν δὲ ἐνοικοῦντα πατέρα, ποτὲ μὲν τῷ Νοητοῦ[2] δόγματι περιρρηγνύμενος[3], ποτὲ δὲ τῷ Θεοδότου, μηδὲν ἀσφαλὲς κρατῶν. Ταῦτα τοίνυν Κάλλιστος.

ἂν βούληται· καὶ τὸν αὐτὸν ἀόρατον εἶναι καὶ ὁρώμενον, καὶ γεννητὸν καὶ ἀγέννητον· ἀγέννητον μὲν ἐξ ἀρχῆς, γεννητὸν δὲ ὅτε ἐκ παρθένου γεννηθῆναι ἠθέλησε· ἀπαθῆ καὶ ἀθάνατον, καὶ πάλιν αὖ παθητὸν καὶ θνητόν. Ἀπαθὴς γὰρ ὢν, φησὶ, τὸ τοῦ σταυροῦ πάθος ἐθελήσας ὑπέμεινε. Τοῦτον καὶ Υἱὸν ὀνομάζουσι καὶ Πατέρα, πρὸς τὰς χρείας τοῦτο κἀκεῖνο καλούμενον. Νοητιανοὶ προσηγορεύθησαν οἱ τήνδε τὴν αἵρεσιν στέρξαντες. Ταύτης μετὰ τὸν Νοητὸν ὑπερήσπισε Κάλλιστος, ἐπιθήκας τινὰς καὶ οὗτος ἐπινοήσας τῇ δυσσεβείᾳ τοῦ δόγματος.

[8] Fort. ἐκτεθείμεθα σαφῶς. Miller. [9] Addidimus ἕν. Miller.
[1] Cod. θέλειν. [2] Cod. Νοητῷ. [3] Cod. περιρηγ . . μενος, duabus literis evanidis.

Philos. p. 330.

῾Ερμογένης δέ τις καὶ αὐτὸς θελήσας τι λέγειν, ἔφη τὸν θεὸν ἐξ ὕλης συγχρόνου καὶ ὑποκειμένης τὰ πάντα πεποιηκέναι· ἀδυνάτως γὰρ ἔχειν τὸν θεὸν μὴ οὐχὶ ἐξ ὄντων τὰ γενόμενα ποιεῖν.

Theodoret ii. 19.

῾Ο δὲ ῾Ερμογένης ἐξ ὑποκειμένης ὕλης καὶ συναγεννήτου τὸν Θεὸν ἔφη δημιουργῆσαι τὰ πάντα. ᾿Αδύνατον γὰρ ὑπέλαβεν ὁ ἐμβρόντητος καὶ τῷ Θεῷ τῶν ὅλων, ἐκ μὴ ὄντων δημιουργεῖν.

Philos. p. 330.

῞Ετεροι δέ τινες ὡς καινόν τι παρεισάγοντες ἐκ πασῶν αἱρέσεων ἐρανισάμενοι ξένην βίβλον σκευάσαντες ᾿Ηλχασαΐ [4] τινος ἐπονομαζομένην, οὗτοι τὰς μὲν ἀρχὰς τοῦ παντὸς ὁμοίως ὁμολογοῦσιν ὑπὸ τοῦ θεοῦ γεγονέναι, Χριστὸν δὲ ἕνα οὐχ ὁμολογοῦσιν, ἀλλ' εἶναι τὸν μὲν ἄνω ἕνα, αὐτὸν δὲ μεταγγιζόμενον ἐν σώμασι [πολλοῖς [5]] πολλάκις, καὶ νῦν δὲ ἐν τῷ ᾿Ιησοῦ ὁμοίως [π]οτὲ μὲν ἐκ τοῦ θεοῦ γεγενῆσθαι, ποτὲ δὲ πνεῦμα γεγονέναι, ποτὲ δὲ ἐκ παρθένου, ποτὲ δὲ οὔ. Καὶ τοῦτον δὲ μετέπειτα ἀεὶ ἐν σώμασι μεταγγίζεσθαι καὶ ἐν πολλοῖς κατὰ καιροὺς δείκνυσθαι.

Χρῶνται δὲ ἐπα[οι]δαῖς καὶ βαπτίσμασιν ἐπὶ τῇ τῶν στοιχείων ὁμολογίᾳ. Σεσόβηνται δὲ περὶ ἀστρολογίαν καὶ μαθημα-

Theodoret ii. 7.

Οἱ δὲ ᾿Ελκεσαῖοι, ἔκ τινος ᾿Ελκεσαῒ τῆς αἱρέσεως ἄρξαντος τὴν προσηγορίαν λαβόντες, ἐκ διαφόρων αἱρέσεων μύθους ἐρανισάμενοι, τὴν οἰκείαν συντεθείκασι πλάνην. Καὶ περὶ μὲν τὴν τῶν ὅλων ἀρχὴν συμφωνοῦσιν ἡμῖν. ῞Ενα γὰρ ἀγέννητον λέγουσι, καὶ τοῦτον τῶν ἁπάντων καλοῦσι δημιουργόν. Χριστὸν δὲ οὐχ ἕνα λέγουσιν, ἀλλὰ τὸν μὲν ἄνω, τὸν δὲ κάτω. Καὶ τοῦτον πάλαι πολλοῖς ἐνῳκηκέναι, ὕστερον δὲ κατεληλυθέναι· τὸν δὲ ᾿Ιησοῦν, ποτὲ μὲν ἐκ τοῦ Θεοῦ εἶναι φησὶ, ποτὲ δὲ πνεῦμα καλεῖ, ποτὲ δὲ παρθένον ἐσχηκέναι μητέρα. ᾿Εν ἄλλοις δὲ συγγράμμασιν οὐδὲ τοῦτο. Καὶ τοῦτον δὲ πάλιν μετενσωματοῦσθαι, καὶ εἰς ἄλλα ἰέναι σώματα λέγει, καὶ καθ' ἕκαστον καιρὸν διαφόρως δείκνυσθαι. ᾿Επῳδαῖς δὲ καὶ δαιμόνων ἐπικλήσεσι καὶ οὗτοι κέχρηνται, καὶ βαπτίσμάσιν ἐπὶ τῇ τῶν στοιχείων ὁμολογίᾳ. ᾿Αστρολογίαν δὲ, καὶ μαγικὴν, καὶ μαθηματικὴν ἠσπά-

[4] Titulus rubricatus ᾿Ελχασαΐται. sed non prorsus certa. Miller.

[5] Vocis πολλοῖς vestigia exstant

τικὴν, καὶ μαγικοῖς[6]. Προγνωστικοὺς δὲ ἑαυτοὺς λέγουσιν.

ζοντο πλάνην, καὶ Προγνωστικοὺς ἑαυτοὺς προσηγόρευον. Τὸν δὲ ἀπόστολον παντελῶς ἠρνήθησαν· καὶ βίβλον δέ τινα συντεθείκασιν, ἣν ἐκ τῶν οὐρανῶν ἔφασαν πεπτωκέναι. Ταύτης τὸν ἀκηκοότα ἄφεσιν ἁμαρτιῶν λαμβάνειν παρ' ἣν ὁ Χριστὸς ἐδωρήσατο.

[6] Literæ ἀστρ plane evanidæ. Post μαγικοῖς excidit fortasse ἐπτόηνται. Miller.

APPENDIX C.

The mention of St. Polycarp, the disciple of St. John, and Bishop of Smyrna and Martyr, whose name occurs not unfrequently in the foregoing pages, suggests an occasion for submitting a question to the consideration of the reader, in reference to the History of his Martyrdom, as narrated in the contemporary Letter of the Church of Smyrna, and transcribed by Caius, supposed by some (e. g. by Ussher) to be, perhaps, Caius the Roman Presbyter (mentioned above, chap. iii.), from the copy of St. Irenæus, who had conversed with St. Polycarp. (See Eccl. Smyrn. Epistola de S. Polycarpi Martyrio in Petr. Apostol. Coteler. ii. p. 204, Amstel. 1724, or Jacobson ii. p. 595, ed. 1838.)

In that interesting narrative of St. Polycarp's Martyrdom it is related (cap. 16.), that the body of the venerable Bishop not being consumed by the fire which was kindled by the heathen officers, in order that he might be burnt therein, orders were given to the executioner to pierce him with a short sword. The original words of the Letter are as follows, *πέρας οὖν ἰδόντες οἱ ἄνομοι οὐ δυνάμενον αὐτοῦ τὸ σῶμα ὑπὸ τοῦ πυρὸς δαπανηθῆναι, ἐκέλευσαν προσελθόντα αὐτῷ κομφέκτορα παραβῦσαι ξιφίδιον.* The Letter then proceeds to say,—according to the received reading of the passage,—*καὶ τοῦτο ποιήσαντος, ἐξῆλθε* ΠΕΡΙΣΤΕΡΑ ΚΑΙ *πλῆθος αἵματος, ὥστε κατασβέσαι τὸ πῦρ i. e.* "a Dove came forth, and a stream of blood, so as to quench the fire."

The old Latin version is as follows, "Quumque hoc ita fuisset effectum, ecce subito fluente sanguinis copia Columba processit de corpore, statim sopitum cruore cessit incendium." But the Dove, which is so strangely combined in this passage with the stream of blood, appears to owe its origin to an erroneous reading.

Eusebius had it not in his copy. He has transcribed the LETTER, nearly verbatim into his History, and writes thus (Euseb. iv. 15), *ἐκέλευσαν κομφέκτορα παραβῦσαι ξίφος, καὶ τοῦτο ποιήσαντος ἐξῆλθε πλῆθος αἵματος.* Nor had Nicephorus any mention of the Dove in his MS. of the LETTER. His words are (iii. 35) *ἐκέλευόν τινα νύξαι ξίφει τὸν ἅγιον ἔξωθεν· οὗ δὴ γενομένου πλῆθος αἵματος ἐξεῤῥύη, ὡς ἱκανῶς ἔχειν καταμαραίνειν τὴν ἀκμὴν τοῦ πυρός.* If the Dove had been mentioned in the Letter, as read by Eusebius and Nicephorus, it is not likely that they would have omitted to notice it.

In short, the words ΠΕΡΙΣΤΕΡΑ` ΚΑΙ` appear to be corrupt, and ought, probably, to be amended to ΠΕΡΙ` ΣΤΥ΄ΡΑΚΑ, *i. e.* "about the haft." "No sooner did the executioner pierce the body with his steel, than a stream of blood flowed *upon the haft* of the weapon, so as to quench the fire." The word *στύραξ* signifies *ξύλον τοῦ ἀκοντίου* (Ammon. Valckenaer, p. 133), and the handle of a smaller weapon,—as here.

THE END.